FIRST OFF
THE TEE

FIRST OFF THE TEE

PRESIDENTIAL HACKERS, DUFFERS, AND CHEATERS FROM TAFT TO BUSH

DON VAN NATTA JR.

PublicAffairs
New York

Published in the United States by PublicAffairs™,
a member of the Perseus Books Group.

Book design by Jane Raese
Text set in 12 pt Bembo

Library of Congress Cataloging-in-Publication Data
Van Natta, Don, 1964-
First off the tee : presidential hackers, duffers, and cheaters from Taft to Bush /
Don Van Natta Jr.
p. cm.
Includes index.
ISBN 1-58648-265-3
1. Golf—Political aspects—United States. 2. Presidents—Sports—United States.
3. Sports and state—United States. I. Title.
GV981.V36 2003
796.352'0973—dc21
2002037085

FIRST EDITION
2 4 6 8 10 9 7 5 3 1

For Lizette

*"On the golf course, the ball doesn't know if
your first name is Mr. President or not."*
—Bob Farmer, American consul general in Bermuda
during the Clinton administration

CONTENTS

CONTENTS

PROLOGUE

BILL, GEORGE, JERRY, AND BOB

Golf is fatal.
—Theodore Roosevelt

O N THE FIRST TEE, the three men pace around in tight semi-circles, take jagged practice swings, and wear smiles that barely conceal their collective panic. It is a glorious February morning at Indian Wells Country Club, one of those routinely beautiful California desert winter days embraced by warm sunshine and kissed by a coy breeze. But the three golfers do not blink appreciatively at the deep blue sky. Instead, each man grimaces into the sunshine's glare at the enormous gallery and squints at the platoon of NBC television cameras focusing on their every move and the boom microphones eavesdropping on their every word. For each man, the day conjures a private vision of a very public horror.

The goal of these three famous men, after all, is not to win this historic round. The goal is to escape a nationally televised humiliation.

Bill worries that he may be doomed to shoot triple digits without his old putter. He had broken in that putter back in Arkansas a long time ago—what was it, thirty-five years ago? Then, just two nights ago, as he packed his bags, he discovered his beloved Titleist Bullseye putter was missing from his golf bag. His house on Pennsylvania Avenue is a big one, and things do tend to get misplaced, but a frantic two-hour search failed to turn up that trusty, beat-up putter with the green handle, the one that looks like a club you might find lying around at a faded miniature golf course. He must have inadvertently stuck it in the bag of one of his golfing partners. Could the timing be any worse?

George's palms are sweaty. Here is another intimidating first hole, the province of muffed shots and quick ridicule. He is anxious to dispense with the preliminary chitchat as quickly as possible, and take that first swing, always the hardest of any round, and just get the bustling gallery of this first hole behind him. George's least favorite place on a golf course is the first tee, while his favorite is the final green or, more precisely, the downward slope from the 18th hole to the safety of the clubhouse. It will be impossible to enforce the "no laughing rule" here. He harbors a modest goal: "Just try to get it in the air."

Jerry, the oldest and yet the most athletic of the three men, feels jittery, too, though he manages to conceal it from his playing partners. He hopes to be able to survive this first hole without launching a golf ball into the crowd nestled along the first fairway. If he can't, that will confirm a generation-old stereotype about his game and provide the late-night comedians with enough new material to carry them into the next century.

Sure, the men are smiling now, projecting a cool confidence. This comes easily to them; after all, they have spent their entire public lives smiling and appearing unflappable. But the first tee, on this day, is a stage that they have never had to occupy. They have grown accustomed to playing golf far from the crowds and the cameras, and even farther from one another. Until today, the golf course was one of the few places on earth where these men could escape scrutiny and judgment.

Bob, the ninety-one-year-old host of this charity golf tournament, the Thirty-Sixth Annual Bob Hope Chrysler Classic, is also pacing around the first tee with a 3-wood. In the winter of 1995, it was Bob Hope's idea to persuade President Bill Clinton and two of his predecessors, George Herbert Walker Bush and Gerald R. Ford, to get together to play a round of golf in a PGA Tour event. Three American presidents playing golf together was a spectacle that had never been attempted, or even imagined. Hope is the fourth golfer

George Bush, Gerald Ford, and Bill Clinton stand side by side at the Bob Hope Chrysler Classic Pro-Am on February 15, 1995, at Indian Wells Country Club in California. It was the first and only time three American presidents played a round of golf together.

in the presidential group that also includes a fifth, the professional golfer Scott Hoch, the winner of the previous year's Bob Hope Pro-Am tournament.

One of the television cameras moves in. "Well, a historic foursome," Dick Enberg, the NBC commentator, announces to Bob Hope and the three presidents. "How do you put this group together to play a game of golf?"

"Well, it's damned lucky, I think, you know," Bob Hope says. "Because I called President Clinton and asked him, and he finally said, 'Yes, I'd like to do that.' Then I got President Ford, President Bush, and we got—and me.

"Three presidents, and a hacker."

Everyone chuckles, but the quip—*presidents and a hacker*—hangs in the air for a painfully long moment, posing the awful question that will soon be answered: Which president will distinguish himself as the worst hacker?

"You're without your thirty-five-year-old putter," Dick Enberg tells Clinton. "I hope the rumors aren't true that Mr. Ford confiscated that."

Clinton winces at this pointed reminder about his misplaced Bullseye. Ford jumps in: "Well, Dick, I've played here seventeen years with Bob and it's always a great, great thrill. He's kind of a scoundrel, but he's fun to play with, and it's a great cause."

Bush is asked if wagers have been placed. "I don't know," he says with the impatient shrug he often flashes when he wants the pace to quicken. "We haven't gotten to that."

Clinton tries to put aside any old political bruises by extending a peace offering to Bush, the man he defeated for the presidency in 1992. "We're on the same side," Clinton offers. In a way, Clinton is right: The three men are united by the rawest emotion—fear of failure. "We're going to try to stay out of—we're going to avoid out of bounds, he and I are. We're not going to go too far right or too far left," Clinton says. "We're going to play political golf today."

This gambit does not seem to be working. Bush stares at his shoes. Old campaign scars never fade, and Ford senses that Bush and Clinton simply do not like each other. Ford observes that Clinton seems to be trying too hard, Bush seems not to be trying at all, and both men are tense and uneasy with each other.

Perhaps Dick Enberg senses it, too. He asks, "Have you been in this close an association in recent terms, or have you played before?"

Clinton keeps trying. "We've never played golf together before," he says, "but President Bush has been good enough to support a lot of things we've done together on trade and issues, for example, things he started that I tried to finish. So we've been together on several occasions."

Dick Enberg asks, "Isn't it interesting that in these complicated times, this sport brings this unusual group together?"

Clinton, never quite forgetting that he is up for reelection the next year, clutches the question like a lifeline. Talking brilliantly, off-the-cuff, has always come easily to him; swinging a golf club, well, that's another thing.

"One of the nicest things about golf is that it's really becoming a sport for every man and woman in America," Clinton says, his eyes gleaming as he embarks on the impromptu stump speech. "All kinds of people, all these new courses coming up, public courses, people able to play who never could have played ten, twenty years ago. And that's very rewarding, because it's a sport that you can play throughout your life and at all different skill levels. It's really a perfect sport for our people."

"Well," Dick Enberg says, "you gentlemen are used to high pressure. I can't think of anything in sports that has more anxiety and pressure than that first hit."

Everyone laughs again. President Clinton confesses, "We are as nervous as cats. We were just talking about it." He slaps Bush on the elbow. "We're just as nervous as can be."

"Dick," Jerry Ford says, "I would advise people they should stay behind us."

This line gets the biggest laugh of them all, but Ford's warning should not be ignored. In a matter of minutes, the former presidents take their first swings of the Bob Hope Chrysler Classic, with Clinton, the sitting president, teeing off first. He grabs his Big Bertha driver from his bag, which contains nineteen clubs. (Five more than are allowed according to the PGA Tour rules, but who's counting?)

Clinton's tee shot flies far right.

"Go! Go!" the President shouts before the ball crash-lands in a sand trap.

Ford smashes his tee shot, and yells "Fore! Fore!" But his shot is so high and far left that no one in the jammed gallery even bothers to move as the ball soars far above their heads and lands somewhere behind them.

Bush's first tee shot stops on the fairway's left fringe. He uses a 4-iron to hit his second ball, a spectacularly high shot that appears headed for the flag but then fades near the green and smacks a tree.

"And at right angles, like a bullet, the ball went in the crowd," Bush would later recall. "When I got to the scene of the crime, a lady lay bleeding."

THE GAME SAYS NO.
Nearly every person in a president's privileged life says yes. *Yes, Mr. President. What can I do for you, Mr. President? Yes, it would be my pleasure to get that done for you, Mr. President. Would you like more choco-late syrup on your sundae, Mr. President?*

Only the game of golf says no. It says the word bluntly and it says the word repeatedly, with no chance for negotiation and no room for compromise. It is a brutal game that can be counted on to dis-appoint, enrage, and humble anyone who attempts to play it, even the most powerful man in the world. *No, Mr. President, you can't have that double-bogey. No, Mr. President, you will never solve that slice. Sorry, Mr. President, sir, you will never rid yourself of that nagging urge to hurl your golf bag in the creek.*

That simple admonishment—*no*—has attracted so many American presidents to the game of golf. It is that single word that encouraged the presidents to continue to play despite the game's innumerable, heartless embarrassments and humiliations, some even becoming so hopelessly obsessed that they willingly sacrificed political capital to play. And if they were willing to shed a few points in the public opin-ion polls for the game, what would stop some presidents from cheat-ing and lying openly to try to persuade the world they were better golfers than they really were?

Just as a bully accords respect to the kid who dares to stand up to him, a president respects the harsh game that not only stands up to him but reduces him to a nervous wreck, to tears even. It is the im-movable game's uncompromising difficulty that has appealed most of all to the American presidents. Golf cannot be stage-managed or spun, it cannot be tailored by image makers or tallied by pollsters, it cannot be buttonholed or lobbied, and it certainly cannot be wowed by the trappings of the Office of the President of the United States.

The game said no to Dwight D. Eisenhower, the most enduring symbol of the golfing president, a man who left his cleat marks on the wooden floorboards in the Oval Office. Eisenhower, who joined Augusta National Golf Club in 1948, had been regularly bedeviled by a tall Loblolly pine tree, located left-center of the famed course's 17th fairway, about 195 yards from the green. The tree interfered with Eisenhower's sliced shots so often that he actively campaigned to have it removed. At an Augusta governors' meeting in 1956, Eisenhower proposed having the tree chopped down. Without hesitation, the board chairman, Clifford Roberts, ruled the President out of order and immediately adjourned the meeting. The pine still stands tall today, and it is appropriately—and even a bit snidely— called the Eisenhower Tree. During Augusta's renovation, completed in 2001, the board moved the 17th hole's tee box back twenty-five yards. The lengthening of the hole turned the Eisenhower Tree into an even more perilous hazard for the green-jacketed members and the men who compete every April for the honor of wearing one.

The game said no to Ronald Reagan, an infrequent White House golfer who practiced his putting down the wide aisle of Air Force One and on the rich carpet in the Oval Office. Usually, he played just once a year, on New Year's Eve, at Walter Annenberg's estate in southern California. When Reagan was a B-movie actor in Hollywood, he tried to force the Lakeside Country Club in Burbank, California, to accept blacks and Jewish golfers into its ranks. Reagan said he would be forced to quit the club if it refused. The members of the Board of Directors did not waver. They pinned Reagan's letter to a dartboard in the clubhouse. Before long, Ronald Reagan's admonishing letter was full of holes.

And the game said an emphatic no to Bill Clinton, the forty-second president, whose tastes embraced the country club lifestyle but whose manner and style of play belonged on the well-worn public tracks where he learned to play growing up in Hot Springs, Arkansas. After leaving office in January 2001, Clinton moved to another white house in Chappaqua, New York, just after his wife had been sworn in as the state's junior U.S. senator. Clinton learned, much to his surprise and dismay, that none of the country clubs near his home wanted him as a member. Every club said no, all refusing to let him jump ahead dozens of names parked for years on lengthy waiting lists. Some clubs said no to Clinton far less politely than others, with unstated motives. Bill Clinton was the second president to be impeached and the first golfing ex-president to fail to find a local country club to hang his spikes.

Some presidents could not resist trying to say no to the game. They sidearmed golf balls from the woods back into the fairway. They grabbed gimme putts—"made" putts given by playing partners without having to take the trouble to swing the putter—as if they were entitlements. They shaved a few strokes from their score, writing a "5" on their scorecards when everyone saw a "7." Richard M. Nixon could not improve quickly enough to impress Ike, his boss, and so he resorted to rescuing his golf balls from out of bounds without taking penalty strokes. Bill Clinton, an unlit cigar in his mouth (a habit of his political idol, John F. Kennedy), yearned to play the game as flawlessly as Kennedy, too; if you read Clinton's scorecards, you might even think he was capable of keeping up with his hero. Lyndon Baines Johnson hit 300 golf balls a round, but it was not a clumsy attempt to enhance his score. He was just searching for that one elusive perfect shot.

These presidents tried to say no to the game, trampling and twisting the game's Official Rules, despite irritating some of their playing partners and many of their golf-playing constituents.

But golf never takes no for an answer.

It is the cruelest game of them all, the great equalizer that gracefully invents diabolical ways to infuriate players while it gradually reveals their true character. Golf is the only sport where there is no referee and honor is hard-earned; the player must obey and enforce the rules at the same time. The game is so maddeningly difficult and yet so gorgeously seductive, a pursuit where perfection is impossible and mediocrity is something to strive for.

For all those reasons, golf is the game that fourteen American presidents have played, a game that revealed as much—and in some cases, even more—about their personalities, their character, and even their presidencies as the words they chose, the bills they signed, or the legacies they imagined for themselves.

"If the people wish to determine the best candidate [for president], put all the contenders on a golf course," the golf pro Jimmy Demaret once said. "The one who can take five or six bad holes in a row without blowing his stack is capable of handling the affairs of the nation."

There were some, however, who thought so little of golf that they wanted the U.S. Constitution amended to bar golfers from public service, apparently believing that the game's tumult would torment an officeholder to the point of distraction. "If I had my way," the curmudgeon H. L. Mencken wrote, "no man guilty of golf would be eligible to any office of trust under the United States."

Almost everything is revealed on a golf course—a player's shortcomings and strengths, most of all, but other subtleties of personality and foibles of character that you may never see across a desk or a conference room table or in the dim light of the situation room. Over eighteen holes, you discover if a player is blessed with patience or intolerance, a sense of humor or a streak of envy, a long or short fuse—all of it. And because so few presidents could play with any consistency, the game presents itself as a clear prism to view how these powerful men tried to cope with all that can go wrong from the first tee to the final green.

Ken Raynor, the golf professional at Cape Arundel Golf Club in Kennebunkport, Maine, who is a close friend of the Bush family, put it this way: "You get to know a man, standing together with him in waders and on the first tee."

Yes, you do. You most certainly do.

THE IDEA FOR THIS BOOK arrived during the summer of 1999, after Bill Clinton survived the second impeachment trial of a president in the history of the republic. It was an exhausting period in American history. The President had dragged the nation, his aides, his friends, and his family through a year of lies and recriminations. It had been as exhausting and as frustrating for the American people as it had been for Clinton. And so in late August, just six months after he escaped removal from office, the President decided to recharge his batteries by going to Martha's Vineyard for two weeks to raise a boatload of campaign cash for the Democratic Party and to cheat his way around the Farm Neck Golf Club.

Several times in the 1990s, I was fortunate enough to play that beautiful little gemstone of a course on the island's edge. I learned the hard way that Farm Neck is one of the nation's more unforgiving public courses, especially for a duffer like me who aspires to break 100. The course has small rolling hills that are usually lashed by powerful wind gusts off the Atlantic. Most of the dogleg holes make sharp turns that avoid cranberry bogs, forcing your approach shots to sail right into the snarl of the sea wind. The stiffer the wind, the easier it is to deposit at least a half-dozen balls in the tall weeds or among the shoreline's rocks.

But each day, on the wires, I read that Clinton had managed to conquer Farm Neck. He put up an 82, an 84, and then an 81. A veteran reporter told me that two years earlier, Clinton had claimed to have shot a 79 at Farm Neck.

It was the 79 that got me.

Breaking 80 had been an elusive goal of Clinton's, but he managed the feat in the most suspect way. Clinton took credit for this 79 on an especially blustery day in August 1997 after reporters observed that he needed three shots off the first tee to hit a playable ball. The first shot soared into the trees, the second zipped into a nearby fairway, and only the third shot landed in play. And, of course, the President decided to play the third ball. If the rules had been strictly followed—a very big if, in Clinton's case—he would have started the round with a 5, meaning he would have needed to hit two over par over the eighteen holes to card that 79. And that was impossible. But even if you grant him the two mulligans as warm-up shots (it's just a friendly game, right?), he'd still have to shoot 7 over par for the course! And *that* was impossible.

Of course, the reporters were forbidden from following the President around the eighteen holes with scorecards and little pencils. After the round, Mike McCurry, the White House press secretary, dutifully announced that the President had indeed shot a 79, only the third time in his life that he crossed the magical 80 mark. By contrast, Ike, who was a far more disciplined player than Clinton, managed to break 80 fewer than a dozen times during his lifetime.

First, reporters howled with laughter at the 79, but the laughs quickly gave way to a smoldering anger. Perhaps the reporters' fury was fueled by boredom; there is nothing worse for a White House correspondent than trying to gin up stories during a president's August vacation when the desk back home is ravenous for copy. There was something about the 79 that inspired an anger that other Washington boondoggles had never inspired. So the press corps fired prickly questions at McCurry about the score, but the President's spokesman declined to describe how Clinton had pulled it off. In Washington, "no comment" is often translated to mean, "Guilty as charged."

I work as an investigative reporter for the *New York Times*. At the time, I had spent two and a half years covering Bill Clinton. I had written hundreds of stories chronicling the many political traps that Clinton had built for himself, and his Houdini-like way of escaping them while leaving his political enemies looking ridiculously overmatched. I knew, from experience, that Clinton often succumbed to the urge to stretch the truth like taffy or, worse, tell preposterously baroque lies. Clinton's natural ability to glide from misstatement to misstatement, with few consequences, had confounded his enemies and frustrated some members of the press. Yet even as the denials mounted and the revelations piled up, the President's approval ratings spiraled merrily higher and higher.

In hindsight, Clinton's claim of 79 should not have surprised anyone. The 79 was nothing, really, compared to the morning at the White House in January 1998 when Clinton fixed a furious glare on the cameras, shook his index finger for emphasis, and hissed: "I did not have sexual relations with that woman, Miss Lewinsky." Then, of course, there was Clinton's infamous under-oath truth-dodging response to a potentially incriminating question before the grand jury, "It depends on what the meaning of is . . . is." With a record like that, did it really matter if the President lied about shooting a 79 on the golf course?

To quite a few Americans, it did matter. Cheat us here, they seemed to say, and he'll cheat us over there. Perhaps it was the brazenness of the claim. Golfers understand: It is one thing to acknowledge your score was enhanced by a few mulligans (the notorious do-over shots often taken by amateur golfers but forbidden by the United States Golf Association's *Rules of Golf*). It is quite another thing to take mulligans and tell the world your score is legitimate. A golfing friend called me on the phone, a pal who had helped me tear up Farm Neck. "Can you believe these scores Clinton is taking credit for?" my friend asked.

A similar indignant buzz ricocheted around clubhouses and practice greens all over the country. Rob Duca, the golf columnist for the *Cape Cod Times,* wrote, "Seventy-nine really isn't all that difficult when you've got guys with Uzis guarding the woods and playing partners who consider anything inside 75 yards to be a gimme."

It was late August in Washington, the streets were empty, and it was the slowest of news weeks. I didn't have much to do except wonder about the President's 79. And so I called a few honest people (by Washington standards) who had played a round or two with Clinton.

"Have you ever seen the President shoot a legitimate 79?" I asked four Friends of Bill.

The answers were: no, nope, no way, and one of those hysterical laughs that sounds as if it might last all afternoon.

Then I asked them how the President managed to shoot in the low 80s, the range that he claimed. "Mulligans and gimmes," one of his friends told me. "The President treats himself to lots of mulligans and gimmes. He likes to say he grants presidential pardons to the bad balls." This same friend added, "I haven't seen him shoot a legitimate round in the 80s. Without all the mulligans and gimmes, he'd be in the 90s—okay, maybe the low 90s. Maybe."

So I wrote a piece about Clinton's quaint habit of bending the rules a bit on the golf course, as nearly every weekend golfer does and many past presidents have also done. It was all intended to be some harmless late summer fun. The story was published in the newspaper's Week in Review section, and it was reprinted in newspapers around the country.

Clinton hated my story, but to this day, I am convinced he was most offended by the photographs that accompanied it. On the front page of the Week in Review, a three-column, full-color photograph depicted the President in the horrible throes of what could only be charitably described as a painfully wild swing off the tee. His eyes were bulging, his cheeks were puffed, and you just knew that after the President was done creaming the ball, a brigade of Secret Service agents accompanied by bomb-sniffing dogs was not going to find it. Inside the section, a second photograph wasn't much better. This one showed the President sheepishly hunting for his lost ball along a stand of evergreen trees.

I wrote that President Clinton was addicted to mulligans, saying he often "pardoned" a bad ball without even bothering to ask the permission of his playing partners, a practice that offended more than one playing partner. As Clinton neared the end of the back nine of his time in the White House, I presented the mulligan as the perfect metaphor for his presidency. The voters, the Congress and, yes, even the First Lady had all granted the President a few mulligans.

"Cynics in the gallery continue to believe that President Clinton's golf scores—he claims to shoot around 80 and as low as 75—are enhanced by at least a half-dozen mulligans," I wrote. "Sure, the President is a pretty good golfer, the cynics say. He's just not *that* good. Skepticism is, of course, understandable. Mr. Clinton, after all, claimed that he did not inhale, and that he did not have sexual relations with that woman. Why wouldn't the President also put the spin on his golf score?"

But it was this observation that annoyed the President most of all: "Apparently being president means never having to say double-bogey."

Perhaps not surprisingly, I heard the presidential verdict from one of Clinton's closest friends, Terry McAuliffe, a gregarious and prolific Democratic fund-raiser who happened to be a frequent golfing partner of the President. McAuliffe called me at home on a Sunday afternoon, one week after the article was published. "Don," he said, his tone signaling the gravity of his assignment. "The President is furious with you. Your piece was horrible. You wrote some very damaging things." He went on to tell me that I managed to "badly hurt" the President's feelings.

"It's all I heard about for five straight days," groaned McAuliffe, who had spent much of the past week with the Clintons during the last leg of their late-summer vacation outside Syracuse, New York. "The President is so mad at you. He will never forgive you."

I quickly reminded McAuliffe that the golf piece paled in comparison to some other unflattering things that I had written about Clinton—his excesses with Monica Lewinsky, his leasing of the Lincoln Bedroom to wealthy political donors, and the many indignities heaped upon him by Independent Counsel Kenneth W. Starr, including the fact that Starr ordered a doctor to take blood out of the President's arm, in the White House Map Room, in August 1998, to prove once and for all that the leader of the free world had left incriminating evidence on a certain navy blue dress purchased at the Gap.

And I gently reminded McAuliffe that my articles, published in the *New York Times* and newspapers all over the world, had portrayed President Clinton as a habitual liar, an adulterer, and a cad.

"Those things bothered him, too, but this is different!" McAuliffe shot back. "This is much, much worse. You called him a cheater! The President takes his golf game . . . *very* seriously."

Later, it occurred to me that McAuliffe never disputed a single fact in the article. He never simply said, "The President does not cheat at golf." It was only after McAuliffe had slammed the telephone down that I began to wonder why Bill Clinton was angrier about getting caught cheating at golf than cheating on his wife.

What is it about this crazy game that causes so many people, even the president of the United States, to care more about it than almost everything else?

OVER A SPAN OF NEARLY 100 YEARS of American history, from William Howard Taft to George Walker Bush, there have been seventeen presidents. Fourteen of those men played golf, which qualifies it as the most cherished sport among the White House occupants over the past century. Most of the presidents played the game as recklessly and as joyously and sometimes even as guiltily as millions of their constituents.

Yet even as golf surged in popularity through the latter half of the twentieth century, the presidents recognized potential political peril on the golf course, and it was not necessarily lurking in the bunkers or the rough. Sometimes, the potential political costs were envisioned as the ball soared straight at the pin.

John F. Kennedy was one who cringed at his own beautiful shot. Despite a bad back, Kennedy possessed a graceful, effortless swing, which allowed him to easily rank as the best player among the fourteen presidential golfers. But he was obsessively secretive about his love of the game, just as he was obsessively secretive about the other extracurricular activities that he participated in during his 1,000 days in the White House. And some members of the press, many of whom adored Kennedy, enabled the President to keep his passion for women—and, to a lesser extent, golf—hidden from the public.

As he ran for president in 1960, Kennedy was acutely aware that some Americans had become disenchanted with President Dwight D. Eisenhower's methodical devotion to golf. Kennedy was almost maniacal about his refusal to allow photographers to snap his picture while holding a driver or a putter.

Just a few days before the Democratic National Convention, Kennedy teed off on the par-3, 154-yard 15th hole at the breathtaking Cypress Point Golf Club on California's Monterey Peninsula. Kennedy's ball landed on the green and rolled straight toward the hole. It looked almost certain that the ball would glide into the cup.

"I was yelling, 'Go in! Go in!'" recalled Paul B. "Red" Fay Jr., who would later serve as undersecretary of the navy in the Kennedy administration. But Jack Kennedy looked stricken with terror. The ball stopped just six inches short of the hole.

Kennedy exhaled, then told Fay: "You're yelling for that damn ball to go in the hole and I'm watching a promising political career coming to an end. If that ball had gone into that hole, in less than an hour the word would be out to the nation that another golfer was trying to get into the White House."

Harry S Truman was one of the three presidents in the past century who never picked up a golf club; the other two were Herbert Hoover and Jimmy Carter. Poker was Truman's game. He dismissed golf as a dangerous political noose that was perceived by middle-class voters to be a rich man's indulgence. Truman became furious when a newspaper published an article accusing him of hitting a spectator with a wild shot off the tee at a course in his hometown of Independence, Missouri. "For your information," Truman wrote to the newspaper, "I have never played golf in my life, never had a golf club in my hands, except to look at it—so I couldn't possibly have fired a ball on the Independence golf course and hit anybody on the head."

Despite the persistent worries that golf reminded most voters that presidents felt comfortable among the elite and their gated, private country clubs, no president was ever encouraged to quit because of a disappointing poll number or a commentator's barb. In fact, the first presidential golfer enthusiastically played through his campaign, despite a warning that the game itself could keep him from winning the White House.

While serving as secretary of war to Theodore Roosevelt, William Howard Taft was mercilessly lampooned for his obsession with the game, and not just because of his 350-pound girth and his awkward, almost comical stance on the tee. Swinging a driver, Taft resembled a sumo wrestler trying to swat a gnat. On the campaign trail, Taft often took breaks from the flesh pressing to play a quick round. And he delivered sermons to anyone who would listen about the wonders of the relatively new game that had debuted in the United States just twenty years earlier, in the 1880s.

Theodore Roosevelt had no taste or patience for golf; he tried it once, and that was enough. He dismissed it as "too tame," which for him was synonymous with weak. Roosevelt was the first president to conclude that a politician was at risk if he whittled away too many afternoons chasing a little white ball around a wide expanse of land better viewed from horseback. Perhaps more important, Roosevelt was aware that many Americans had laughed at Taft for having the audacity to play the silly game and, even worse, look silly while doing it.

In 1908, Roosevelt had selected Taft to succeed him for the Republican nomination and the presidency. As Election Day approached, T.R. was bothered by the torrent of criticism of Taft's love of golf. The newspapers gleefully published embarrassing photographs and cartoons of Taft, squatting heavily over a small stick and a miniscule white ball. The images sickened Roosevelt, who felt compelled to give his pupil one final lesson down the campaign stretch. "I myself play tennis, but that game is a little more familiar; besides, you never saw a photograph of me playing tennis," Roosevelt wrote in a private letter to Taft. "I'm careful about that; photographs on horseback, yes; tennis, no. And golf is fatal."

Golf is fatal. For a century, Theodore Roosevelt's grim warning has echoed down the halls of the West Wing, worrying a century of his successors and their aides. But Taft did not care—the game was too important to him. Taft did more than discard the advice of Roosevelt, his political mentor. Taft thumbed his nose at the notion that the love of golf should be political suicide, and he was committed to using a presidential election as a referendum to test whether it was a myth. In a subtler way, Taft's rejection of Roosevelt's advice was an attempt to take a small step out of his mentor's gargantuan shadow. And in doing so, Taft was the trailblazer for all the Oval Office golf nuts to come.

At a campaign event in South Dakota, Taft told the crowd, "They said that I have been playing golf this summer, and that it's a rich man's game, and that it indicated I was out of sympathy with the plain people." He then asked to be heard "before the bar of public opinion" on the subject of golf. His stump speech on the game sounded as passionate as any he had delivered on more pressing issues. "It is a game for people who are not active enough for baseball or tennis, or who have too much weight to carry around to play those games," Taft declared.

Taft believed it was better to attempt to win the crowd's sympathy by acknowledging his obesity.

"And yet when a man weighs 295 pounds," he continued, shaving more than a few pounds from his actual weight, "you have to give him some opportunity to make his legs and muscles move, and golf offers that opportunity." Golf was exercise!

Americans accepted the explanation and handed the White House to Taft. Was it an important precedent? Perhaps. But Taft's easy victory may be partially attributed to the fact that Americans simply had too much fun laughing at those cartoons of a very big man chasing a very small ball.

GEORGE H. W. BUSH SPEED-WALKS down the left-hand fringe of Indian Wells' first fairway, making a beeline to "the scene of the crime," and he sees a few TV cameramen running their lungs out to get there ahead of him. With his mouth agape and his skull suddenly pounding, the forty-first president of the United States thinks: *Now I know why I prefer to play golf in Kennebunkport. No spectators, no casualties.*

Beneath a cluster of palm trees, Bush is confronted with his first victim of the day. Mr. President, meet Norma Earley, a seventy-one-year-old woman from Vista, California, whom you just happened to bean in the head with a golf ball—and she voted for you, twice! Mrs. Earley is on the ground, her bloody right hand covering a deep gash on the bridge of her nose that stretches over her left eye. Bush thinks: *Geez, there's blood everywhere. Is this lady still trying to smile at me?* Bush's ball knocked the sunglasses off her face. In the grass at the poor woman's feet, Bush spots a single lens, dislodged from the frames, that catches a glint of the high sun.

A blood-stained spectator is something that Bush had not even imagined during those panic-spiked moments on the first tee just five minutes ago. *Oh, golly, it's even worse,* Bush thinks. Turns out Mrs. Earley is the wife of the Indian Wells Country Club golf marshal, the man charged with enforcing the course's rules and etiquette. *It's like smacking the police chief's bride with a tire iron.*

"I leaned over to console her," Bush would later recall. "She recognized me and tried to smile." *Poor lady, trying to bail me out, pretending we were just introduced at the White House Christmas Party.*

Bush says, "I am sorry." *What else can I say?* A few nearby spectators have the nerve to laugh, but they are in the minority. Most fans, no doubt Republicans, just glare at Bush, wondering how they could have voted for this hacker.

"I'm sorry I got in the way of your shot," Mrs. Earley tells Bush.

She thinks it's her fault! What do I do now? What would Mr. Smooth do? Do I wait for the medical-evacuation chopper and escort Mrs. Earley on board? Or should I just play on?

"I played on," Bush would later recall. By now, Ford and Clinton—and, it seems, dozens of swarming, sunglasses-wearing Secret Service agents—have shown up, but who is in danger now? Don't the agents have it backward? *Perhaps the Secret Service guys should be protecting the fans from us. Hand out fencing helmets to everybody.* Bush would later recall the indignity of "confessing to President Clinton that I had dobbered Mrs. Earley. I won't say he seemed happy. Maybe it was a 'There but for the grace of God go I' feeling." Ford shoots a sympathetic glance at Bush. *Well,* Bush thinks, *Ford is well seasoned in these matters.*

A golf cart, with a blue flashing light atop its roof, whisks Mrs. Earley off the course and to a nearby hospital.

After the first hole, the presidents have tallied three triple-bogeys and one fan in need of ten stitches. Even a president, especially a president, cannot take a mulligan on a shot that bloodies a spectator.

On the second tee, none of the three presidents manage to put the ball in bounds. It is as if everyone is rattled by the sight of blood. Bush, clearly shaken, bangs his ball far left; this time, it rolls harmlessly beneath the feet of some fans. Clinton hits a soaring drive— "No, no, no!" he yells—that smacks a house with a loud crack. Ford's drive clears the house that Clinton's ball hit.

And, as often happens in golf, the presidential round degenerates from bloody to "bloody embarrassing," as a London tabloid would put it.

Over the next few holes, Clinton's iron shot strikes a palm tree and ricochets back toward him. He ducks. Another Clinton ball soars into the Santa Rosa hillside. "Ugh!" he groans. On one green, Clinton attempts a twenty-five-foot putt, but he slams the ball at least twenty-five feet past the hole. Scott Hoch tosses his putter on the green in an attempt to stop the ball from rolling off the back of the green. Clinton hurls his head backward, gulps, and looks as if he wants to dig a ditch and climb into it.

On the 11th hole, Clinton's ball skitters off the green, clears two bunkers and a water hazard. Somehow, the ball kicks up and knocks a piece of watermelon out of the hand of a small boy standing on the edge of a nearby fairway.

Poor Bush. He is so flummoxed by the first hole that he imagines Mrs. Earley is stalking him. On the 12th tee, Bush spots a rather angry-looking elderly woman, sitting in a folding chair, with "an ugly cut above her eye," he'd say later. And this woman is glaring at Bush.

"I said, 'Mrs. Earley, I am glad to see you here. I am so sorry.' She looked confused," Bush would later say. "She mumbled something. She nodded as if in terrible pain. I held her hand. I wanted her to know that I felt awful. As I was walking down the 12th fairway, a stranger said to me, 'That wasn't the lady you hit. That woman was hit by Clint Eastwood.'"

Ford is all over the course, confirming the bumbling image that the comedian Chevy Chase had pinned on him during the halcyon days of *Saturday Night Live.* His ball almost never goes straight, except straight up. "Oh no, I popped it up!" Ford groans. The baseball metaphor is appropriate: the ball goes 200 yards, straight up, then lands just thirty yards ahead of him. Infield fly rule in effect.

Off another tee, after another spectacularly bad tee shot by Clinton, Ford outdoes him by slamming a ball that clocks a golf cart with a loud pop.

More victims: On the 14th hole, Bush's ball zips into a crowd of people. Mr. President, sir, meet John C. Rynd, of Chula Vista, California, whom you just smacked in the rear end with your golf ball. *Not again.*

"How's the wound?" Bush asks Rynd with a nervous giggle.

"No blood, no problem," says Rynd. "Sorry, sir, I wasn't looking." Rynd has just one request—an autograph. Bush autographs the offensive ball and then flees.

Ford rips a ball off the 17th tee that sends another gallery scattering. Mr. President, please say hello to Geraldine Grommesh of Fargo,

North Dakota, whom you just hit in the left index finger with your ball. Mrs. Grommesh apologizes to Ford for tampering with the trajectory of his shot.

A truism of presidential golf emerges from the carnage: The unfortunate people hit by presidential golf balls apologize for getting in the way. They put aside the pain and, with a smile, hustle a few souvenirs to commemorate the honor. Mrs. Grommesh later tells reporters, "I'm just glad it was a former president who hit me." She would likely not have appreciated being hit by some less famous golfer who had played that day, like Yogi Berra or Alice Cooper.

The presidential trio plays on, finding this kind of talk not even remotely funny. Bob Hope has not floated a lame joke for some time; he is busy enough keeping his head down. But the golf writers are convulsing with laughter at the wild play. "It's the funniest thing I've ever seen," says Geoff Russell of *Golf World* magazine. "They're doing *reeeeeally* bad."

Wasn't this the ultimate fear of these three presidents? To be snickered at and sneered at? Their games have been dissected, their first tee behavior studied, their level of play assumed to be much worse than they claim. But rarely do the cameras get to follow them off the first tee all over the course. It is even more unusual for the presidents to be forced to play narrow holes, flanked by 20,000 spectators on each side. If you can't hit straight—and these three men often cannot—that's a big problem.

It's a combat zone out here, thinks Bush, the old navy pilot and war hero who knows one when he sees one.

An NBC interviewer catches up with Bush as he walks down the final fairway. The interviewer asks if Bush is enjoying himself. "I had a good time, a good time," he says grimly. "I'm not carved out for celebrity golf. I'm a man who likes to cruise it in about two hours max—eighteen, nobody watching. It's a stupid thing. I spoke to a million people in Czechoslovakia, with Václav Havel. I didn't feel one qualm, one nervousness. You get up here in front of a funnel full of spectators, and every muscle tightens up. It's crazy." And then a confession, said under his breath and yet still audible, barely, to the TV audience: "And it shows you are not a real good golfer."

President Clinton salutes former President Ford on the 18th green at Indian Wells Country Club. Ford sank a 40-foot putt on the final hole to card a 100 for the afternoon, but the presidential trio of Clinton, Ford, and Bush played a chaotic round that all three men would much rather forget.

As the presidential round finally ends, after six and a half tortured hours, several of the golf writers who had watched the historic round say they had never seen such poor play at a PGA event. "Absolutely terrible," one veteran writer says about the presidents' performances.

The final scores: Bush 92, Clinton 93, Ford 100. The presidents' scores "should be taken with a grain of salt," one of the golf writers says. But in the press accounts of the first presidential threesome in golf history the next day, a few other counts will be published, and these will be coldly accurate and remembered far longer than these scores. Hit spectators: Bush 2, Ford 2, Clinton 0. Trips to the hospital: 1. Stitches: 10.

"Bad Golf Is Par for the Course," the *Buffalo News* says in a typical headline, "As Clinton, Ford, Bush Hit the Links—and Some Fans."

After the round, Ford and Bush do not have much to say, but they aren't dreaming of another term in office. Clinton is obligated to say something, to offer some kind of defense or excuse. "This is the worst I've played in three or four years," Clinton says, trying to justify his 93 when he has been telling everyone that he is flirting with breaking 80. "But it didn't bother me. I had a great time. This was beautiful. This was wonderful."

Bush hears this description and thinks: *Beautiful? Wonderful? This guy is clearly running for reelection.*

When the game is finally, mercifully, over, George Bush searches the clubhouse for his wife. He has a simple wish—to get out of there. Barbara Bush has watched the ugly play from the calm of the press box, her smile dissolving into that famous judgmental scowl. She shakes her head, sighs heavily, and then says into a reporter's microphone: "As if we don't have enough violence on television."

From her bed at Eisenhower Medical Center in Rancho Mirage, where she will spend the next five days, Norma Earley is suddenly granted that peculiar, momentary brand of American fame. They have to get the golf ball victim on the air. And the lady is game for it all. She grants interviews with NBC Sports and *Inside Edition,* and a half-dozen early morning radio programs whose hosts cannot crack enough jokes about the presidents' wild golf games. The producers are thrilled; the video is gold. Both of Mrs. Earley's eyes are blackened, and the gash above her left eye is bandaged. Bush would place a sheepish call a couple days later. "He just said he was sorry that it happened and that it was just one of those things," she says. "I told him he made me an instant celebrity, and he said that is not the way to become a celebrity, and I agree with him."

Next time she gets the opportunity to watch a current or former American president hit a golf ball, Mrs. Earley knows what she will do: "I think I will start watching from behind instead of on the side."

PART ONE

THE PURISTS

Hole	1	2	3	4	5	6	7	8	9	Out	In	Tot
Distance	410	160	300	520	360	195	396	451	356	3148	3100	6248
Par	4	3	4	5	4	3	4	5	4	36	36	72
JFK	5	4	4	6	4	2	5	5	5	40	40	80
Ike	5	4	5	7	5	3	4	6	4	43	45	88
Ford	6	3	5	6	5	4	4	6	5	44	41	85
FDR	4	3	5	7	5	1	3	7	2	14		
Handicap	5	15	13	4	1	3	7	2	14			

*average scores while president (FDR did not play when president)

[Signatures: John F. Kennedy; Dwight D. Eisenhower; Gerald R. Ford; Franklin D. Roosevelt]

WHEN HE ASSUMED NO ONE WAS LOOKING, Dwight D. Eisenhower would sometimes quickly and quietly nudge his golf ball to improve its position.

John F. Kennedy would say almost anything to jangle his opponent's nerves. He warned about the dangers of sand traps, out-of-bounds markers and other unseen hazards—a "courtesy that would have taken the confidence out of a Ben Hogan," his press secretary, Pierre Salinger, said.

Franklin D. Roosevelt would take a mulligan or two, or even three, before the polio snatched one of his great pleasures.

If someone said, "Mr. President, pick up the putt, that's an easy one," Gerald R. Ford would grab his ball without a moment's hesitation, even if the cup was a tricky six-foot stroke away.

And yet by the golf standards and on-course behavior of America's fourteen golfing presidents, Ike, JFK, FDR, and Ford qualify as the purists. They comprise a presidential dream foursome that played the game better than their White House predecessors and successors and, more important, did so with a contagious enthusiasm bordering on passion and even obsession. Each of these four men harbored a deep affection for the game, though "affection" does not come close to capturing the depth of their feelings. Playing golf was among their greatest pleasures in life, not cherished as much as their families and their country, of course, but at times it seemed the game ranked a not-so-distant third.

These four competitive men played well enough to win more matches than they lost, which was a good thing because they hated to lose on the links. Almost always, the members of this foursome had wagers riding on their rounds—modest stakes, no more than a few bucks changing hands. Far more important were the bragging rights that were on the line. As much as they wanted to win, these four men respected the game, its traditions, and its rules.

Well, most of the time, anyway.

They did accept gimme putts, if offered, but so did nearly all the golfing presidents. One of the great perks of being president is that your playing partners are absolutely certain you can sink a putt from almost any distance on the green. Golfers lavished presidents with gimmes the same way that foreign leaders visiting the White House showered their hosts with baubles. The gifts were almost never refused. Most presidents dutifully picked up their putts, feeling relieved to be spared the potential embarrassment of missing a tap-in. Besides, you should always try to grant a constituent's wish.

After Ike left the White House, he was asked how his life had changed, and he responded, "I notice people don't give me as many short putts."

Ike, JFK, FDR, and Ford were never caught lying about a score, or hitting three or four balls from the tee box, or tossing a ball out of the woods back onto the fairway when no one was looking. This foursome represents the best of White House golf; each man possessed that mix of competitiveness and companionship necessary to a president's physical and mental health. These four men played the purest games of the golfing presidents.

And no one played better than Jack Kennedy.

John F. Kennedy

A Private Passion

*With a nearly perfect swing, John F. Kennedy hits a drive off
the first tee at the Hyannis Port Country Club on July 20,
1963. Kennedy qualifies as the finest golfer to live in the
White House. He zealously kept his love of the game hidden
from the public, worrying that the voters would not tolerate
another golfer after Eisenhower's eight golf-obsessed years.*

It is true that my predecessor did not object,
as I do, to pictures of one's golf skill in action.
But neither, on the other hand,
did he ever bean a Secret Service man.
—John F. Kennedy

A SUDDEN AND STUBBORN WINTER FOG engulfed the White House on an unseasonably warm Saturday morning in early February 1961, dropping an immovable white curtain between Pennsylvania Avenue and the executive mansion. Inside, the nation's new young president was forced to cancel his first scheduled round of golf since taking the oath of office. Two of his playing partners, Senator George A. Smathers of Florida and Senator Stuart Symington of Missouri, were sent home. But on this miserable Saturday, John F. Kennedy possessed a president's unshakable urge to do what he wanted to do despite the mountain of roadblocks. And Jack Kennedy wanted to hit a few golf balls.

"Why don't we go out here in the Rose Garden and hit some?" Kennedy asked Undersecretary of the Navy Red Fay, an old friend and frequent golfing companion, who had been an ensign on Kennedy's boat, PT-109, during World War II. "They say that Ike used to come out here and practice his irons," Kennedy said.

Golf was Kennedy's closely guarded private passion. He maintained a lifelong love affair with the game, but he managed to keep it hidden from the public until he was elected president. And even then, he revealed his affection for the game gradually and carefully, and never completely.

During his campaign for president, Kennedy was extremely sensitive about some voters' distaste for Dwight Eisenhower's widely known golf addiction. As Kennedy quietly asked his friends: Would it be appropriate for someone aspiring to be the champion of the people to indulge in a rich man's game? Besides, Kennedy, a fan of

Ian Fleming's spy novels, loved keeping secrets (almost as much as he loved hearing them). Before his election, Kennedy devised ways to insure that the public knew little or nothing about his love of golf, the patrician game that would only serve to remind the public that the Democratic presidential nominee was an ambassador's son, a product of Choate and Harvard with a trust fund in his hip pocket. Kennedy knew Americans would instantly detect the hypocrisy if they discovered that he, too, stalked country club courses with as much zeal as President Eisenhower. The revelation would deprive the Democrats of the opportunity to criticize Ike, a Republican, for caring more about improving his golf score than improving the lives of all Americans.

Golf was just one of Kennedy's secrets, of course. There was an enormous stockpile of secrets, but according to Richard Nixon (an authority on such things), the game amounted to nothing less than Jack Kennedy's "secret vice."

Throughout his 1,000 days in office, most Americans had no idea that their president was not just an enthusiastic golfer but a talented golfer. Most Americans knew that Kennedy was devoted to playing a ferociously competitive game of touch football with his large, rambunctious family at their compound in Hyannis Port, Massachusetts. And the newspapers were full of pictures of Kennedy taking wind-buffeted yacht rides in the *Honey Fitz* off the coast of Palm Beach. But golf? Very few knew. This was fine with Kennedy.

On the edge of the Rose Garden that foggy February morning in 1961, Kennedy presented an impromptu assignment to a security aide, Muggsy O'Leary, a former senior officer on the Massachusetts Capitol Police Force. "Muggsy, of all the people who have cherished this opportunity," the President said, "you have been selected to be the first person to shag for the thirty-fifth president of the United States."

"What is shag?" Muggsy asked tentatively, clearly sensing that the assignment carried some risks.

Muggsy and Fay followed the President out into the Rose Garden. "Muggsy," the President said, pointing at a bag of balls, "dump the balls here on the lawn. Then take the bag and go out a ways, and we'll hit some iron shots at you."

"From the expression on Muggsy's face," Fay recalled, "I wasn't convinced that Muggsy didn't see himself as the first true martyr of the New Frontier. In the fog that surrounded the White House that morning, even a skilled ball hawk would have had his problems tracking the golf balls. With Muggsy at the helm it looked to me as though the only possible result would be a lot of lost balls and Muggsy in the nearest hospital as a result of taking too many golf balls on the head and body."

Fay and Kennedy watched Muggsy trudge about twenty yards away from them, slowly turn around and wait for the hailstorm of golf balls to begin. In a hushed voice, Kennedy told Fay, "Don't you get the impression that Muggsy hasn't quite grasped the true art of shagging?"

Then, the President shouted more instructions to the shagging appointee: "Muggsy, you have to go out farther. Go across the road to the South Lawn."

Kennedy and Fay grabbed their 9-irons and began to fire beautifully hit golf shots into the fog. "The balls would rise, disappear in the fog and then drop somewhere in the vicinity of Muggsy," Fay recalled.

After just a few minutes of play, the pair stopped. Both men were convinced that it was only a matter of time before Muggsy would indeed become the first casualty of the new administration. The President called into the fog, "Muggsy, you're too valuable to this administration to risk you out there. Go back under cover. We'll have someone go out when the fog clears and pick up the balls."

After Muggsy was out of danger, Kennedy and Fay hit dozens of balls, working on their 8-irons and 9-irons, then moving to their 3-irons and 4-irons and concluding with their 3-woods. Balls soared into the trees near the East Gate. With the fog, it was impossible to know where the balls ended up.

The mystery appealed to Kennedy, who asked Fay, "If you hit a driver or brassie with everything you have, right on the screws, do you think you could hit one out of the grounds?"

"There's only one way to find out," Fay replied. He smashed a few drives with everything he had. Kennedy watched as the balls soared over the Rose Garden, across the South Lawn and cleared the tree line before disappearing. "Because of the fog," Fay recalled, "it was hard to tell if I ever made it."

Fay laughed as he told Kennedy, "Can't you see the expression on the face of some farmer in from Dubuque, Iowa, with his wife, strolling around their White House for the first time when suddenly a golf ball drops out of the fog and bounces down the street?"

This scenario greatly amused the President. Confronted with a golf ball bouncing down Pennsylvania Avenue, the farmer would have undoubtedly told his wife: "I thought Ike moved out of the White House last month!"

Jack Kennedy felt right at home smacking those golf balls into a wall of fog. He could play his beloved game of golf, right there in his own backyard, and no one could see.

OF THE FOURTEEN AMERICAN PRESIDENTS who played golf, no one looked more comfortable and relaxed on the links than John F. Kennedy. It was not an act: He was relaxed because he knew he could play. Kennedy glided from hole to hole, making impossible shots look easy, flashing that winning smile in the face of the game's treacherous snarl. As he tamed nearly every course that confronted him, he played with the smoothness of someone who applied a daily shine to his game's scuffs and rough edges.

No president played the game better. But Kennedy did not play every day. He played only on occasion and even then there was almost always some pain. Kennedy was born with an "unstable back," in the words of a family physician. (Biographers say that later stories about heroic football and wartime back injuries were fictitious.) His chronic back pain from osteoporosis—as well as a host of other ailments, including Addison's disease—kept him off the golf course for several long stretches of his life. Watching him swing a golf club, though, you would never know he was hurting.

Like so many things, the game just came easily to him. Kennedy possessed an effortless, graceful swing that his friends watched with wonder. His swing was textbook perfect—relaxed, slow, and smooth, and the ball usually ended up not far from where he intended it to go. From the tee, he crushed the ball, driving it straight and true and as long as 275 yards (one playing partner said he saw Kennedy hit a drive that exceeded 300 yards). And he owned a deadly touch on the greens. If there was a weak club in his bag, it was probably a long-distance iron, but even with a 3-iron or 4-iron from a rough patch off the fairway, Kennedy rarely embarrassed himself.

Kennedy's doctors were concerned that his chronically bad back would not withstand the wear and tear of even a few swings of a golf club. But Kennedy showed his doctors that he could swing a club without straining certain muscles and vertebrae in his back. In the Kennedy Library, a series of photographs depict close-ups of Kennedy's back as he was swinging a club, demonstrated for his doctors. The President's medical team was persuaded that he could isolate muscles in his back in such a way that he would not worsen his condition. They allowed Kennedy to play golf, at least during some periods of his 1,000 days in office. It is remarkable that Kennedy was able to play golf with a textbook-perfect swing when he was swinging a club in a convoluted motion to keep the doctors satisfied.

He almost never played eighteen holes. He was an accomplished drive-by golfer, spending ninety minutes or two hours on the course, racing through five or seven or eleven holes and always avoiding any holes deemed easily accessible to spectators or photographers. If he had played regularly—and played a full eighteen holes—he would easily have shot in the high 70s, possibly even in the mid-70s, according to people who were familiar with his game. Still, even with his sporadic play, Kennedy's estimated average score of 80 easily qualifies him as the most talented of the golfing presidents. During his short presidency, Kennedy would have shot in the low 80s (again, if he played all eighteen holes)—and they would be legitimate scores not enhanced by mulligans and gimmes.

Most of all, Kennedy maintained his composure on the golf course, even when things did not go his way. He was as cool playing golf as he was debating or delivering smart, impromptu answers to questions at press conferences. "His concentration is wonderful," Walter F. Hill, the club professional at Kennedy's home course in Hyannis Port, Massachusetts, said at the time. "He really moves the ball. He hits a longer drive than I do. And he's a real competitor. If he did play full rounds about three times a week, I'm positive he would be in the 70s."

So why was Kennedy so committed to keeping his natural golf talent as quiet as possible? The answer is a single word: Ike.

Jack did not want to be like Ike.

As the junior senator from Massachusetts, Kennedy had heard dozens of Eisenhower golfer-in-chief jokes; everyone in the capital gleefully laughed at the punch lines. In Kennedy's view, Ike had turned himself into a caricature of the golf-obsessed chief executive, and more than once on the campaign trail, Kennedy and his political strategists used golf to dismiss Eisenhower as a relic from a long-ago past. Golf presented itself as a politically useful symbol of Eisenhower's passiveness and old age. When Eisenhower left office, he was seventy years old, the oldest man to have served as president. At forty-three, Kennedy was the youngest man to have won election to the office. A new president always tries to distance himself from his predecessor's worst habits and traits, so it is not surprising that Kennedy worked hard not to be seen as yet another president rushing from the Oval Office to make another tee time with his country club pals.

Hours after taking the oath of office, Kennedy was astonished to discover thousands of small cleat marks in the Oval Office's wooden floor, leading a pockmarked trail from behind the desk to the double doors that opened to the portico, the South Lawn, and Ike's famous custom-built putting green. For weeks afterward, Kennedy would show visitors the trail of spike marks. The old man's golf obsession was worse than anyone thought, Kennedy told friends. Ike had treated the Oval Office as a clubhouse locker room, leaving a duffer's trail in the floorboards of the most powerful office on earth. What a legacy!

One of Kennedy's first acts as president was to order the removal of Dwight Eisenhower's beloved putting green, a bit of White

House groundskeeping that *was* revealed at a press conference (technically, the green was not removed; it was just no longer meticulously maintained). The symbolism was obvious: The old golfing general–president was gone, and so was his custom-made putting green where he whiled away an incalculable number of hours. And the new, young president was determined not to play games now that he had a nation to run.

Several weeks before the inauguration, a few Kennedy "associates" made this pledge to the press: The new president would not play golf during working hours. It would be only a matter of weeks before Kennedy broke that promise.

M ore than anything, Jack Kennedy despised losing. He was as competitive as any president, on and off the golf course.

There was a rare round in the summer of 1963 when the President was losing all his bets. Nothing was going right for Kennedy or his partner, General Chester V. Clifton, his military aide. On the 18th green, trailing by only one stroke, Clifton had to sink a straight four-foot putt to even the match and erase the day's financial losses. The general felt the pressure, taking a long time to line up the putt. Finally, he tapped the ball—actually, it was a love tap—and the ball trickled to a stop a full two feet shy of the target.

Kennedy shook his head and said, "Nice putt, *Sergeant.*"

Everyone, except Kennedy, laughed.

During a round at Seminole Country Club just north of Palm Beach, Florida, Kennedy played with Bob Hope and an old friend named Chris Dunphy, who was nearly a scratch golfer.

When Kennedy arrived twenty minutes late on the first tee, Dunphy immediately needled his old pal for the tardiness. "I've been working on important things," Kennedy said.

The two men wagered $10 a hole, an unusually high amount for the President. On the first green, Kennedy had a three-foot putt to make par. Kennedy waited a moment for the gimme, and when it was not offered, he asked, "You're going to give me this putt, aren't you, Chris?"

"No, it will develop your character," Dunphy replied.

With exaggerated exasperation, Kennedy said, "You mean to tell me I fly all the way down here to play with you and you won't give me a putt that long?"

"That's right," Dunphy replied. "If you make this, it's going to give you confidence."

As Kennedy lined up the putt, he said over his shoulder to Dunphy, "I've got an appointment with Mortimer Kaplan, the head of the IRS, at 5:30. So we'd better finish this game in a hurry."

"Pick it up," Dunphy said.

John F. Kennedy inherited his passion for golf and winning from his father, Joseph P. Kennedy, a financier and former ambassador to Great Britain who insisted that his children learn at a young age to be aggressive, think clearly, and never settle for second place. "We want winners," Joe Kennedy told his children, often. "We don't want losers here." Eunice Kennedy often said that the Kennedy family motto was "Finish First."

Kennedy's father taught this win-at-all-costs lesson not just with words but with actions. He often hurled his putter in anger when he missed a sinkable putt at the Hyannis Port Club. Joe Kennedy was a high-stakes golf gambler, wagering as much as $20,000 for a nine-hole round in Palm Beach. So the ambassador, who was only a mediocre golfer, had a lot to be upset about when things did not go his way on the links, and quite often, they did not.

But in the first round that he played in Great Britain after being sworn in as the U.S. ambassador, Joseph P. Kennedy shot a hole-in-one. The feat splashed onto the front pages of England's newspapers; it was quite a debut for the new ambassador. Jack Kennedy and his older brother, Joe Jr., could not resist sending their father a telegram that read, "Dubious about the hole-in-one." And for years afterward, the elder Kennedy used the hole-in-one as a way to remind audiences about his large family. "I am much happier being the father of nine children and making a hole-in-one," he often said, "than I would be as the father of one making a hole-in-nine."

To be accepted by the Kennedys, one had to excel at the family's unique brand of hard-knocks touch football. "It's 'touch,' but it's murder," said a family friend. "If you don't want to play, don't come. If you do come, play, or you'll be fed in the kitchen and nobody will speak to you. Don't let the girls fool you. Even pregnant, they can make you look silly."

Jack Kennedy took that competitive zeal with him to prep school at Choate, where he played golf during his senior year. And at Harvard, he earned a letter playing for the freshman golf team, which completed a short, disappointing campaign with no wins, two losses, and a tie. Kennedy played in the match against Yale, but both his twosome and foursome teams were defeated by wide margins.

Golf was also the backdrop during his courtship of Jacqueline Bouvier, the beautiful debutante who was engaged to be married to Kennedy in 1953. During a visit with Jackie's family at their estate in Rhode Island, Kennedy's wartime pal, Red Fay, tried to tempt Kennedy to play a round of golf at Newport Country Club. Fay recalled that Jack was "half tempted" to play but also "half resigned" at the inevitable consequences if he tried to play golf rather than spend some time with the family of his bride-to-be.

"Can't you see how well it will be received by the hopeful bride and her sheltering mother if the ardent husband-to-be spends his first day at her home playing golf with some old wartime buddy?" Kennedy said. "For the sake of future marital bliss and cordial mother-in-law relationship, I'll forgo the privilege of watching that big game of yours."

Instead, Kennedy agreed to drive Fay and another friend to the Newport Country Club. When they arrived, Kennedy told the men in the pro shop: "We'd like to get in a fast eighteen holes. Which will be the fastest, the front or the back nine?"

Kennedy hit a few shots off the first tee, but decided not to join them. When Fay and his friend walked off the 18th green, Kennedy was waiting for them, but he seemed distressed. "I hope you two enjoyed your game of golf," he said, "because as a result of it there was almost a total breakdown of relations between the mother of the bride and her dashing prospective son-in-law. It seems that there is a rule that non-members can play only when accompanied by a member there to sanction the match.

"I'm afraid that they feel that their worst fears are being realized. The invasion by the Irish Catholic hordes into one of the last strongholds of America's socially elite is being led by two chunky red-haired friends of the groom."

THROUGHOUT THE 1960 PRESIDENTIAL CAMPAIGN, Kennedy himself set the sports parameters: Details of his daily swims and frequent sailing excursions could be distributed to reporters, including a photograph of a young, muscular Kennedy preparing to dive into the Harvard pool. Talk of golf was strictly forbidden.

Several profiles portrayed the young Senator Kennedy as a talented athlete, but the pieces always highlighted his love of swimming and sailing. Most of the profiles were written in the glowing, gauzy language of fan magazines; it is not a stretch to imagine that some of the sentences were dictated by the press secretary or even the candidate himself. One profile began: "John F. Kennedy, a lithe, trim 43-year-old former Harvard athlete, has had to cut down on his physical activities because of the demands of his job and the rigors of campaigning but still manages some sailing and swimming."

Golf was buried deep in one lengthy profile, near the bottom and almost as an afterthought: "Since the war, he's played golf and tennis but doesn't have the time to keep up either game." Then a hint of Kennedy's golfing talent, but only a hint: "I used to shoot in the 70s," Kennedy was quoted as saying, "but not anymore."

Not anymore. That became the stock answer when reporters asked about his golf game. The profiles said nothing about Kennedy's numerous health problems.

For Kennedy, keeping his golf game out of the newspapers was quite an accomplishment because he played at least two dozen times during the presidential campaign, both on the trail and near his family's compounds in Hyannis Port and Palm Beach. Kennedy would arrive at the country club with a limited number of security men, and usually just one playing partner. He preferred to begin playing on the 7th or 8th hole and usually ended on the 15th or 16th. Kennedy almost always avoided the first, 9th, 10th, and 18th holes, which were near the clubhouse populated by snooping club members (assumed to be Republicans who would not hesitate to snitch about what they saw) and photographers armed with long-range lenses.

The most famous anecdote about Kennedy's golf phobia was the near hole-in-one he shot in July 1960, when he begged the ball to stay out of the cup at Cypress Point. Kennedy was so rattled by the near feat that he figured hush money would have been needed to safeguard the secret. "I wonder what it would have cost me to have our two trusted caddies keep quiet 'til after the convention?" he asked Red Fay.

After his razor-thin election victory over Vice President Richard M. Nixon that November, Kennedy played golf nearly two dozen times in the ten weeks before his inauguration. Early on the morning of November 15, Kennedy arrived on the first tee at the Palm Beach Country Club, a forgiving, par-68 course. It was the first time Kennedy had played in three months.

On the 18th green, one of Kennedy's playing partners, Governor Abraham A. Ribicoff of Connecticut, was asked by reporters if the president-elect had recruited him to serve as attorney general, as rumors were suggesting. Ribicoff declined to say whether Kennedy had offered him a position with his administration. When he was asked how the president-elect had played over the nine holes, Ribicoff said simply, "I shot a 43, and he beat me one up."

This was a lie. Kennedy had indeed shot a 42, but Ribicoff had shot a 38. When the president-elect saw the fib in the next day's newspaper, he sent this telegram to Ribicoff: *President deeply disturbed at newspaper report of your golf score, insists that anyone connected with his administration be clean as a hound's tooth. Write if you get work.*

Kennedy was kidding, of course. A few weeks later, Ribicoff was nominated to be the secretary of health, education, and welfare.

Every time Kennedy played golf during this transition period, the wires moved three-paragraph dispatches with almost no details, except the names of the courses where the President-elect played and the names of those he had played with. Most important, the stories were never accompanied by photographs. Think of the missed photo opportunity: The handsome, suntanned president-elect was playing golf in beautiful Palm Beach, at the height of that posh island's social season, and yet there were no images. This was Kennedy's choice. He had forbidden photographers from taking his picture on the first tee or anywhere on the golf course.

But soon there were whispers that Kennedy was playing too much golf. The week after Christmas, Salinger put out a story that Kennedy "does not plan to play golf after he enters the White House unless he's on an out-and-out vacation." The story was intended to dispel worries that the nation had replaced one duffer-in-chief with another.

"In other words, no Wednesday and Saturday afternoons at Burning Tree; no quick weekends to another course," the United Press International reported. President Eisenhower played at Burning Tree, every Wednesday and Saturday afternoon, and his "quick weekends" to other courses, particularly Augusta, were world famous. The UPI story could not have been any less subtle.

ALMOST IMMEDIATELY after moving into the White House, the President pined to play golf, despite the chilly Washington winter. Kennedy had been bitten by the golf bug down in Palm Beach.

On February 20, 1961, with patches of snow still on the ground, Kennedy finally played his first round of golf as president at the Chevy Chase Club with Red Fay, Senator Smathers, and Senator Symington. Fay explained that the foursome began on a tee far from the first "to avoid any photographers who might have been tipped off that the President was going to play golf."

"If the word leaks out," Kennedy said that day, "I can just see some eager reporter writing, 'The new President couldn't even wait until the snow was off the ground before engaging in his first game of golf as President. At this rate President Kennedy could devote more time to the golf links than his predecessor.'"

Fay recalled that during Eisenhower's presidency, newspapers had published photographs of Secret Service men walking on the edge of the fairways carrying golf bags, and visible from the top were not woods and irons but the butts of rifles and machine guns. That morning at the Chevy Chase club, Fay noticed the same Secret Service men trying to look inconspicuous, wearing golf attire and keeping their weapons concealed. Because they spent most of their time in the sand traps, they appeared to be bad golfers, Fay said. "They were as conspicuous out on the course as someone attending a formal dinner in a sport shirt," he said.

Before the foursome teed off, Kennedy informed Fay that for the purposes of wagering, they would be on the same team, playing against Smathers and Symington. And the Kennedy "con," as some friends called it, began. Kennedy's greatest weapon was not in his golf bag; it was his conniving, competitive mind.

From before the first tee to moments before the final putt, Kennedy used a running commentary to exploit any of his playing partners' weaknesses. Kennedy often persuaded playing partners to give him a generous handicap or fat odds.

It was this "con," usually delivered on the first tee, that was "the smoothest part of his game," his press secretary, Pierre Salinger, recalled.

"As golf is a mind game, he was incredible against any kind of competitor," said Ethel Kennedy, JFK's sister-in-law. "Even if they were a very low handicap, he could sort of talk them out of the hole."

"Never more than $4 or $5 would change hands in a match," Salinger recalled, "but JFK would play for it as if it were the national debt." He said the secret to the JFK con was the wagering. "Through a complex system of betting, which only he understood fully, JFK won most of his matches before the first ball was even hit," Salinger said. "There were bets not only on who won the hole, but for the longest drive, first on the green, closet to the pin, and first in the

President Kennedy grabs a presidential golf ball from a young caddy before setting up the "con" and then teeing off at Hyannis Port Country Club in August 1963. The "con" was Kennedy's ability to persuade his playing partners to give him fat odds, or a generous handicap, almost always to their regret by the final hole.

hole. In addition, there were automatic press bets whenever one team fell two holes behind and bonus points for birdies and tee shots holding the green on par-3s. Just keeping track of the bets gave his opponents little time to concentrate on their game. But the President was also a master psychologist."

And on this day at Chevy Chase, President Kennedy wasted no time looking for that edge.

"Smathers," the President said, "it is common knowledge that you are probably the finest golfer on the Hill, which in no way implies the slightest dereliction of duty. Stu is one of those few naturally gifted golfers, but in spite of the obvious overwhelming odds, Red and I will still take you on." The President did not wait for an answer.

"Because of the snow, we weren't permitted to go onto the greens," Fay said. "Large six-inch diameter cans had been embedded in the turf in front of the regular greens and the grass had been clipped as short as possible so these areas could serve as temporary greens. To keep some distance from the clubhouse, we made up our holes as we went along, sometimes hitting from one tee across several fairways to the hole of another fairway."

As the foursome played, they ran into Phyllis Dillon, the wife of Secretary of the Treasury Douglas Dillon. Mrs. Dillon was completely unnerved by having to tee off while President Kennedy watched. "If I could have picked up my ball and run, I would have been a lot happier," she said later. "I'm just not accustomed to holding up the play of the President of the United States."

Later in the match, Kennedy said he needed to get in touch with Stewart Udall, the secretary of the interior. A Secret Service man with a walkie-talkie was summoned and transmitted the President's urgent message, but Udall could not be found. Kennedy could not pass up the moment, asking with a trace of mock indignation: "How are we supposed to run a government if the people in positions of responsibility aren't available when needed?"

Trouble awaited the foursome on the 7th green, where a platoon of photographers and reporters had camped out. Kennedy called an audible; the game was over. "The presidential limousine was called, and soon appeared on the course," Fay said. "Almost before those waiting for him were conscious of it, he was in his limousine and gone. Just as suddenly, the bond was broken between the two senators and myself. We didn't even bother to play out the hole, but instead went our separate ways. The excitement of our game had also disappeared in that limousine."

Ben Bradlee, Kennedy's friend who later became the legendary editor of the *Washington Post*, said the President was "fun to play golf with, once you get out of sight of the sightseers, primarily because he doesn't take the game seriously and keeps up a running conversation." In his book, *Conversations with Kennedy,* Bradlee wrote:

If he shanks one into the drink, he could let go with a broad-A "bah-stard," but he would be teeing up his next shot instantly. With his opponent comfortably home in two and facing a tough approach, he might say, "No profile needed here, just courage," a self-deprecating reference to his book, *Profiles in Courage.* When he was losing, he would play the old warrior at the end of a brilliant career, asking only that his faithful caddy point him in the right direction, and let instinct take over. He could play TV golf commentator as he hits the ball, saying, "With barely a glance at the packed gallery, he whips out a four iron and slaps it dead to the pin." He is competitive as hell, with a natural swing, but erratic through lack of steady play.

In the weeks after that first round in the snow, Kennedy continued to sneak out to Burning Tree or Chevy Chase to play quick, partial rounds, hoping to avoid the press and the public by bringing along as few Secret Service agents as possible. Despite all the precautions, the President's arrival at a country club was as covert as a presidential motorcade can be.

RUMORS ABOUT WOMEN DOGGED KENNEDY, first in the Senate after his marriage to Jacqueline Bouvier, then on the campaign trail, and finally into the White House. In the first days of his administration, some reporters assumed Kennedy was spending time with beautiful young women when in fact he was innocently puttering around Burning Tree on weekday afternoons. Reporters had no idea that Kennedy was "sneaking over to the Burning Tree Club to play golf on the sly," as Salinger put it.

"Only after Kennedy's afternoon disappearances became the subject of wild rumors was the story officially confirmed," Salinger observed. Salinger was forced to admit to reporters, "Yes, Kennedy was a pretty good golfer."

It took these wild early rumors about Kennedy's affairs with women to force Salinger to confirm the truth: Kennedy was golfing and, yes, even on weekday afternoons, just as Ike had done. Of course, playing golf on weekday afternoons violated the President's own pledge only to play golf during "an out-and-out vacation."

But was Kennedy really playing golf? Was golf just a cover story?

"The less said about it the better," Salinger said, referring to the golf, not the women, "lest he be compared with 'The Great Golfer,' as Kennedy's chum Gore Vidal had tabbed Eisenhower. Even after his 'addiction to golf' was disclosed, Kennedy refused to be photographed swinging a Number Five Iron." Salinger explained that this No Five Iron rule was simple: "Photographs could be taken of the President standing on the first tee, but not swinging a club."

On April 5, 1961, Americans got their first glimpse of President Kennedy, the golfer, in a photograph published on the front page of the *New York Times* and other newspapers. The photograph shows President Kennedy, dressed in a white polo shirt, khaki pants, and loafers, standing on the first tee of the Palm Beach Country Club. It was the final day of Kennedy's Easter weekend in Florida, where he played golf every day. With a somewhat sheepish smile, Kennedy stands talking to his father, who holds a wooden driver in his right hand. Father and son are flanked by two of JFK's brothers-in-law, Stephen Smith and Peter Lawford.

But instantly, the photo seems odd, as if something is missing. Kennedy stands awkwardly, almost ramrod straight, with his hands by his side. The President is not holding a golf club. Neither is Lawford, and neither is Smith. How often do you see a foursome on the first tee, and three players are not holding golf clubs? It looks as if Jack Kennedy and his two pals are on the first tee to do nothing more than wish the old man some luck before he tees off, by himself.

"For reasons he never made clear," the *Times* reported, "the President has been unwilling to allow news photographers near him while he was on the links." After the photographers were sent home and the round began, Kennedy hit a golf ball that struck a Secret Service agent in the head. The ball bounced once before hitting the agent, who told Kennedy he was not hurt. However, the President insisted that the agent be taken to a local hospital for a checkup. Three holes later, the agent, who was never identified, returned to the links.

But Kennedy used the incident for one of his favorite golf quips: "It is true that my predecessor did not object, as I do, to pictures of one's golf skill in action. But neither, on the other hand, did he ever bean a Secret Service man." As usual, Kennedy used humor to defuse even a minor issue and disarm the critics. "One boon result" to these stories, according to Victor Lasky, the author of *JFK: The Man and the Myth*, "was that political pitchmen who used to worry lest the nation be lost on the back nine weren't worrying out loud any more."

As it turned out, the public was never critical of Kennedy's golf playing. Kennedy was careful not to play too often, and the public never thought of him as a golfer, first. Even after his death, Kennedy was remembered fondly for tossing footballs, not hitting golf balls.

THEODORE SORENSEN, Kennedy's speechwriter, observed, "This administration is going to do for sex what the previous one did for golf." That first published photo of Kennedy-the-golfer allowed golf to come out of the closet—partly, anyway. The photo squelched some of the rumors that swirled around the White House. Reporters continued to wonder, and whisper, about other games the President was undoubtedly playing.

Fidel Castro probably saw the stories in the winter of 1961 about Kennedy and his golf game. Castro had criticized Eisenhower for playing golf and had heaped scorn on the game, saying it appealed only to "the idle rich and exploiters of the people." But even Castro could not resist dipping into the game, despite its connection to capitalist imperialism. In March, after playing his first round of golf in years, Castro stated flatly that he could defeat Kennedy.

Accompanied by two other government officials, Castro played at the Colinas de Villareal Golf Club, just across the bay from Havana. For the round, Castro and his playing partners wore olive-green army uniforms, big black boots, and civilian militia berets.

"I could win over Kennedy easily," Castro, a gifted athlete, declared afterward. But he did not stop there. He said he could also beat Eisenhower, and the president of the United Fruit Company.

According to a dispatch from Havana in the *New York Times*, Castro claimed to have won the first hole, and Che Guevara, who said he had been a caddy in his native Argentina, won the second. But "there were no further details about the game," reporter R. Hart Phillips wrote.

An enterprising Associated Press reporter extracted the truth from a sixteen-year-old caddy who had carried Castro's golf bag. Castro's score easily exceeded 150, the caddy said. Guevara defeated the dictator by shooting a 127.

There was no comment from the Americans about Castro's boast. But in a matter of weeks, Castro would have the last laugh. Kennedy approved the Bay of Pigs invasion, a disaster that would turn out to be the worst moment of his presidency.

The day after the failed military operation, Kennedy played a round of golf with his friend Charles Spalding. "We were just knocking golf balls aimlessly," Spalding said. "And all he'd say is, 'How could I do it? How could I?'"

Once it became widely known that Kennedy not only played golf but played relatively well, it did not take long for reporters to begin pining for a head-to-head match between Kennedy and Eisenhower. An article in the *Washington Evening Star* carried a headline that tantalized readers with a promise it could not deliver: "Big Golf Day A-Coming, Eisenhower Vs. Kennedy."

An unnamed source who had played with both men confided to the Associated Press that a match between Ike and JFK would be close, though Kennedy would likely win. "If Kennedy played as frequently as did Eisenhower," the source said, "there'd be no contest." The source also said this about Kennedy's ability: "When he's on his game, he's as tough as a cop."

The Associated Press sent an army of reporters to find out whether Kennedy was better than Eisenhower. "Not all the returns are in," the AP reported, "but from what old-hand White House reporters have learned from authoritative stories, we are led inescapably to the conclusion: Yes, he probably is."

Kennedy dismissed the notion that he play a match against Eisenhower as a "frivolous idea." But on April 21, Ike and JFK had lunch together at Camp David, the wooded presidential retreat in western Maryland's Catoctin Mountain Park. The former president was harshly critical of the new president; Eisenhower spent several long

*Not long after the disastrous Bay of Pigs invasion of Cuba,
President Kennedy was upbraided by former President
Eisenhower as they walked down a wooded path at Camp
David. At the end of their frosty visit on April 21, 1961, Kennedy
suggested a future golf game to his predecessor. But JFK had no
intention of playing a round with Ike.*

minutes berating some of the bad decisionmaking that had led to
the botched Bay of Pigs invasion in Cuba a few days earlier.

"No one knows how tough this job is until after he has been in it
a few months," Kennedy told Ike.

"Mr. President," Eisenhower said, "if you will forgive me, I think I
mentioned that to you three months ago."

"I certainly have learned a lot since," Kennedy said.

That night, Eisenhower wrote in his diary: "He took me in his car
to the heliport and suggested a golf game in the near future."

By the end of their long day together, President Kennedy was still stung by the harsh criticism leveled by the old general. Kennedy had probably run out of things to say, and the suggestion of a future golf game undoubtedly was an attempt to lighten the mood. But Kennedy had no intention of ever playing golf with Ike, whom he often privately called "that old asshole."

Two weeks after Kennedy and Ike's frosty meeting, the White House was confronted with a potential scandal over golf. (Kennedy must have thought: Aha! My worries about golf were well founded after all!) Newspapers, still digesting the news about Kennedy's affection for the game, were full of breathless reports that Mrs. Kennedy had given the President, as a birthday gift, a private golf course at Glen Ora, an estate near Middleburg, Virginia. The Kennedys had occasionally visited Glen Ora on weekends.

Kennedy seethed over the stories of the private golf course and demanded that his press aides knock it down. Even Ike did not own a private golf course.

"The story is ridiculous and untrue," Andrew Hatcher, the associate press secretary, told reporters. Hatcher pointed out that the cattle on the course constituted real, four-legged hazards. One biography, however, said the White House denials "seemed to protest too much."

Like so much with Kennedy, there was a bit of truth to it.

Ben Bradlee recalled playing the course with Kennedy. "It consisted of about 9,000 square yards of pasture, filled with small hills, big rocks and even a swamp, quickly dubbed 'the water hole' by Kennedy," he wrote in *Conversations with Kennedy*. "Jackie persuaded a hunt-country friend to reduce the wiry grass from about sixteen inches to four inches with a brush hog, and in each corner of the pasture they cut small plots down to two inches. These are both the tees and the greens, which require a five iron instead of a putter to negotiate."

Bradlee called it a "golf course," with the quotation marks included. And he said he observed the President shooting the course record—a 37 for four holes. The 37 was a feat, however, because each of the four holes was a par-9; Kennedy shot a 1-over-par on a cow pasture!

Kennedy was frustrated not just with the cow pasture course. He was restless and bored during those weekends at Glen Ora. He was there because Jackie loved riding her horses across the lush Virginia countryside.

On a few Virginia weekends, Kennedy would sneak off for a few holes of real golf at the nearby Fauquier Springs Country Club. He spent most of his time at Glen Ora slumped in front of the television—watching college and pro football games, and the Sunday morning talk shows *Meet the Press* and *Face the Nation*.

IN MAY 1961, Kennedy shoveled dirt too rapidly during a tree-planting ceremony in Ottawa and injured his back, knocking him off the links for more than two years. The injury put the President on crutches, though he was never seen with them in public. To rehabilitate his back, he swam every day in the White House swimming pool, but he did not play golf again until July 5, 1963, at Hyannis Port. Kennedy played only five holes, but this time he did not seem to worry about the photographers. He played the "inside five"—the first, second, 16th, 17th, and 18th holes, all easily visible by anyone watching from the clubhouse. Aides declined to divulge his score, but it was reported that he shot a 5 on the par-4 18th hole.

Kennedy had desperately missed playing golf, his friends said, and he was committed to playing as much as possible and even wanted to get his score into the mid-70s.

A week later, Kennedy played with Red Fay; Sir David Ormsby-Gore, the British ambassador to the United States; his brother, Senator Edward M. Kennedy of Massachusetts; and Stephen Smith, his brother-in-law. For three consecutive summer evenings, Kennedy

*On occasion, Jacqueline Kennedy joined her husband on
the golf course, and on rarer occasions, they were able to steal
a private moment, such as this one at Hyannis Port on
September 13, 1963. This photograph was taken during one
of the last rounds that Kennedy played.*

played the challenging Hyannis Port club course, hitting powerful
drives and showing no signs of his back ailment.

Late that summer, Kennedy hired Cecil Stoughton, the White
House photographer, to take some 8-millimeter film of him as he
played at Hyannis Port. The film, broadcast in 2001 on the Golf
Channel for the first time, shows the beauty of the President's full
swing off the tee, as well as his putting stroke and smooth chipping
stroke. Stoughton's camera also captured Kennedy addressing the
ball, stroking it, and then watching it, usually with a big smile.

The film was intended for Arnold Palmer, the professional golfer

Kennedy most admired. "He said he wanted to show it to someone like Arnie," Stoughton said. "It was natural—you only go to the top to get that kind of critique."

President Kennedy had planned to invite Palmer to the White House late in 1963 to watch the film and help tinker with the mechanics of the presidential swing. Stoughton said there were plans to do it sometime in December, after a quick trip to Texas.

After Kennedy was assassinated in Dallas on November 22, 1963, most of the tributes to the fallen president focused on his verve and vision, the way he inspired the nation. Some also described him the way Kennedy himself had once described his older brother, Joe Jr.: Even when he was standing still, JFK seemed to be in motion.

"This is a time when the heart is heavy and tears come unbidden to the eyes," wrote Pulitzer Prize–winning sportswriter Arthur Daley in the *New York Times* after that long weekend when the nation mourned its slain president. "Only the mind can see and it still carries the image of a buoyant, laughing and vibrantly alive John Fitzgerald Kennedy in attendance at baseball games and football games. It brings back pictures of him as a golfer, a swimmer, a sailor, a lover of all sports."

Daley continued, "He was quite a man, even when viewed from the circumscribed world of sports. Another sports term kept flickering to mind during television's remarkable portrayal of the events of the last few days. The word is: Thoroughbred. It can be applied in its most majestic connotations to his widow. Class always will tell. John Fitzgerald Kennedy had it, too."

Dwight D. Eisenhower

"Don't Ask What I Shot"

*Everyone at the White House knew when Dwight D.
Eisenhower had shot a good round of golf by reading the
expression on his face. It was the only way to learn how he
was swinging the clubs because Ike ordered his playing
partners and aides to keep the tiny digits on his scorecards a
secret.*

I love the game, no matter how badly I play.
—Dwight D. Eisenhower

I T ALL BEGAN WITH IKE.
Before Dwight D. Eisenhower moved into the White House in 1953, Americans viewed a president hitting a golf ball with a mixture of bemusement and bewilderment. Something just did not seem right about it. Ike changed that perception forever.

Ike's enthusiasm for the game far exceeded the affection demonstrated two generations earlier by his most avid golfing predecessors, Woodrow Wilson and William Howard Taft. Wilson played the highest number of rounds of any president, but Ike was obsessed. Even off the fairways and greens, Ike devoted countless hours to thinking about golf, contemplating the game's intricacies and intangibles, worrying over the kinks in his putting stroke, dissecting his latest round's highs and lows, meditating over the mechanics of that perfect sand wedge swing, plotting a quick getaway to his next round, and dreaming—*always* dreaming—about shooting a hole-in-one.

Unlike his predecessors, Ike played the game well, finishing often in the 80s and managing, on nearly a dozen glorious occasions, to shoot legitimate scores in the high 70s.

On the first Saturday in February 1953, one of Ike's first weekends living in the White House, Eisenhower awakened to a drizzly, bone-chilling morning. Gloomily gazing out the second-floor window, the President was as crushed as a child is on a snowless Christmas morning. "Today, the President wanted to play golf very, very badly," Ike's secretary, Ann Whitman, wrote in her diary. "He peered at the sky during the morning and finally after another excursion out to the porch announced, 'Sometimes I feel so sorry for myself I could cry!'"

Only a washed-out golf outing carried the power to push the wizened old general to the edge of tears.

He was not just a student and fan of the game; he was its most devout evangelist. In a letter to "golfers and fellow duffers" on May 1, 1953, Eisenhower wrote: "While I know that I speak with the partisanship of an enthusiast, golf obviously provides one of our best forms of healthful exercise accompanied by good fellowship and companionship. It is a sport in which the whole American family can participate—fathers and mothers, sons and daughters alike. It offers healthy respite from daily toil, refreshment of body and mind."

Leaders of the golf industry could not have written a more enthusiastic endorsement for the game. After playing nearly 800 rounds of golf across eight years in the White House, Ike did more to boost the fortunes of America's fledgling golf industry than any other special interest group seeking favors from the administration. Ike made the game cool and accessible, lifting the game's popularity to unimaginable heights. And he did it almost single-handedly—though in his second term he was assisted by the emergence of Arnold Palmer. In particular, the President motivated millions of men who were age forty or older to try the game for the first time.

Not long after Ike lavished the presidential seal of approval on the game, the chief of the capital's public courses exclaimed, "Ever since he went into the White House, all you hear is golf, golf, golf. People like to follow the leader."

Oh, how they followed. In 1953, when Eisenhower took office, an estimated 3.2 million Americans played golf on the 5,045 courses in the United States. By 1961, the number of American golfers had doubled, and there were too few tee times to meet the surging demand. Fred Corcoran, a senior official of the Professional Golfers Association of America, said that Eisenhower's dedication to golf was "the greatest thing that ever happened to the game."

"Whatever remained to be done to remove the last traces of the average man's carefully nurtured prejudice against a game originally linked with the wealthy and aloof was done by President Eisenhower," wrote the historian Herbert Warren Wind. "Probably few men in the long history of the game have ever been bitten by the golf bug quite as badly as the President."

The golf bug placed Ike completely and helplessly at the game's mercy. His ups and downs on the course were directly responsible for dramatic swings in his mood during his workdays. His aides never asked his score—that information was off limits. But they could venture a good guess, just by looking at the expression on his face or reading his body language. When his putting was at its worst, Ike was insufferably irritable and short-tempered, glowering his way through meetings with aides. When he discovered a temporary solution to his slice or his putting woes, he bounced from meeting to meeting, always with a quick quip and a warm smile, and the gloominess at the White House lifted for everyone.

His aides and friends prayed for good golf. And they became convinced the game was as necessary to Ike's mental health as a good night's sleep. "Without golf now," Major General Howard Snyder, the President's personal physician said, "he'd be like a caged lion, with all these tensions building up inside him. If this fellow couldn't play golf, I'd have a nut case on my hands."

His love of golf was so complete that it has endured across the decades. Exactly a half century after taking the oath of office, Dwight Eisenhower is remembered as much for being a golf fanatic as he is for his war heroics and his eight-year stewardship of a placid and prosperous era in American history.

ALMOST EVERY MORNING, golf was among the first things on Eisenhower's mind. Moments after lifting his head off the pillow, he grabbed a pitching wedge and started swinging it repeatedly to warm up his wrists and arms. He carried the club from the White House private residence to the Oval Office, where it rested against a credenza, though never for too long.

At certain moments of every day, Ike treated the Oval Office with the casualness of a country club locker room. Sometimes, while dictating letters to his secretary, he took practice swings with an 8-iron. After word of this practice was whispered around the capital, Ike's aides adamantly denied it, though they acknowledged that the President had taken practice swings while dictating letters during a summit meeting of the North Atlantic Treaty Organization in Paris. Still, few Washington insiders believed the denials because it was so easy to envision Ike taking practice swings in the Oval Office.

Near the end of almost every afternoon, Eisenhower sat in his high-backed chair, behind Theodore Roosevelt's old, battered desk, and slipped on his golf cleats. He then grabbed his putter, his wedge, and his favorite club, the 8-iron, and walked toward the French doors leading out to the South Lawn, his cleats clacking loudly while leaving a trail of tiny holes in the wooden floorboards.

Ike had been in office less than a month when he slipped into his backyard with his golf clubs one sleepy Saturday afternoon and began spraying iron shots around the South Lawn. With the majestic White House as a backdrop, the President's valet, John Moaney, shagged the balls and replenished the President's supply.

A reporter just happened to be walking along the executive mansion's iron gates, spotted the President, and dashed into the White House press room with the news: "Guess what he's doing—playing golf on the south grounds!" Every member of the press corps ran out to the street for a first glimpse of Eisenhower chipping balls at an imaginary green. Within minutes, a dozen still photographers pointed large telephoto lenses to capture the moment. Newsreel cameramen shot film footage, which was seen by millions of Americans in movie theaters the following week. Traffic slowed to a crawl around the White House.

Wearing a sweater and cap, Ike practiced for fifty-five minutes. Two photographers for *Life* magazine, Mark Kauffman and Hank Walker, captured some of the first images of President Eisenhower swinging his 8-iron on the South Lawn. Under the headline "Ike Finds a Fairway," *Life* reported that "the President's eyes fell on what others would have always thought of as the South Lawn of the White House but which his golfer's eye instantly re-identified."

Ike did not seem to object to the attention that first day, though the crowds and the noise eventually became an annoyance, forcing him to hide in a police shack on the White House grounds until the spectators dispersed. "You know," the President said, "once in a while I get to the point, with everybody staring at me, where I want to go way back indoors and pull down the curtain."

Ike persevered. By late spring, the leaves on the trees shielded the President from the street. Eventually, the novelty wore off. By autumn, Eisenhower's golf practice attracted the attention of only a handful of passing tourists who waved a friendly hello to their president.

In the gymnasium in the White House basement, Ike ordered the construction of a netted practice range so he could hit hundreds of tee shots. And just outside his office door, Ike practiced his putting on a custom-built putting green, funded in the spring of 1954 by private donations and constructed with the assistance of the United States Golf Association. The green had two undersized holes, designed to help the President improve his putting, and a small sand trap. White House gardeners became skilled at repairing the dozens of divots surrounding the green.

Over the years, some impediments complicated Ike's backyard practice regimen. In the spring of 1955, an unruly gang of gray squirrels defaced the President's White House putting green with unnatural divots composed of scratch marks and buried acorns. "The next time you see a squirrel go near my putting green, take a gun and shoot it!" Ike ordered several Secret Service agents. Of course, murdering the squirrels was never a serious option. Instead, the Secret Service agents trapped three of them; two were relocated to the capital's Rock Creek Park, and the third was released in the Virginia woods.

Secret Service agents were less worried about the squirrels and more concerned that an assassin might try to shoot the President as he practiced on the South Lawn, or even while he was putting around on his more secluded practice green.

"Point out one of those fellers to me," Ike told the agents, "and I'll show you a direct hit at 250 yards."

DWIGHT D. EISENHOWER WAS BORN on October 14, 1890, in Denison, Texas, and before he turned two, the family moved to Abilene, Kansas, a small town that introduced him to the pleasures of the outdoors. As a young boy, he learned to fish in Mud Creek, located seven blocks from his house, and the Smoky Hill River, just two miles south of town. Eisenhower loved all sports, but his favorites were baseball and football, which he played at Abilene High School. Eisenhower was a center fielder with a big bat—his baseball team lost only one game during his senior year and that was to a team of freshmen from the University of Kansas. On the high school football team, he played right defensive end and had a reputation for tough, aggressive play.

Eisenhower went on to the United States Military Academy at West Point, where he played linebacker for the varsity football team. At five feet eleven inches and 180 pounds, Ike's hard-hitting tackles and hustle earned him the nickname "the Kansas Cyclone." Some fans believed Ike possessed enough talent to qualify for the All-American team.

During Ike's short stint on the varsity team, West Point played tiny Carlisle Indian School, whose team was led by Jim Thorpe, the All-American halfback and future Olympic hero. Eisenhower and teammate Charles Benedict managed to halt one Carlisle scoring drive by gang tackling Thorpe. But later in the game, Thorpe bowled over Eisenhower and Benedict, who crashed headfirst into each other. Both men had to be removed from the game. Carlisle went on to rout Army, 27–6.

In the next game, against Tufts University, Ike injured his knee and then further damaged it when he attempted to get on a horse, forcing him to end his football career. The injury devastated Eisenhower; his roommate said he lost his will to live. He stayed close to the game as an assistant coach for Army, watching glumly from the sidelines as Notre Dame, led by legendary coach Knute Rockne, used the innovative forward pass to embarrass Army in November 1913, in a game that marked a turning point in the sport's history.

In 1925, at the age of thirty-five, Eisenhower played his first round of golf while attending the army's Command and General Staff

School at Fort Leavenworth, Kansas. His wife, Mamie, encouraged him to try the game as a way to relieve stress. Golf immediately rekindled Eisenhower's competitive fire. At an Eisenhower family reunion in June 1926, Dwight and his three brothers played at the Abilene Country Club, where Ike managed to shoot in the 80s just a year after first picking up the clubs.

Ike continued to play through the 1930s while stationed in Washington and in the Philippines. Even while serving as a general in Europe during World War II, Supreme Allied Commander Eisenhower found time to play a few holes of golf. His rural hideaway south of London, Telegraph Cottage, was located within walking distance of two golf courses. Ike and his naval aide, Captain Harry C. Butcher, worked hard to avoid the course's war-made hazards—deep craters cut into the earth by German bombs.

After the war, Eisenhower became the army chief of staff and began playing golf four or five times a week at Burning Tree Country Club just outside Washington, D.C. He also played the game often as president of Columbia University and then as the supreme commander of the North Atlantic Treaty Organization.

On a vacation following World War II, Eisenhower played eighteen holes at the Augusta National Golf Club, and the visit would change his life. Ike and Mamie fell in love with the place and knew early on during that first stay that they wanted to become members. In 1948, Ike joined the exclusive club, and he remained a dues-paying member until his death in 1969. Ike's association with Augusta was a major boost to the Masters tournament, the club's professional tournament, because he was one of its biggest fans, often visiting the course the week following the tournament to congratulate its champion.

Eisenhower resigned from NATO to run for president in 1952. Most profiles of the Republican nominee described his love of golf, but Ike's playing was curtailed by the rigors of the campaign. Even so, he managed to shoot a few good rounds, including an 84 at one of his favorite courses, the Cherry Hills Country Club in Denver.

Voter turnout by golfers was astounding, and golfers liked to think that it propelled Eisenhower to the White House, though their support was not really needed as Eisenhower cruised to victory over Democrat Adlai Stevenson. Maury Luxford, who ran the Bing Crosby golf tournament at Pebble Beach, created an organization called the National Golfers Committee for Ike. Luxford pledged to recruit three Republican members in every country club in the United States to "get golfers out of the clubhouse on Election Day," an Ike campaign aide wrote in a memorandum.

The first thing Ike did after winning the presidency was fly to Augusta, where he played golf every day during a ten-day celebratory vacation with aides and more than one future member of his administration.

Several weeks before Ike's inauguration, a nationally syndicated columnist named Henry McLemore wrote a prescient column: "I can picture the changes that will take place at the White House when the Eisenhowers move in. The General probably will build an 18-hole course on the lawn and drain the swimming pool for a putting green. And I'll bet you that the Cabinet will have to wait more than once while the President practices chip shots or tries to improve his swing."

SHORTLY AFTER 7:30 ONE EVENING in May 1953, one of Eisenhower's top aides was notified that the President had just left the White House grounds for the Burning Tree Country Club.

"Good Lord," the aide exclaimed. "He's not using luminous golf balls, is he?"

No, the aide was told, the President was headed to the club for a dinner party with a group of Republican senators. If luminous golf balls had been invented, of course, Ike would have played until midnight.

The aide's worry about Ike's all-consuming devotion to golf was well placed. From the earliest days of the first term, golf loomed as a potential political hazard. Ike's golf made an irresistible target for the Democrats because enough Americans were uncomfortable with the idea that their president was hopelessly obsessed with a game, especially one that catered to the rich. In fact, Ike helped cement the long-held opinion that golf was a Republican game.

Eisenhower's political opponents portrayed him as a full-time golfer who moonlighted as president. And most of the harshest criticism dripped with condescension. The President was written off as "a nice old gentleman in a golf cart" by Joseph and Stewart Alsop, the nationally syndicated columnists.

Senator Wayne Morse, an Oregon Independent, proclaimed on the floor of the Senate that Eisenhower should demonstrate "more interest in increasing employment and less interest in his golf score."

Political satirists and comedians found golf was one way that audiences did not mind seeing their president skewered. One joke had the President and his playing partners asking a slow foursome ahead of them if they could play through.

"What's your hurry?" Ike was asked.

"The Russians have just bombed New York."

Another quip: "I suppose that we'll have a national holiday if the President ever makes a hole-in-one."

In 1956, a bumper sticker declared: "Ben Hogan for President. If we're going to have a golfer, let's have a good one."

Shortly after Ike's first few trips to the Burning Tree Country Club, officials at the Democratic Party's national headquarters announced that they were tabulating Eisenhower's golf rounds, and they vowed to share the statistics with the voters, presumably in the fall of 1956. Several labor unions also began counting Ike's visits to the golf course.

At a press conference during a bitter federal budget crisis, a reporter asked Eisenhower if he was going to undergo some cost cutting himself by forgoing the "pair of helicopters that have been proposed for getting you out to the golf course a little faster than you can make it by car." "Well," said Ike, his eyes fixed with fury at the inquisitor, "I don't think much of the question because no helicopters have been procured for me to go to a golf course." When the reporter attempted to pose a follow-up question, Ike snapped,

"Thank you—that is all." Later, he seethed over the question, telling aides it was both inappropriate and disrespectful. (After playing eighteen holes at Burning Tree Country Club on June 9, 1960, Eisenhower was ferried back to the White House on an army helicopter. By then, the press made only a passing mention of the President's post-golf helicopter ride.)

In the spring of 1955, several congressmen criticized Ike's decision to evict squirrels from the White House grounds after the animals tampered with the presidential putting green. A few Democrats started the "Save the White House Squirrels Fund" to pay for an aluminum fence to ring the green.

Senator Richard L. Neuberger, Democrat of Oregon, asked President Eisenhower to spare the White House squirrels. "Tolerate a few scratches and bumps on your private putting green in order to continue a fine and colorful heritage of White House squirrels," Neuberger beseeched the President from the Senate floor.

The White House had no comment, but the issue simmered for several weeks. A conservationist was caught releasing a new pack of squirrels on the White House lawn. Ike's aides announced that they would no longer trap the squirrels. Senator Neuberger donated the $202.48 raised in the Save the White House Squirrels Fund to the Wildlife Management Institute. While scoffing at the creation of yet another Washington special interest group, Ike could not pass up an opportunity to joke about the controversy, saying he envied the relocated squirrels their freedom. "A freedom I would personally dearly love," he said, somewhat sadly.

Democrats joked that Ike had devised a thirty-six-hole work week. It was literally true, at least when Eisenhower was in the capital. He played thirty-six holes a week at Burning Tree, a round on Wednesday afternoon and another on Saturday morning. The greens fee at the club was raised on those two days, and some club members suspected the higher fee was intended to discourage play to keep the course less congested for the President.

Ike invited much of the criticism with his own golf-crazed remarks. He blamed the pressures of the office on adding eight strokes

To commemorate Ike's famous admonition against divulging his golf score, Golf Digest *distributed buttons that the President, more than once, was happy to pin on his chest, along with a wide grin.*

to his score shortly after becoming President. After shooting a 96 at Burning Tree, Ike snapped, "If I don't improve, I'm going to pass a law that no one can ask me my golf score."

"Don't Ask What I Shot," was emblazoned on thousands of buttons by *Golf Digest.* More than once, Ike wore the button as he played.

He grumbled that his worries about the affairs of state had undermined his confidence with the clubs. Sometimes, a government problem entered his mind "right in the middle of my backswing," and, needless to say, the ball never ended up where it was aimed. Ike was also distracted by his worries about the plight of American farmers, telling reporters, "My golf would be a lot better if somebody would do something about the price of beef."

A journalist visiting the Oval Office observed that Eisenhower was wearing a bandage on his left wrist. The President explained it was intended to mend an arthritic condition. The visitor said at least it was not a serious injury. "I should say it is serious!" Eisenhower boomed. "It means that I can't play golf!"

Those remarks sent a powerful message to the people that golf was near the top of the President's list of priorities.

In early September 1953, Ike completed a work-and-play vacation in Denver, but he seemed to devote more time to play than work, carding eighteen holes every day, sometimes twenty-seven holes. Reporters estimated that he played a total of nearly twenty rounds in two weeks. Senior White House aides were becoming increasingly uneasy over all the chatter about Ike's golf. When he returned to Washington, Ike did not play for nearly two months. There were two cover stories released by the White House: One was that Ike had a sore elbow. The other was that the President simply wanted to spend extra time with his grandchildren, who were visiting. But Merriman Smith, a White House correspondent for United Press International, discovered that Ike's golfing hiatus was "definitely because of the anti-golf reaction."

Then something unexpected happened. Harry S Truman rushed to Ike's defense. Truman and Eisenhower had had a strained relationship, in part because Ike's 1952 campaign had been deeply critical of Truman's leadership. But now Truman proclaimed that the criticism of Ike's golf-playing was ridiculous and unpatriotic. "To criticize the President because he uses a helicopter to fly to his home, to yap at him because he plays a game of golf is unfair and downright picayunish," President Truman said. "He has the same right to relax from the heavy burdens of the greatest office as any other man."

After Truman's declaration, several leading Democratic senators privately put out the word to other party strategists that it was time to "back off" their golf criticism. There was deep concern that the criticism of the popular president would backfire and would damage the Democrats. One senator told his colleagues that the "fence in" Ike strategy would impose "unnecessary psychological burdens" on him.

But not all Democrats agreed to back off. Some senior Democratic strategists were convinced that golf made Eisenhower vulnerable. Perplexed by the criticism, senior White House aides and Republican strategists complained to reporters that Truman's frequent poker playing and rides on the government yacht up the Potomac merited almost no criticism by the press. "Justifiably or not, much of the public associate golf with country clubs and country clubs with high society and snobbery—something most people cannot afford," wrote Merriman Smith.

Ike suffered a heart attack while vacationing in Denver on September 24, 1955. The day before, he had played twenty-seven holes of golf. Eisenhower stayed in the hospital nearly three months, and nearly five months elapsed before Ike played his next round—nine holes at Thomasville, Georgia, in February 1956. Doctors had asked the President to try to play less intensively, and, on the first tee, Ike warned his playing partners, "You're going to hear a heck of a lot of laughter today. My doctor has given me orders that if I don't start laughing instead of cussing when I miss those shots, he's going to stop me from playing golf. So every time I miss a shot, you're going to hear a haw-haw-haw."

Eisenhower's aides told reporters that Ike's speedy return to the links demonstrated that he had made a quick and complete recovery from his heart attack. Ike had to undergo surgery for inflammation of a portion of his small intestine in June 1956, and he suffered a mild stroke in November 1957. But each time he bounced back, returning to the golf course the moment his doctors gave him the green light. "Golf is a tonic for the President," said Howard Snyder, Ike's personal physician. "I say he should play whenever he gets a chance. He doesn't get away from the office nearly as much as I'd like him to do."

The White House suddenly embraced Ike's golf as a savvy way to defuse a potential health issue during the 1956 presidential campaign. And it worked. After Ike coasted to his reelection victory in November, his aides told reporters that they were convinced the voters agreed with Truman and understood that golf was good for the President's physical and mental health.

But it still did not stop the capital's golf quips and whispers. The quiet criticism molded a generation of politicians' view of the game—John F. Kennedy and Richard M. Nixon, for example, both believed playing golf was politically risky.

At a press conference in October 1958, Eisenhower was asked why he enjoyed playing golf so much.

"Well, a funny thing," he replied. "There are three that I like all for the same reason—golf, fishing and shooting. . . . They take you into the fields. There is mild exercise, the kind that an older individual probably should have. And on top of it, it induces you to take at any one time two or three hours, if you can, where you are thinking of the bird or that ball or the wily trout." He went on to describe golf as "a very healthful, beneficial kind of thing, and I do it whenever I get a chance, as you well know."

Jacob Potofsky, the blunt, bearded president of the Amalgamated Clothing Workers of America, told the President as he left the Oval Office, "You know, Mr. President, we're keeping track of the number of times you play golf."

A few aides winced at the remark, but Ike just smiled and said, "You go right ahead. I only wish that I could play more."

EARLY IN HIS MARRIED LIFE, Ike tried tennis. He played with Mamie, but he struggled to master the game and to control his temper. After double-faulting or muffing an easy baseline return, Ike would become so furious that he stormed off the court and, more than once, he slammed his head against the nearest tree. Needless to say, Mamie did not enjoy these episodes, and they did not play the game very long.

During World War II, Eisenhower became enraged after being asked to host a luncheon for a group of touring congressmen. His blood pressure shot so high that his physical examination that day had to be postponed. He also suffered a lifetime of battles with his stomach, which doctors blamed on severe tension.

In the book *Eisenhower Was My Boss,* the general's wartime secretary, Kay Summersby, chronicled a dozen unhappy episodes of what she called "the Eisenhower temper," always spiked by a torrent of profanities. Ike's temper was ignited by such trivial things as a reporter being told the brand of cigarettes he smoked. Summersby said that Ike once launched himself into "the granddaddy of all tempers," but it was like a sudden summer storm. It came suddenly and ended just as quickly.

As president, however, Eisenhower controlled his anger, though there were still unfortunate flashes of it, often on the golf course when he could not solve his slice or tame his wild putter. When things went wrong, "his face turned just as red as could be," observed Norman Palmer, the club pro at the Newport Country Club, in Rhode Island, where Ike played frequently during his second term. The President looked "annoyed" when he missed an easy shot, Palmer said. "But he plodded ahead and the next good shot brought a smile back to his face," he said. "It put a spring in his step and he was just as chipper as ever. He never went into any prolonged sulking moods."

"Ike was a golfer to warm every weekender's heart," said Bob Hope, "playing with gusto and determination. He fumed over his bad shots and exulted over his good ones, scrapping for every dollar on the line."

Bob Hope once played a round with Ike at Burning Tree against General Omar Bradley and Senator Stuart Symington. They discussed the stakes on the first tee. "Well," Ike said, "I just loaned Bolivia $2 million. I'll play for a dollar Nassau," a $1 wager won by the lowest scorer on the front nine, the back nine, and the entire eighteen holes.

Unfortunately for Ike, he was teamed with Bob Hope. "I played terribly," Hope said, "and we lost. The next day I teamed with Senator Prescott Bush against Ike and General Bradley. I was back on my game and shot 75. I beat Ike for $4.00 and I'll never forget the sour look on his face when he pulled out his money clip and paid off. He looked me in the eye and grumbled, 'Why didn't you play this well yesterday?' He wasn't laughing, either."

Another playing partner observed, "He gets pretty steamed when he misses a shot, and he curses a little under his breath." The President would say to himself, "Boy, I sure made an ass of myself on that one."

But if he rolled in a long birdie putt, he would shout, "Well, even a blind pig finds an acorn now and then!" And Ike liked to tell golf stories. One of his favorites was about two golfers standing in front of the green. One lay there in eight, the other in nine. The one who had taken nine strokes said, "It's your hole. My short game is lousy."

Ike always paused on the course to greet people, especially young people. One morning at Newport, a little girl with a box camera stepped to the edge of the 9th green to snap a picture of the President. Ike saw her and stopped walking. The girl quickly snapped the picture, but nervously realized she had not advanced the film. "That's all right, dear, don't hurry," Ike told her, removing his hat and stopping to pose. The girl advanced the film and snapped the President's picture again.

The caddies adored him. He treated them as equals, as teammates and counselors. He blamed himself for failing to execute their advice. When things went right, he often told them, "We did all right on that shot." He tipped his caddies $5 apiece, plus a more valuable bonus: two of his Dunlop Dot golf balls, engraved with the words "Mr. President."

And yet, nothing angered Ike more on a golf course than finding a professional photographer lurking in the woods along the course, waiting to ambush the presidential foursome. The White House barred picture taking of Ike and his playing partners on the golf course, and the Secret Service agents kept busy enforcing this rule. On a warm spring day in 1953, a print photographer set up his long-lens camera on the front lawn of a house right across the street from a Burning Tree green. A slight hill on the lawn provided a perfect vantage point for a long-range picture of Eisenhower. But the photographer had the bad luck of selecting a house owned by a Central Intelligence Agency official, who immediately called the club to report the interloper with a lens. Within moments, a grim Secret Service agent removed the photographer from his perch.

During a presidential round at Augusta, an enterprising photographer was almost shot by a Secret Service agent. An agent walking ahead of the President on the fringes of the fairway saw a man hiding in the brush in the woods, holding what appeared to be a gun barrel. The agent darted into the woods, quickly reaching for his revolver in his coat pocket. With his hand grasping the gun, the agent realized that the would-be gunman was armed only with several cameras and a long lens mount that had appeared, from a long distance, to be a rifle.

For months, photo editors at newspapers and magazines complained to the White House about the limited access, saying their readers clamored for something other than the customary first tee shot image. In August 1953, Eisenhower relented, for a day, and invited dozens of photographers and film crews to follow him as he played a midmorning round at Cherry Hills Country Club in Denver, where he was vacationing. With photographers kneeling behind him, squatting in the sand traps, and flanking both sides of the first tee, Ike showed no signs of nerves as he hit a beautiful drive off the tee and scored a birdie on the first hole.

Eisenhower was dressed sharply for the occasion. He wore a checked shirt, fawn slacks, and tan-and-white shoes, topped off by a straw hat. Several times, newsreel photographers nearly blocked Ike's path to the green. "I hope this doesn't bother you, Mr. President," one of them said.

"Oh, you won't bother me," the President replied as he lined up his shot, "but I may bother you."

The White House established strict rules about all the information related to Ike's game—his score, his club selection, the advice he tried to put into practice. Everything was off limits. Playing partners and caddies were forbidden from discussing his score or any details about his rounds. Norman Palmer, the Newport pro, joined Ike's foursome forty-five of the forty-six times that the President played at Newport. After most rounds, Palmer tore up the President's scorecard. If the scorecard was worth saving, Palmer slipped it to Ike. Palmer dismissed the speculation that Ike had forbidden talk of his game because of the criticism that he played too frequently.

"This, obviously, was false," Palmer wrote in his book, *Five Star Golf*. "The real fact is that he is such a conscientious golfer that he realized people reading about him or watching him play would always be rooting for him to play a great game. Consequently, he felt

At the Newport Country Club, where he played often during his second term, President Eisenhower hits practice balls in front of a crowd of onlookers and photographers in August 1958. Ike's swing looks picture-perfect.

that if the scores were published, he had to have a good game—and that wasn't possible. In other words, he couldn't go off and relax, not worrying if he missed a shot. He felt that if the public had knowledge of every score, he would not be able to enjoy the game."

In 1958, Palmer was accused of divulging every detail about a round with Ike, including his score and club selections, to a newspaper in Boston. "We found out that a newsman had paid one of the caddies ten dollars to give him a rundown on the President's game," Palmer said.

Ike enforced another rule on the golf course: no talk of government business or politics by his playing partners. Golf was the only permissible subject. Too often, however, Ike had no choice. A Secret Service man accompanying Ike carried a walkie-talkie, and the President was often forced to attend to official duties. Inevitably, the official interruption destroyed his concentration. And several times, Ike became furious when he stopped his game to pick up the walkie-talkie only to find no voice on the line.

"He'll be going along playing really well—par, par, bogey, par, bogey," said Jim Hagerty, Ike's press secretary. "All of a sudden his mind comes off golf. You can see it. Suddenly he's thinking about Quemoy, or Lebanon, or Berlin. Then its triple bogey, triple bogey, and we all might as well go home. It isn't going to be any more fun that day."

In an article published in *Golf* magazine, "Take a Mulligan, Mr. President!" Roger Kahn reported that Ike, on occasion, took a mulligan off the first tee. And others reported that Ike, on occasion, used the club face to gently alter the lie of his ball. But almost always, Ike played a straight game, rejecting offers for three-foot gimme putts.

Eisenhower's strength was his short irons, from about 80 to 100 yards away. His weakness was a putting affliction that bedeviled him throughout his life. "He has a million putters, but what he doesn't have is the touch," one friend said. Ike tried everything, experimenting with new putters, changing his grip and alternating his stance. Pointing to a putter, he said grimly, "If I could just make this darn thing work, I'd enjoy the game a whole lot more." From ten feet in, he could sink them, though not consistently. Beyond that, Ike struggled with measuring the proper distance.

Frequent playing partners knew that Ike usually did not like getting tips while playing because it made him press too hard, guaranteeing an even higher score. During a round at Greenbrier, Sam Snead gave Eisenhower an unsolicited, entirely unorthodox lesson that the President never forgot. "Ike never asked for tips, he had his own game," Snead explained. "It seemed Ike was losing sleep over the fact that his short backswing was causing him to lose power on his drives. The problem was so obvious I didn't hesitate to give him my advice: 'You've got to stick your butt out more, Mr. President.'"

"His bodyguards couldn't believe I'd said that to the President of the United States. I couldn't believe it either, but Ike was too intent on his game to notice."

Ike said plaintively, "I thought it was out."

Later in that round, Ike was jubilant as he hit several long straight drives more than 200 yards. Ike later thanked Snead for realigning the presidential butt.

IF EISENHOWER HAD BEEN ASKED to describe what his own personal heaven would look like, he might have responded, "Augusta." One of America's most exclusive country clubs offered Ike everything he needed—a lush golf course, competitive nighttime bridge games and, most of all, a private sanctuary far removed from the whirlwind of political life.

While president, Ike made twenty-nine trips to Augusta National Golf Club, an extraordinarily high number that amounts to an average of almost one trip per season, including winters. Eisenhower was a dues-paying member at Augusta for twenty-one years, proudly wearing the club's signature emerald-green blazer with gray slacks. Presidential records show he played 210 rounds on the famous course during his eight years in office.

Before he became President, Ike often borrowed the cottage belonging to his old friend Bobby Jones, the immortal amateur champion and a longtime president of Augusta. Two months after his inauguration, Eisenhower, who was also an amateur painter, presented Jones with a portrait of the golfer concluding a swing with his driver.

Around the same time, the club's members paid $150,000 to build a spacious, three-story country house for the President and his family, nestled in a stand of pine trees not far from the 10th tee.

The club also built a pond for Eisenhower. During his second visit to Augusta, after the war, General Eisenhower walked through the woods on the eastern edge of the club's land, later telling Augusta chairman Cliff Roberts that he had found the perfect location to build a dam if the club wanted to have a fishpond. The club built the spring-fed pond, on a three-acre patch of land, precisely where Eisenhower suggested it should be placed, and it is named "Ike's Pond." Eisenhower often fished in the pond after playing golf.

In June 1954, the President wrote an excited letter to Roberts, describing his first eagle. It came on a day at Burning Tree when Ike had missed a twenty-inch putt for an eagle earlier in the round. "This eagle might not be important to anyone else, but it is my first," he wrote. "I was hitting the ball fairly long and straight the other day and on Burning Tree's 10th, I banged my second one about six feet from the pin. This time I decided to take no chances so I shut my eyes, gave it a prayerful stab—and sure enough, there it was."

A hole-in-one still eluded Ike; it was the one thing he still had not done on a golf course.

AFTER LEAVING OFFICE IN 1961, Ike retired to his beloved farm in Gettysburg, Pennsylvania. He continued to play golf at Eldorado Country Club in Palm Springs, California, at Augusta, and on several courses in Pennsylvania. He was asked how his life had changed as a former President.

"I don't get as many short putts," Ike said.

Eisenhower thanked Richard Nixon for a note in 1966 congratulating Ike on his seventy-sixth birthday. "Seventy-six is a formidable number," Eisenhower wrote, "and I would like it to be my golf score rather than my age."

In retirement, Eisenhower became the crotchety conscience of presidential golf, frowning on the mulligans taken by President Lyndon B. Johnson during a round in 1968 in California. And with the pressures of the presidency lifted, Ike actually improved his putting and had a few memorable rounds in the 1960s. One of his most memorable was the afternoon in 1963 when he and golf legend Arnold Palmer teamed up to play together in a charity match against golf professional Jimmy Demaret and singer Ray Bolger at the Merion Golf Club in Ardmore, Pennsylvania.

Ike and Palmer enjoyed a special friendship. They often sat on Ike's porch at his farm in Gettysburg, swapping stories while sipping coffee or a few cold beers. "I spent a good bit of time away from the golf course with Eisenhower," Palmer recalled in his usual understated way. But he also said that he played with Ike "at Gettysburg all the time," as well as at Burning Tree, Eldorado, and Cherry Hills.

Ike was in awe of Palmer's talent. But on this day at Merion, Palmer was lucky to have Ike as a partner. "The General carried me," Palmer said later.

It was the first time Eisenhower had played before a large gallery, but he showed no nerves on the first tee, banging the ball 220 yards perfectly straight down the fairway. "Hustler," Bolger yelled.

The format was alternate shot. So Palmer then deposited Ike's ball on the green, and Eisenhower sank a seven-foot putt for the birdie. Through the afternoon, Eisenhower suddenly found his short game.

"That man came to play," Palmer marveled after Ike chipped the ball just two feet from the 8th hole.

Eisenhower and Palmer had the match won by the 16th hole. That evening, Ike was scheduled to appear at a dinner event at the nearby Valley Forge Military Academy. An aide asked the former President if he wanted to end the round early.

"The heck with it," Ike said. "Let's finish it."

On the 17th hole, Eisenhower sank a nearly impossible forty-five-foot putt for another birdie. As the gallery shrieked, Eisenhower "beamed like a boy with a new bicycle," *Golf* magazine reported. It was one of Ike's finest performances on the golf course.

In 1968, at the age of seventy-seven, Ike played at the Seven Lakes Country Club in Palm Springs with one of his closest friends, Freeman Gosden, who had played Amos on the popular *Amos 'n' Andy* radio show. On the 13th hole—par-3, 104 yards—Eisenhower chose a 9-iron. The ball soared straight at the pin, landed softly on the green, and rolled neatly into the cup. Ike finally had his hole-in-one.

"The thrill of a lifetime," he called it.

A few months later, he was in the hospital.

That November, Eisenhower's vice president, Richard Nixon, was elected president. As Nixon began to select his Cabinet, one nominee, labor secretary-designate George P. Shultz, met with Eisenhower at Walter Reed Hospital in Washington, D.C.

"Here was this genial man in bed," Shultz said. "I was astonished about how much he knew about the Department of Labor. He was a very sociable guy and fun, and we talked about a lot of things, including golf.

"The doctor came in to tell me it was time to go. And then this genial man, Ike, got adamant. He wagged his finger in my face, and he said, 'Young man, let me tell you something. You are going to work fourteen hours a day, seven days a week for the government, and you are going to think you are doing your job. Here is what I want you to know. If that's what you do, there is no way you'll be able to do your job. Everybody needs to get their mind off the job. If you don't get out to that golf course twice a week, there is no way you will be able to do your job.'"

Eisenhower died four months later.

A week after Ike's death, the 1969 Masters tournament began. It was Eisenhower's favorite tournament during his favorite time of year. Cliff Roberts delivered a loving golf eulogy to Ike by breaking the club's official silence on the state of his game.

Eisenhower had failed to overcome a "congenital slice" and an untrustworthy putter, Roberts told the sportswriters, but the late president still managed to break 80 four times on the Augusta course. "He was ready to start swinging the minute he set foot on the club grounds," Roberts said, "always anxious to hit the next shot and he never quieted down on the course."

Roberts declared, "Very few contributed as much as General Eisenhower toward the enhancement of the popularity of the game of golf." He announced that the club intended to make a shrine of the home where Eisenhower stayed during most of his visits to Augusta—the white cottage with green shutters, located about a mid-iron shot from the 10th tee.

"We've always called it Mamie's Cabin for Mrs. Eisenhower," Roberts said, "and the name will never be changed."

Before long, most members of the all-male Augusta National Golf Club started referring to it simply as the Eisenhower Cottage, and that was the name that stuck.

GERALD R. FORD

HERE COMES JERRY . . .

FORE!

Gerald R. Ford fondly remembers this 270-yard tee shot on the first hole at Pinehurst Country Club's No. 2 course at the grand opening of the World Golf Hall of Fame on September 13, 1974. Ford played with nearly a dozen golfing legends that day. Ford said this tee shot was the first and only good shot that he would hit that day.

I know I'm getting better at golf
because I'm hitting fewer spectators.
—Gerald R. Ford

O N THE SOUTH LAWN of the White House, Gerald R. Ford wore a grim smile as he waved farewell to Richard M. Nixon. The disgraced President stood in the helicopter doorway, mustering a grin and that awkward V-for-victory wave, one last time. After Nixon was gone, Ford walked arm-in-arm with his wife, Betty, back to the White House. In the East Room, with his right hand raised high and his left hand resting on the family Bible, Ford swore to preserve, protect, and defend the Constitution, so help me God. "My fellow Americans," Ford declared, "our long national nightmare is over."

That night, Ford thought how surreal the day had been, how exhausted he felt but also how much work there was to do.

Less than forty-eight hours later, Jerry Ford went golfing, playing eighteen holes at the Burning Tree Country Club. Years later, I asked him why he felt he needed to go hit the golf ball so soon after becoming president. He laughed.

"With all of the hectic publicity about Nixon's resignation and my taking over," he said, "I thought I needed a little breather."

In a way, Ford played that first round for the badly shaken American people, who were still reeling from the unprecedented political upheaval of the previous week. He thought a round of golf by their new president would send a comforting message that it was time to try to return to "our normal lives, and try to have a little fun."

Golf was always Gerald Ford's favorite way to have a little fun. His closest friends were not at all surprised that on the first three weekends after taking the oath of office in August 1974, Jerry Ford, the accidental president, spent long afternoons chasing the little white ball. The game was Ford's favorite escape hatch, both as president for two and a half years and following his forced retirement in 1977, when he played a dozen Pro-Am tournaments annually, all for charitable causes.

"I was on the tour," Ford told me about those first two years after he moved out of the White House. "It was a lot of fun."

As president and also as an ex-president, Ford always instructed his playing partners to grant him no breaks, no special favors, no cut corners. He demanded no mulligans, no gimmes, and he insisted that no one call him "Mr. President." Of course, nearly everyone still did.

On the first tee, Ford liked to say, "Out here, I'm just Jerry Ford."

ON HIS FIRST FULL DAY IN THE OVAL OFFICE, Ford was confronted with two questions. One was very serious and the other was trivial by comparison. But the new president would devote considerable time and thought to figuring out the best way to resolve both.

The first question was whether Ford should grant a pardon to Richard Nixon for the crimes he might have committed in the Watergate cover-up. Everything rested on this decision—the nation's ability to move beyond the crisis, of course, but also Ford's political future.

The second question was whether Ford should honor a commitment he had made while vice president to attend the opening ceremony in September of the World Golf Hall of Fame at the Pinehurst Country Club in Pinehurst, North Carolina. Now that he had suddenly become president, Ford had the perfect excuse to cancel his appearance.

That was certainly the fear of the planners of the hall's opening ceremony. They worried that it would be impossible for the new president to fly down to Pinehurst on a workday for a ribbon-cutting ceremony, nine holes of golf, and a black-tie dinner. There were, after all, so many more important things on Ford's agenda now.

The dreaded cancellation phone call was received by the Pinehurst committee before Ford had been living in the White House for a full week. A White House aide expressed President Ford's regrets, saying he no longer had the time to honor the commitment. The Pinehurst committee began scrambling to find someone to replace him.

Then something odd happened. Two hours later, the White House aide called back with a question: Had the President's cancellation been made public yet?

The answer was no. Then the White House aide asked if all the inductees into the new Hall of Fame would be present at the ceremony. The Pinehurst official reeled off the names on the golfing legends' list, all of whom had agreed to attend: Arnold Palmer, Jack Nicklaus, Gene Sarazen, Sam Snead, Byron Nelson, Gary Player and—

"Ben Hogan?" the White House aide asked. "Is he still coming, too?"

"Yes. Hogan will be here."

The White House said: Stand by. We'll get back to you soon.

An hour later, the phone rang again, and this time the commitment was confirmed, with no waffling: The President of the United States would indeed attend the event, just as planned. Jerry Ford would keep his word.

A committee member breathed a sigh of relief, saying, "He must know how hard it is to get Ben Hogan out of Texas."

Three days before going to Pinehurst, President Ford announced to the nation that he had signed an unconditional pardon of former President Nixon. "It is believed that a trial of Richard Nixon, if it became necessary, could not fairly begin until a year or more has elapsed," Ford proclaimed in the pardon document. "In the meantime, the tranquility to which this nation has been restored by the events of recent weeks could be irreparably lost by the prospects of bringing to trial a former President of the United States. The prospects of such trial will cause prolonged and divisive debate over the propriety of exposing to further punishment and degradation a man who has already paid the unprecedented penalty of relinquishing the highest elective office of the United States."

Ford insisted that the pardon of Nixon was necessary if Americans had any hope of putting Watergate behind them. But the decision was instantly and angrily criticized by millions of people. When he arrived at Pinehurst on Wednesday, September 11, 1974, dozens of young protesters greeted him. They shouted angry chants and waved placards proclaiming, "Is Nixon Above the Law?" and "Be a Ford, Not an Edsel."

For Ford, the protest stood as a pointed reminder of the controversy that he had left behind in the capital. And yet, almost immediately, the President seemed far more comfortable at Pinehurst than he had been just that morning in the capital. Golf courses always had that effect on Jerry Ford. They relaxed him.

Golf writer John M. Ross described the opening of the World Golf Hall of Fame as "golf's day of days." Ross wrote, "There on the ceremonial platform to the rear of the new $2.5 million World Golf Hall of Fame, the greatest collection of golf talent ever had assembled. Any one of them would be the star attraction at any golf gathering. But now all waited and watched for the arrival of a weekend hacker."

Prior to Ford's arrival, Max Elbin, the former president of the Professional Golfers Association and the club professional at Burning Tree, Ford's club, was introduced to the crowd. Elbin had flown down with Ford on Air Force One, even helping the President edit his remarks. "Boy, that's class," a golf writer marveled. "Who else would think to bring their club pro to a party like this?"

Then the band played "Hail to the Chief," and President Ford walked on the stage. The crowd unleashed an enormous roar, nearly as loud as the one that had greeted Arnold Palmer.

One by one, Ford shook hands and patted the backs of the golfing legends assembled on stage, many of whom he had played rounds with in the past. When he spoke, the President made no mention of his controversial pardon of Nixon. But when Ford talked about one of the game's great lessons, he was clearly applying it to Nixon's pardon.

"I have never seen a tournament, regardless of how much money or fame or prestige or emotion was involved, that didn't end with the victor extending his hand to the vanquished," Ford said. "The pat on the back, the arm around the shoulder, the praise for what was done right and the sympathetic nod for what wasn't are as much a part of golf as life itself."

Ford paused a moment. Then, in an obvious allusion to his decision to pardon Nixon, he said, "I would hope that understanding and reconciliation are not limited to the 19th hole alone."

The President could not pass up the chance to poke fun at his own wild golf game, which was quickly becoming a favorite target of comedians around the country. Ford, then an 18 handicap, recalled the time when Ben Hogan, Patty Berg, and Byron Nelson approached him at Burning Tree and said they needed a fourth great golfer to complete their foursome.

"Well, here I am," Ford replied.

They said, "Good, you can help us look."

Ford also praised the tremendous array of golfing talent assembled in a row behind him. He then said, "I think there's another great golfer watching us today, and I'm referring to Ike Eisenhower who, I think, had as much to do as anyone in making the game what it is today."

As he returned to his seat, a button popped off Ford's jacket sleeve, and Ben Hogan quickly retrieved it from the stage and delivered it to the President. An observer said, "Hogan should have kept it. It'd make a great ball marker."

Ford then ran a pair of scissors through an enormous red ribbon, officially opening the World Golf Hall of Fame. After a quick tour of the hall, he prepared for a historic nine holes of golf with the new inductees on the Pinehurst No. 2 course.

In the clubhouse, Ford quickly traded his wrinkled gray business suit for an electric-green, loose-fitting golf shirt bearing the Burning Tree crest, dark green slacks, and a pair of well-worn white golf shoes.

An enormous crowd of several thousand people was jammed into the bleachers surrounding the famed course's first tee. The plan was for Ford to play a total of nine holes—three holes with three different foursomes of legendary golfers. The first group to join Ford was a fivesome—Palmer, Nicklaus, Player, and PGA Commissioner

President Ford is joined by Jack Nicklaus, Gary Player, and Arnold Palmer to complete a famous foursome at Pinehurst Country Club on September 13, 1974. Years later, Ford said he was pleased that he was able to honor a commitment to play a round of golf that day to commemorate the opening of the World Golf Hall of Fame.

Deane Beman. As the men took their practice swings on the first tee, Nicklaus said, "Why don't you start it off, Mr. President? We're looking to you to lead us all the way."

Ford smiled, adjusted his eyeglasses, and teed up the ball. Without delay, the President crushed the ball more than 270 yards down the right side of the fairway. The crowd roared, and several pros jokingly grabbed their bags, indicating they had seen enough and were going home.

Player and Palmer hooked their drives into the left rough. Beman was short. Nicklaus was the only pro to outdrive the President, by about ten yards. In the fairway, Palmer and Player continued to walk past Ford's ball, pretending they had hit longer drives than his.

Pinehurst No. 2's first hole was a 405-yard, par-4. Ford's second shot ricocheted off the green. He put a perfectly executed chip shot within three feet of the hole, but his par putt lipped out, forcing him to settle for an unsatisfying bogey.

Ford behaved as any weekend hacker would, baby-talking his ball on the greens and yelling "Up, up!" after his iron shots from the fairways and bunkers. But it was all downhill after the missed par putt on the first hole. When the nine holes were over, Ford finished with a 48. He had missed some easy chips, and some easier putts.

Even though Ford ripped up the course, the pro golfers clearly enjoyed their time with the new president. Gene Sarazen, the veteran professional whose experience with presidential golf stretched back to Warren G. Harding, was especially impressed with Ford's demeanor. "He's a lot like Eisenhower, the same kind of charm," Sarazen told a few friends. "People like him right away."

Someone said, "But it's hard to be a hero in the White House these days."

"Yes, but this fellow's a big hitter," Sarazen said, "and all the world loves a big hitter."

That evening at the Pinehurst Hotel, Ford relaxed at the black-tie dinner, puffing on his pipe and laughing at the golf stories told by the new inductees. When it was his turn to speak, the President had the audience roaring by telling jokes with Jerry Ford as the punch line. "They say you can always tell a good player by the number of people in his gallery," the President said. "We've all heard of Arnie's Army. Well, my group is called Ford's Few."

And he said, "I have a very wild swing and I demonstrated it on a number of occasions this afternoon. Back on my home course in Grand Rapids, they don't yell 'Fore.' They yell 'Ford.'"

He concluded his remarks with another reference to the outcry that awaited him in the nation's capital: "This afternoon, for a few hours, quite unsuccessfully, I tried to make a hole-in-one. Tomorrow morning, I will be back in Washington trying to get out of one."

I asked Ford what he remembered about that day, twenty-eight years later.

What else? The drive.

"It was such a wonderful experience, I'm very glad I went ahead and did it," Ford said. "And I had a helluva drive on the first tee. I was out there with the pros, *past* the pros." Then he stopped himself. Jerry Ford never liked to brag.

"That was the last good shot I played all day," he said.

GROWING UP in Grand Rapids, Michigan, Gerald Ford carried golf clubs for his stepfather. Working as a caddy at the Masonic Country Club was the last thing young Jerry wanted to do.

"My father was about a 20 handicapper, and I used to caddy for him," Ford told me. "That's where I got started. My father kept trying to get me to go out and be a caddy at one of the local country clubs. I was much more interested in football, basketball, and baseball. I never really did what they were trying to get me to do, which was learn golf. I wish I had, in retrospect."

Ford was a terrific athlete, playing baseball and football and basketball. Years later, as president, he confided to an audience that his lifelong dream was to play pro baseball. "But nobody would sign me," he said. Ford's best sport, by far, was football, and many people in his hometown predicted he would go on to play the game professionally. In high school, he was recruited to play for Michigan, Harvard, and Northwestern, all national collegiate football powers. He decided to stay close to home and attend Michigan, where he won the team's most valuable player award in his senior year as the team's center and linebacker.

Ford played his best game in a losing effort against archrival Northwestern, whose star guard, Rip Whalen, told the Michigan coach, "Ford was the best blocking center I ever played against." On the strength of that compliment alone, Northwestern's coach, Dick Hanley, recommended Ford to be chosen for the East-West Shrine Game in San Francisco on New Year's Day of 1935. "I still cherish that remark," Ford said years later. Ford played a total of fifty-eight minutes on both sides of the ball, impressing pro scouts with his toughness and quickness.

That summer, the Green Bay Packers and the Detroit Lions offered Ford contracts to play football: $200 a game, for a fourteen-game season. "Pro football did not have the allure it has now," Ford explained, "and though my interest was piqued I didn't lose any sleep over my decision."

Instead, Ford decided to accept an invitation to coach both foot-ball and boxing at Yale. "I saw the chance to realize two dreams at once—to stay in football and to pursue a long-nurtured aspiration for law school," Ford said. "Of boxing, I knew next to nothing. No, that's not right. I knew absolutely nothing."

For three years, Ford had more than enough spare time to play golf on the famous Yale golf course designed by Charles B. Mac-Donald. But in 1938 he entered Yale Law School, and until his grad-uation three years later, Ford did not play a single round of golf. He left Yale and went home to Grand Rapids, where he started a law practice that was not very busy, so he had plenty of time to get back out on the golf course. His law career was interrupted by a stint in the navy during World War II. When he returned to Grand Rapids, he was a thirty-three-year-old lawyer-bachelor who set out to be-come a good golfer.

Those plans were sidelined, however, after Ford was elected to Congress in 1948. There was just no time for golf; Ford committed himself to his new political career. He did not play serious golf again until 1965, the year that he was elected the House minority leader and joined the Burning Tree Country Club.

When he started playing again, his game was erratic. He had some horrible rounds, but he also managed to break 80, playing with his old friend Bill White, at The Homestead in Hot Springs, Virginia. "That's a pretty tough golf course," Ford told me. "And I got a 79. He made a scorecard, got me to sign it, and he framed it for me."

Ford, who stood six feet one inch and weighed 190 pounds, was always a big hitter off the tee, though he was prone to slicing the ball. But his short game bedeviled him. "He couldn't putt for sour apples," observed Max Elbin, the Burning Tree pro.

While Ford was the minority leader in the House, he opposed President Lyndon B. Johnson's Great Society program, which made Johnson furious. Jerry Ford had "played football too long without a helmet," Johnson said, a quip that greatly amused official Washing-ton. When Ford opposed the President's Model Cities legislation, Johnson told an aide that Ford needed to be coddled "like a little baby boy."

"Well, you take his little building blocks," LBJ said, "and go up and explain to Jerry Ford what we're trying to do."

Publicly, Ford laughed easily at himself, but the President's jabs grated on his feelings. He felt compelled to remind some people in the capital that he had graduated in the top third of his class at both the University of Michigan and the Yale Law School. Is this the cost of public life? Ford asked himself. Do I have to defend my ability to think?

He knew the best way to defuse such talk was with humor, especially the self-effacing kind. At a Gridiron Dinner in 1968, Ford stood up and struggled to slip on the old leather football helmet that he had worn in the Shrine Game back in 1935. He said nothing about the LBJ remark, but everyone just knew. The helmet's flaps did not fit over his ears.

"Heads tend to swell in Washington," he said, and the packed house laughed, then cheered.

Ford continued to toil in Congress until the fall of 1973, when a string of unlikely rapid-fire political events shuttled him, over the course of just ten months, from relative political obscurity to the most powerful office on earth. Vice President Spiro Agnew resigned in October after pleading no contest to income tax evasion. President Nixon chose Ford to replace Agnew, and Ford was approved by Congress in December. Ford and Nixon had played golf several times in past years, though they did not play together after Ford became vice president. "He wasn't a really good athlete," Ford said. "But he was always pretty competitive."

During the suffocating summer of 1974, Ford played a lot of golf. The anonymity of the vice presidency made it easy to get away. Golf granted him some breathing room—not to mention excuses to get out of town—while Nixon was struggling, practically alone, to save his presidency from imploding.

Seven days before he became president, Jerry Ford played in a Pro-Am tournament as a guest of his friend, House Majority Leader Thomas P. (Tip) O'Neill, the Massachusetts congressman who would later become Speaker of the House. But it was not easy, because Ford needed to be in San Diego the day before to give a

For a golfer, there are few pleasures as glorious as limbering up the old joints on a sparkling spring day in your own backyard. President Ford practiced his wedge shots on the south lawn of the White House on May 9, 1975.

speech and attend a fund-raiser. To keep this golf commitment, Ford had to zigzag across the country. He took a red-eye flight from San Diego to Washington, D.C., arriving at 5:30 A.M. Ford expected to be able to take a quick flight up to Boston for the tournament, but he was told by the White House that he was needed to fill in for President Nixon, reeling from Watergate, at a ceremony honoring a ranking military officer.

Ford raced to his house in Alexandria, Virginia, where he changed clothes, and then dashed into Washington for the ceremony. Then, on the plane ride to Massachusetts, he caught a ninety-minute nap.

When he arrived, he had a bounce in his step and he was ready to play eighteen holes. "Anyone else would have been traveling on one cylinder," said Cosmo "Cuz" Mingolla, the longtime sponsor of the Pleasant Valley tournament. "But he was charged up to play and was gracious to everyone. . . . Of course what I'll always remember is when he took me aside after I had addressed him as 'Mr. Vice President' several times. He gave me a pat on the shoulder and said, 'Out here, Cuz, I'm just Jerry Ford.'"

President Nixon was well known for his telephone calls to locker rooms, usually to congratulate Redskins coach George Allen on another victory. Just ten days after moving into the White House, President Ford placed a congratulatory call of his own, to a golf clubhouse. Dave Stockton, a former PGA champion who had played with Ford at the Pro-Am in Massachusetts, had just signed his scorecard after winning the Sammy Davis Hartford Open when someone told him that an urgent call was waiting for him in the press tent.

He picked up the phone and heard, "Hello, Dave, this is Jerry Ford."

Ford explained to Stockton that he had not watched the telecast of the tournament because he was playing golf at Burning Tree, where he shot five birdies.

"Thanks for calling, Mr. President," Stockton said.

Reporters wanted to know: What kind of golfer was President Ford? It was the first assessment of Ford's play from a pro golfer who knew. Stockton did not dodge the question. "He's a pretty good golfer," he said, "and he could be much better if he could find more time to play." Stockton thought about that response for a moment, then added: "But I hope he doesn't. I'd rather he be a good President than a good golfer."

I ASKED JERRY FORD WHY GOLF WAS THE FAVORITE GAME of American presidents over the past century.

"I think it's the camaraderie," he said. "You make friends and you expand friendships when you play golf. There is a downside—it takes a lot of time. It's a good atmosphere for relaxation and escape from the problems in the Oval Office. And I loved playing the Pro-Am tournaments."

No president played in as many Pro-Am tournaments as Gerald Ford. As president, playing a Pro-Am is much more challenging than playing a round with your pals at a private course. There are enormous crowds, and large galleries line the fairways. Ike and Kennedy, of course, did not even like to be photographed on the golf course, but Jerry Ford did not mind a group of television cameras trailing him from hole to hole. Perhaps it was his college football background, but Ford was always comfortable playing a game in front of the fans.

In fact, he thrived on it. He loved the crowds, fed off their enthusiasm, and they adored him.

In February 1975, Ford played the Pro-Am tournament at the Jackie Gleason Inverrary Classic near Fort Lauderdale, Florida. It was the first time a sitting president played in a Pro-Am tournament. "Kennedy never played in a Pro-Am, Johnson didn't, Nixon didn't," said Richard H. Wammock, the associate director of the tournament.

It took guts. How did the new president agree to play in the tournament? "Well," Wammock said, "we were sitting around one night, talking about who would play, and Jackie Gleason said he would call up Jerry Ford and see if he would play. He just put through a call to the President, and Jerry Ford said, OK, he would see if he could work his schedule out."

Jerry Ford, of course, worked his schedule out. The President had a single request: He wanted Jack Nicklaus to be part of his foursome. And Gleason asked Bob Hope to join them.

So the dream foursome of Ford, Nicklaus, Gleason, and Hope attracted 41,208 golf fans, a record crowd on the pro golfers' tour.

"Look, there's the Prez!" one man shouted as Ford walked up the fairway. On the first tee, Ford swung wildly, his ball sailing over the gallery, and someone said, "Keep your head down, Mr. President!"

Nicklaus shot a 63, a 9-under-par course record. Ford shot a 100,

Jack Nicklaus, Jackie Gleason, President Ford, and Bob Hope discuss the stakes on the first tee of the Jackie Gleason Inverrary Classic near Fort Lauderdale, Florida, on February 26, 1975. A record crowd of 41,208 fans turned out to witness the first time that a sitting president played in a PGA Pro-Am tournament. Nicklaus shot a 9-under-par 63, a course record that eclipsed Ford's score that day by 37 strokes.

28 strokes above par. "He could be a good golfer," Nicklaus said. "He thoroughly enjoyed the round. He doesn't get too much time to enjoy himself."

IT IS ONE THING to have the courage to compete in the Pro-Am tournaments. It is quite another to play well enough to keep from scattering the galleries. Jerry Ford hit a lot of people with golf balls. Even before he became president, his wildness off the tee earned him a label that he never shook—Golfer Hazardous to Your Health.

As vice president, Ford had replaced Spiro Agnew, another wild golfer who had struck half a dozen spectators with golf balls. And very quickly, Ford replaced Agnew as the capital's wildest golfer and the butt of countless jokes.

On the front page of the *New York Times* on June 25, 1974, the headline was: "Ford, Teeing Off Like Agnew, Hits Spectator in Head with Golf Ball." No politician wanted to be compared to the disgraced Agnew; even a golf comparison was humiliating. At a celebrity golf tournament in Minneapolis, Ford struck seventeen-year-old Tom Gerard in the head with a golf ball. And later in the round, another Ford tee shot slammed into a golf cart carrying a police officer, though the officer was not hit.

The Minneapolis mishaps were just the beginning. In the 1970s, Bob Hope told dozens of Gerald Ford golf jokes and, like the LBJ helmet quip, they endured through the years. Among Hope's favorites: "Ford doesn't really have to keep score; he can just look back and count the wounded."

And: "You all know Jerry Ford—the most dangerous driver since Ben Hur."

And: "Ford is easy to spot on the course. He drives the cart with the Red Cross painted on top."

And: "There are forty-two golf courses in the Palm Springs area and nobody knows which one Ford is playing until he hits his tee shot!"

And: "Ford was the first President to use a lethal weapon—a golf club."

And: "One of my most prized possessions is the Purple Heart I received for all the golf I've played with him."

And: "Whenever I play with him, I usually try to make it a foursome—the President, myself, a paramedic, and a faith healer."

Bob Hope had a million of 'em.

I told Ford that it seemed of all the golfing presidents, his game was tagged with a disproportionately high percentage of the jokes. Laughing, he said, "My golf game is such that I don't take it that seriously. If I hit a bad shot, I don't like it, but I accept it."

He accepts it, but not always gracefully. In 1978, at the Bing Crosby National Pro-Am tournament in Pebble Beach, Ford played with Arnold Palmer. Ford blew up on the 18th hole. He hit his tee shot into the ocean. He hit his second tee shot down the fairway but then dribbled his fourth shot. "I just happened to walk by," said

Richard Wammock, the PGA official, "and he turns to me and says, 'You can just tell Bing to take me out of this thing next year. I will not be back.'" Later that afternoon, Ford calmed down, and he played the tournament again the next year.

WHEN GERALD FORD BECAME PRESIDENT, he realized that the old LBJ label about playing without a helmet had shaped the way much of the public viewed him. Ford was furious when he read in news articles that he had "acted presidential" or had "struck a presidential posture" or was "trying to look presidential." One article said that Ford was "going to play President."

These references offended Ford, who always insisted on playing by the rules but sensed that the political rules had somehow changed when they applied to him. He did not try to look or act or sound presidential; he *was* the President. Why didn't they see that?

Ford was soon stuck with another label: stumbling, bumbling klutz. The legend began in May 1975. As the President walked down the ramp of Air Force One in Salzburg, Austria, his shoe caught a bump, and he fell, wildly, to the tarmac. He quickly jumped to his feet, announcing that he had not been hurt by the fall. Much to Ford's surprise, his stumble was covered as if it was a major news event. Later that day, Ford made matters worse by slipping, twice, on a wet and slippery staircase at the Residenz Palace.

Not long after that, he slammed his head into the top of a marine helicopter doorway. From then on, Ford was lampooned as an oaf, endangering himself and others. The newspapers dutifully reported every time Ford fell while skiing, or tripped while walking, or slipped off a diving board, or injured another spectator with a golf ball. The "Ford, Sports" clip file in the *New York Times* archives has a half-dozen photographs of golfers, lying prone, with Ford crouched over them, looking concerned. The captions all read like this one: "Ford's Shot Strikes Spectator: Former president Ford bending over Gene Bartelt, 56, after his golf drive struck the man at Menomonee

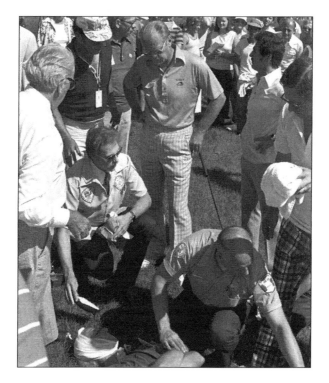

Former President Ford watches as rescue workers care for an injured spectator at the Vince Lombardi Memorial Golf Tournament in Milwaukee on June 25, 1977. Ford struck the victim, Gene Bartelt, fifty-six, in the head with an out-of-bounds tee shot on the first hole. The incident confirmed Ford's reputation as the wildest presidential golfer.

Falls, Wis. Mr. Bartelt, who said he voted for Mr. Ford, suffered a cut." Only the names of the victims and the golf courses change.

Soon, the White House correspondents took note when Ford did not trip over his own feet. CBS told its viewers that Ford had survived a campaign trip and—sounding surprised—the network reported that it was "remarkably free of gaffes."

It seemed as if every night, Johnny Carson told a new round of Ford the Buffoon jokes. And Chevy Chase, on the new, popular NBC television program *Saturday Night Live,* did an imitation of Ford that consisted solely of falling down. Chase did not sound like

Ford, he didn't look like Ford. The only thing he did to evoke Ford was fall on his face. In one skit, Chase played Gerald Ford falling, in a spectacularly awkward way, while trying to put an ornament on top of the White House Christmas tree. The tree broke Chase's fall.

Ron Nessen, the White House press secretary, told reporters that Jerry Ford was perhaps the best athlete to serve in the White House since Theodore Roosevelt. Besides golf, Ford loved to ski, swim, and play tennis. Nessen actually said, "The President . . . is by far the most athletic President in memory." It was an attempt to squelch the criticism, but it was too late.

Ford tried it himself, again hoping that self-effacing humor would work the way it had against LBJ's helmet remark. At the Radio-Television Correspondents Association dinner in March 1976, the traditional evening when a president must be humorous enough to make a few thousand journalists laugh, Ford agreed to share the podium with Chevy Chase.

As the band played "Hail to the Chief," Chase made a bumbling entrance, falling down repeatedly as he made his way through the ballroom and with a flourish slammed his head on the rostrum. "I have asked the Secret Service to remove the salad fork embedded in my left hand," he said.

Everyone laughed, including Ford. When it was the President's turn to speak, Ford imitated Chevy Chase imitating Ford, dropping dishes and silverware, getting the tablecloth tangled in his pants, scattering the pages of his speech all over the place. (They were retrieved by Walter Cronkite and Dan Rather.)

"I'm Gerald Ford, and you're not," Ford said. "Mr. Chevy Chase, you are a very, very funny suburb." The journalists laughed until their sides hurt.

I asked him: Did all that ribbing about the golf hurt you politically and personally? "I thought it was unfair," he said. "But by that time, I had learned whether you are in sports or politics, those things happen. I never complained. It made me a little mad behind a closed door."

Gerald Ford lost the 1976 presidential election to Jimmy Carter, and on his first full day of private life, he played eighteen holes of golf at the Bing Crosby Pro-Am tournament at the Monterey Peninsula Country Club at Pebble Beach. Ford played with Arnold Palmer. Enormous crowds followed the two men around the fairway, and the former president seemed touched by the crowd's warmth. "Go get 'em, Mr. President!" a man yelled near a tee box.

"Where were all these people on Election Day?" Ford wondered aloud.

Ford hit a bunch of bad shots, and a few good ones, particularly a birdie on Pebble Beach's challenging 14th hole. He seemed genuinely content.

"The family's happy, I'm financially in good shape, I'm doing the things that I wanted to do, like play golf," Ford said as the air force jet took him on his final trip, from Washington to Monterey.

Sitting in his shirtsleeves, puffing on a pipe, the former president appeared content as he reflected on his two and a half years in office. "Sure," he said, "we would have loved to, wanted to, be around for another four years."

Ford moved into a home in the exclusive Thunderbird Heights area of Rancho Mirage, California. Ford loved its location, directly across from the Thunderbird Country Club.

The loss of politics left a void. He missed the competition, and the Pro-Am circuit was the next best thing. "I played ten Pro-Ams a year after leaving the White House," Ford told me. "They were all for very good charitable purposes. I always felt good being able to help bona fide charities. And I really treasured my relationship with all of the PGA players that I played with. I never found one who was not a classy guy. I like the competition. The combination made it easy for me to say yes. They were the highlight of my first couple of years out of politics."

Not long after Ford left the White House, the actor Danny Thomas called to invite him to play in his Pro-Am. "Mr. President," Thomas told Ford, "I cannot get the networks to cover us, but they will if you play."

Ford recalled, "That's how I got started down in Memphis—
Danny Thomas was desperate. So I started playing down there with
Danny, and that's where I had my first hole-in-one."

It was on the 5th hole at Colonial Country Club, a par-3, 150-
yard hole. And Ford used a 5-iron. His playing partners, Bob Hope
and Ben Crenshaw, were thrilled. The pro, Dave Stockton, sent Ford
a note of congratulations. It was a sweet reversal of Ford's congratulatory phone call in 1974.

Ford sent Stockton a thank-you poem that reads:

Dear Dave,
'Twas the Danny Thomas Memphis Classic
On Wednesday, June the eight,
The fifth hole and a 5-iron shot
Was flying true and straight.
A hole-in-one, the golfer's dream
For me had now come true.
That thrill is sweeter yet because
A note has come from you.

Ford went on to shoot two more holes-in-one, separated by two
years, on the same golf course, the Tamarisk Country Club and even
on the same par-3, 174-yard 11th hole. And for each hole-in-one, he
used the same 5-iron. He told me about the additional holes-in-one,
but only after I asked. He talked about the feats as if they were really
nothing at all. Modesty is Ford's strong suit.

As he played the Pro-Am circuit, the tournaments named after
Bing Crosby, Sammy Davis Jr., Danny Thomas, and Byron Nelson,
Ford started playing the best golf of his life. "As president, my handicap was 17 or 18," he told me. "The best I ever got was down to
about a 12, after I got out of the White House." With the help of
Arnold Palmer, he managed to improve his putting, that lifelong
nemesis. Palmer recommended that Ford try his own putter, an ex-
tralong forty-five-inch club that is held against the chest and swung
in a pendulum motion with the right hand. "I figured if Arnold
could use it," Ford said, "I should, too."

In the early 1980s, Ford founded his own tournament, the Jerry Ford Invitational in Vail, Colorado, one of Ford's favorite places on earth, where he and his family had vacationed for twenty years. In its first fifteen years, the Jerry Ford Invitational raised more than $1 million for charities in Colorado. Ford often said that the best thing that he did in the golf world was start his own Pro-Am.

I asked Ford whether he ever took mulligans or gimmes. He thought about it for a moment. "Integrity in golf, even among amateurs, is extremely important," Ford said. During our conversation, Ford's voice had sounded shaken and weary. But as he talked about the integrity of the game, he spoke with a sudden firmness. He was almost emphatic.

"Of course, in the professional ranks, it is mandatory," he said. "I think that is a good example for people generally. They know that integrity is a principal guiding point in a positive golfing environment."

Arnold Palmer admired Ford for throwing himself so completely at the game, blaming the President's reputation as a wild golfer on his willingness to play so many Pro-Am tournaments. Palmer also admired Ford's deep respect for the rules. "One indication of his passion is that if you tried to give him a putt, he would never take it but insist on trying to make it," Palmer said in *A Golfer's Life*. "That's a true gamer in my book."

Palmer also observed that Gerald Ford "may not have been a natural at either game, but he threw himself honorably into the fray at crucial points in history, did very good things for this country and his favorite game, and is still out there trying."

Even now, at the age of eighty-nine, Ford is still playing the game. He told me he belongs to the "Nine Holers Club" in Palm Springs, California.

"I've had two total knee joint replacements from football and skiing," said Ford, his voice sounding tired again. "Nine holes are all I can really enjoy right now. That's enough, that's enough."

FRANKLIN D. ROOSEVELT

THE NATURAL

As a young man, Franklin Delano Roosevelt flashes his natural ability off the tee. He learned to play the game as a boy, and in his twenties, there were few public men in Washington, D.C., who could hit the ball straighter or farther than FDR.

Golf was the game that Franklin enjoyed above all others. . . .
After he was stricken with polio,
the one word that he never said again was golf.
—Eleanor Roosevelt

O N   A   T R I P   T O   S O U T H E R N   F R A N C E   in the spring of 1890, Franklin Delano Roosevelt's father, James, learned how to play golf. His discovery was nothing short of an epiphany. Dazzled by the game's emerald beauty and challenged by its beguiling simplicity, he returned home with a travel crate full of golf clubs and golf balls. James Roosevelt imported the game to Hyde Park, New York, in a steamer trunk.

As soon as he returned home, Roosevelt designed a modest six-hole course in the meadows that ringed the family estate. By the summer, he had introduced his wealthy friends to this irresistible game. One of those friends, Colonel Archibald Rogers, became an accomplished player almost overnight. Rogers was talented enough to compete in the first U.S. Amateur Championship, played in October 1895 at the Newport Country Club.

Golf was intertwined with Franklin Roosevelt's family from the beginning. When James Roosevelt broke ground on that golf course, young Franklin was eight years old.

James may have been smitten by the game, but Franklin preferred other sports, at first. The more hard-hitting the sport, the more he liked it. He played football and tennis and loved sailing and horseback riding. He often went on fishing and hunting trips, shooting native birds for his own collection and for the American Museum of Natural History in Manhattan.

He did not become interested in playing golf until he and his friends discovered it for themselves.

When he was twelve years old, Franklin was sailing with friends at his family's summer retreat on Campobello Island in New Brunswick, Canada, on the coast just two miles north of the Maine border. A sudden fog rolled in and forced them to find something else to do, so they tried a round of golf. Golf was easier and safer to play in the fog than sailing a boat, though not by much. When he returned to the summer retreat, Franklin told his father that he was thrilled about this new game of golf. Franklin was tall and lean, the perfect physique for the game.

As his father had done at Hyde Park, Franklin and his friends cleared a patch of the family's four-acre estate on Campobello Island to make room for a rough-hewn golf course. It was a challenging nine-hole course, whose greens were pockmarked with unsightly clumps of crabgrass.

Because Roosevelt's image as a wheelchair-bound president is ingrained in the public's memory, it is difficult to imagine him as a young man chasing a golf ball around a field. "I broke my record on the links yesterday, doing 41, which is within two strokes of the record for the course," Roosevelt wrote in a letter to his parents as a senior at Groton in 1899. Golf had become his favorite game.

By the time he turned twenty, there were few players, anywhere, who could hit the ball as far as Franklin Delano Roosevelt.

ROOSEVELT BROUGHT HIS GOLF CLUBS with him to Harvard, where his initials became his nickname. In college, FDR continued to improve his game, often shooting in the 80s but doing it with finesse around the greens. Roosevelt was a long-ball hitter, though his tee shots were not always accurate.

At Harvard, Roosevelt bragged that he could drive a golf ball at least 300 yards. A classmate challenged him, and they placed a bet. FDR won the wager by waiting until the dead of winter when he drove the ball onto a frozen pond. The ball easily skated more than 300 yards.

During his summers in college, he played every day at Campobello, improving his accuracy by avoiding the living and breathing

At the age of seventeen, Franklin Roosevelt was a fine, devoted golfer who was able to polish his administrative and public-speaking skills as the secretary and treasurer of the Campobello Golf Club on Campobello Island. Roosevelt redesigned the club's scorecards and ordered the greens to be enlarged, which made the members happy.

hazards. Large herds of loud, smelly sheep had free run of the course. The sheep choked the greens and fairways, their bleating a constant intrusion on a player's backswing.

While he was still a student at Groton, at the age of sixteen, Franklin had won a tournament, beating older players. Sara Roosevelt, FDR's mother, joked many years later that "it is difficult now to remember whether the score was recorded in strokes or sheep. As no call of 'fore' penetrated their wooly skulls, the players simply had to aim well over the cropping heads, shut their eyes and hope for the best."

On Campobello Island, the Roosevelt family course, though ragtag, was turned into the centerpiece of the Campobello Golf Club in 1899. James Roosevelt was the club's president, and its members were so impressed with FDR's maturity and energy that they invited him, at the age of seventeen, to serve as the club's first secretary and treasurer. One of Franklin's first acts was to order the greens to be enlarged, but there were many thankless tasks that kept him busy, such as collecting dues and shuffling paperwork. His mother offered to help with the paperwork, but Franklin declined, saying he did not mind the menial tasks that came with the job.

"I intend to hand the position back with the club in as good condition as when I take it," he said in a letter to his mother. One of FDR's contributions to the club was designing and printing new scorecards.

He addressed the members about the proper use of the course, and his presentation was so smooth that Justice Horace Gray of the U.S. Supreme Court, another summer resident, congratulated young Franklin. The job provided FDR with early experience as both an administrator and a public speaker.

In 1900, James Roosevelt died of a heart attack, and Franklin resigned the secretary-treasurer position, having held it just one year. His family had no interest in returning to Campobello without the family patriarch. Instead, they sailed to Europe during that first summer without him.

FDR did not return to the island until the summer of 1904, after his graduation from Harvard. That summer, he achieved his greatest thrill as a golfer, winning the Campobello Golf Club championship. If he had been able to win two more consecutive club championships, he would have won a beautiful silver cup. But he never had the chance to win that cup because the Campobello Golf Club was disbanded the following year. It was replaced, just fifteen miles down the road, by a much more luxurious club, built by the Canadian National Railroad.

Forty years later, when FDR was president, he received a letter that Campobello's never-won silver cup had been handed down by a former member to the Jefferson Islands Club, a Washington group whose well-connected members included Sam Rayburn, the Speaker of the House.

FDR HAD ALWAYS WANTED TO BE A NAVAL OFFICER, but out of respect for his father, he enrolled in Columbia Law School in the fall of 1904. Six months later, on St. Patrick's Day 1905, Roosevelt married his sweetheart, his cousin Eleanor. The two sailed to Europe, where FDR always made time for a game of golf. He played all the best courses, including St. Andrew's in Scotland.

It was on their honeymoon that Eleanor discovered the depth of her husband's love of the game. She worried that she had already become a golf widow.

When they came home, Franklin continued to spend long afternoons at the St. Andrew's Golf Club in Westchester County, New York. Eleanor was frustrated, even a little angry. "Because my husband played golf," she wrote in her memoirs, "I made a valiant effort one year to practice every day, trying to learn how to play." One summer at Campobello, Eleanor secretly took golf lessons and practiced every day for a week before joining her startled husband on the first tee. At first, FDR seemed bemused by Eleanor's attempt to play golf.

"After watching me for a few minutes, he remarked he thought that I might just as well give it up!" Eleanor wrote.

Her husband's laughter at her golf swing devastated Eleanor. "I never again attempted any thing but walking with my husband," she said.

In 1913, FDR was appointed by President Woodrow Wilson to serve as assistant secretary of the navy. He played golf almost every day. "I'm off at 4 P.M. to play golf," FDR wrote in a letter to his mother. "Tomorrow also I am to golf, so you will see that I'm taking care of myself." His golf game may have done wonders for his spirits, but it did little for his marriage. Eleanor had indeed become the classic golf widow, trudging off to church every Sunday with their five children while Franklin played eighteen holes with his buddies.

Then, in 1918, Eleanor discovered that golf was not the only thing keeping her husband away from home. She caught her husband having an affair and confronted him. Although the affair nearly wrecked their marriage, Roosevelt tried to hide the tumult of his home life from his friends. But his golf game gave him away.

He started playing horribly. He was easily angered and clearly distracted. One of his closest friends, a Harvard classmate named Livingston Davis, knew something was wrong because Roosevelt was losing every round. "Never saw FD play so poorly," Davis wrote in his diary. It was after an especially poor round that FDR confessed his infidelity to his pal.

FDR and Eleanor worked out an unsteady truce, but their marriage never fully recovered from Roosevelt's unfaithfulness.

While serving as assistant secretary of the navy, FDR played most often at the Chevy Chase Club, where he was invited to join the exclusive group known as the Senatorial Foursomes. FDR was occasionally paired up with Senator Warren G. Harding of Ohio. It was the first time that a pair of American presidents—past, current, or future—played a round of golf together.

At Chevy Chase, Roosevelt asked his oldest son, James, to carry his clubs. "Father decided I should earn my allowance—25 cents a week—by caddying for him," he wrote in his memoirs. James loved the time he spent carrying his father's clubs; it became one of his most beloved childhood memories. Caddying for Dad also excused James from having to attend church with his mother.

Several times, young James carried the clubs for his father as he played with Harding. "All I remember about Harding was that he seemed amiable, and that Father enjoyed golfing with him," he recalled.

Roosevelt also played often at the Metropolitan Country Club, whose membership included the most powerful men in Washington. Most of them were dazzled by Roosevelt's charm and wit, and FDR made the most of his new admirers. In 1920, he was selected by the Democratic presidential nominee, James M. Cox, to run as his vice presidential candidate. He opposed Harding, his old golfing pal. Neither man gave up the game during the campaign.

On the campaign trail in Billings, Montana, Roosevelt asked someone if there was a nearby golf course. FDR was so starved for a round that he played nine holes in the pouring rain. "I don't remember his score," said J. B. Arnold, a playing partner. "But I do recall he played a fine game."

Harding won in a landslide. FDR's defeat would be the last of his life.

IN AUGUST 1921, Roosevelt returned to Campobello for his first visit in nearly a decade. One day he came down with a high fever and his legs grew extraordinarily weak. "My left leg lagged," he later recalled. "Presently it refused to work, and then the other." At the age of thirty-nine, FDR had contracted polio.

FDR refused to admit that the paralysis was a permanent condition. Surely he would recover fully and walk, and play golf, again. Years later, Eleanor said, "I never heard him mention golf from the day he was taken ill. That game epitomized to him the ability to be out of doors and to enjoy the use of his body."

More likely, FDR never mentioned golf again to Eleanor because it was the source of so much pain in their rocky marriage. Privately, however, FDR never stopped pining to play the game. He wrote a letter in 1923 to the Dutchess Golf and Country Club near Hyde Park, asking to be transferred to an inactive membership. But it would only be temporary. "I am still on crutches," FDR wrote in the letter, "and cannot possibly play golf for a year or two."

FDR fought with courage to strengthen his legs, spending hours swimming vigorously in the pool. In the summer of 1924, he appeared, on crutches, at the Democratic National Convention to nominate Governor Alfred E. Smith of New York, a speech in which he gave Smith the nickname that would remain with him for the rest of his life: the "Happy Warrior."

In 1926, Roosevelt bought a ramshackle resort located in Warm Springs, Georgia, where the hot mineral pools provided him with temporary relief. He was determined to turn the resort into a first-class therapeutic center for polio victims as well as a destination spa for vacationers. He spoke excitedly about building two eighteen-hole championship golf courses, a majestic clubhouse, and a quail-shooting preserve on the property.

Instead of eighteen holes, FDR designed a unique nine-hole course himself. He was the only American president to design a golf course, an extraordinary reflection of his dedication to the game. It had been years since he swung a golf club.

The course featured roads and reinforced bridges, allowing cars to whisk polio victims around the course. Some polio sufferers could still play a few holes if they only had to walk short distances, and the car paths allowed them to play. Roosevelt, however, was unable to play, but he loved to watch. He was often seen in a car, sipping martinis as he offered advice and saluted the finest shots.

FDR WAS ELECTED PRESIDENT IN 1932, promising "a new deal" for the American people who were ravaged by the Great Depression. He was reelected three times, serving the longest tenure of any president in American history.

Although he never played a single round of golf while in office, FDR still loved the game. His affection for golf was most obvious in the verbal jabs he sent to the golf-playing members of his Cabinet. When he learned that an aide, Stephen Early, had scored an eagle in a local tournament, FDR wrote a friend, "Steve came back most unexpectedly with money in his pocket and with a tall tale about how somebody's ball knocked his in a cup. We still think he was in his cups. The FBI is investigating."

A local official wrote FDR to report that Early and two other White House staffers were heard using expletives on the course at Burning Tree. Kiddingly, the friend asked whether the men qualified as golfing "gentlemen."

In his return letter, FDR, wrote, "In the first place, I did not know that any one of the three could be classified as a golfer." And he offered to come to Burning Tree on a Sunday morning "to see for myself just how the Unholy Three conduct themselves on tee, fairway and green."

FDR donated to Burning Tree the golf club that he had played with for years in Washington. "This club, which we used to call a brassie, became mine about 1913 and I used it at Chevy Chase and other Washington courses until I left here in 1920," FDR wrote in a letter to the club president in July 1940. "It was a grand instrument for getting two hundred yards out of the rough with. And, incidentally, the rough in those days was much rougher than the rough today! Don't let anyone try to use it at Burning Tree. Being nearly 30 years old, it might disintegrate."

The club is on display at Burning Tree with the clubs donated by the other golfing presidents, from William Howard Taft to George W. Bush. The club president, Robert V. Fleming, wrote back to FDR, thanking him for the gift and saying, "The club is proud to have this trophy from one of our greatest Presidents who, regardless of the grave responsibilities resting on his shoulders, finds time to do so many kind and thoughtful acts."

In the end, one of FDR's least known but most enduring golf legacies was his administration's public works program that helped the nation endure the depression. During the Roosevelt administration, more than 250 municipal golf courses were built with federal money, making golf accessible to hundreds of thousands of new players.

"Roosevelt has done much to change the complexion of U.S. golf," wrote the syndicated newspaper writer Bob Considine in 1940. The public works projects that built so many new public golf courses had created "a different type of Average Player," Considine wrote. "He is John Doe, successor to John Dough."

Perhaps the most powerful evidence that FDR never relinquished his fond memories of his golfing youth can be seen in one of the most famous photographs of his presidency. On December 8, 1941, the day after the date that will "live in infamy," Roosevelt is sitting at his desk in the Oval Office as he signs the declaration of war against Japan. He is surrounded by senators and congressmen, their grim but purposeful expressions reflecting the immense challenge facing the nation.

Flanked by senators and congressmen, President Franklin Delano Roosevelt signs the declaration of war against Japan on December 8, 1941. Within arm's reach, on his Oval Office desk, sits a cigarette lighter in the shape of a golf ball, a sure sign that FDR never lost his affection for the game.

On Roosevelt's desk, within arm's reach, sits what appears to be a golf ball perched atop a small podium. It is actually a decorative cigarette lighter shaped like a golf ball, a memento that FDR used, again and again, in the Oval Office.

PART TWO

WORST OFF THE TEE

Hole	1	2	3	4	5	6	7	8	9	Out	In	Tot
Distance	410	160	300	520	360	195	396	451	356	3148	3100	6248
Par	4	3	4	5	4	3	4	5	4	36	36	72
Taft	6	6	6	7	8	4	6	7	4	54	51	105
Wilson	8	6	6	8	7	6	6	8	6	61	54	115
Coolidge	7	7	8	7	8	5	6	7	7	62	58	120
Reagan	6	5	6	7	5	4	6	7	5	51	49	100
Handicap	5	15	13	4	1	3	7	2	14			

*average scores while president

W. H. Taft

Woodrow Wilson

Calvin Coolidge

Ronald Reagan

ULYSSES S. GRANT was the first American president to attempt to play golf, a brief, unsuccessful try that, perhaps mercifully, lasted no more than five minutes.

While visiting Great Britain in August 1877, during the first leg of a post-presidency cruise around the world, Grant was invited to watch a round of golf at a time when the centuries-old Scottish game had begun to sweep through England in a sudden blaze of popularity. By all accounts, Grant was bemused by the spectacle. At the time, most people found it absurd that grown men and women would waste an afternoon chasing a little ball with a few odd-shaped sticks all over a piece of land far better suited for farming or cattle grazing. The participants encouraged Grant to try the game, and a caddy handed him a wooden club, probably a driver.

Grant "looked earnestly at the ball, then at his club, and having measured the distance carefully made a strike, his club going six inches above the ball," recalled General John C. Smith, a neighbor of Grant's who witnessed the first presidential swing. "Disappointed at this failure, a more careful estimate was made of length of club and distance to ball and another swing was made, the club striking the ground one foot before reaching the ball."

Grant tried again and again, but he failed to hit the ball even a single time.

"Returning the club to his caddy," Smith said, "General Grant re-marked to the gentleman beside him, 'I have always understood the game of golf was good outdoor exercise and especially for the arms. I fail, however, to see what use there is for a ball in the game.'"

Ulysses S. Grant did not touch a golf club again.

The first sitting president to attempt to play the game was William McKinley, the nation's twenty-fifth president. Like Grant, he gave golf a brief, unsuccessful, and decidedly halfhearted tryout. Unlike Grant, President McKinley played it more than once.

When McKinley took office in 1897, golf in America was barely a decade old. In 1888, the nation's first golf course was built in

Yonkers, New York. John Reid had converted a sliver of his cow pasture into a three-hole golf course, dubbing it St. Andrew's Golf Club in honor of the original golf course in Scotland. Although the game was in its infancy, nearly half of McKinley's Cabinet played golf, the first capital golf clique to embrace the game. According to the *New York Times,* "It is asserted on the authority of a member of the Cabinet that all the real business of the regular Cabinet meeting is disposed of in three minutes and that the rest of it—an hour or an hour and a half—is largely devoted to talk [of] golf."

It was during his summer vacation in 1897, in Bluffs Point, New York, near Lake Champlain, that McKinley first picked up a club. Vice President Garrett Hobart, one of America's most prominent and enthusiastic golf aficionados, persuaded the President to play a few rounds, but McKinley had no success. The few accounts of the game politely do not record the President's first score, but it can be assumed it was deep into triple digits, perhaps even closer to 300 than 200. After a few atrocious rounds that summer, McKinley dumped the game.

"The President was not athletically inclined and could not obtain much satisfaction in following a golf ball around a meadow," wrote H. B. Martin in *Fifty Years of American Golf.*

After giving up the game, McKinley whiled away the rest of his summer vacation sitting under a tree and reading. Every day, he sought the shade of the same tree, "a tall stately oak tree," Martin had described it. It became known as the McKinley tree.

Two years later, during his summer vacation in Hot Springs, Virginia, McKinley surprised his aides when he announced that he would like to take up golf again. He was probably inspired by the endless golf chatter of several men in the government. But his senior advisers were very concerned, telling McKinley that golf was "undignified for a President" and that the American people would likely lose confidence in the administration if he was photographed on the golf course. McKinley's most trusted aides were concerned about their man's reelection prospects in 1900, but they were also just trying to spare the President from humiliating himself.

The question of the appropriateness of a chief executive playing golf was posed to the readers of the *Boston Evening Record.* Half of those polled said there was nothing wrong with a golfing president, and half agreed with McKinley's aides that the game would demean both the office and the man who occupied it. By all accounts, McKinley's second try was utterly forgettable; he had played as poorly in 1899 as he had in 1897. Two whacks at the game, tried over the course of two summers, were enough to persuade President McKinley that the game was impossible to master and a colossal waste of time.

And so that was it. No more golf.

President McKinley was assassinated in 1901, shortly after he had begun his second term. Oddly, the McKinley tree at Bluffs Point was struck by lightning the same month that McKinley was murdered. Tree surgeons managed to save the old oak tree.

Vice President Hobart had died in office in 1899, but if he had survived, he would have become the nation's first presidential golfer. Instead, Theodore Roosevelt, Hobart's successor, became the president, and Roosevelt had no use for the game. It would take a half century before a White House resident played golf with a level of skill that even flirted with mediocrity.

As it happened, the first few presidents to hit the links ranked among the worst White House golfers of the past century, qualifying in the least talented foursome—the men who were worst off the tee, and also consistently bad in the fairways, in the traps, and on the greens, too.

William Howard Taft
The Fat and Happy Hacker

William Howard Taft was the pioneer of presidential golf, playing often while living in the White House despite being lampooned for his 350-pound girth and an awkward swing. He refused to cancel a round of golf to visit with a dignitary from Chile at the White House. "I'll be damned if I will give up my golf game to see this fellow," Taft said.

*The beauty of golf to me is that you cannot play
if you permit yourself to think of anything else.*
—William Howard Taft

IF HE HAD EVER STOPPED TO THINK ABOUT IT—and there is no evidence or even a hint that he had—William Howard Taft could easily have come up with quite a few fine reasons *not* to step within a country mile of a golf course.

For one thing, the game seriously endangered his political career. Theodore Roosevelt admonished Taft not to play and practically begged him to quit the game just as Taft launched his campaign for president in 1908. In the western United States, in particular, the game was viewed with profound mistrust. If you continue to play golf, Roosevelt warned Taft, it will amount to nothing short of a ghastly political suicide. Playing that damn silly game, he said, could keep a qualified man out of the Oval Office. In a heartfelt letter to Taft, Roosevelt wrote that Americans view the presidency as "a very serious business and we want to be careful that your opponents do not get the chance to misrepresent you as not taking it with sufficient seriousness."

Taft ignored his political mentor's advice. Perhaps he wanted to prove Roosevelt's theory wrong. Or perhaps Taft knew Roosevelt was right and he figured golf would keep him out of the White House, which would have been just fine with him. Taft didn't much want to be president; he had to be cajoled into seeking the office. And so perhaps golf was a political death wish. The public did not hold the game-playing against Taft, who rode to victory mostly on the coattails of the immensely popular Roosevelt. And once he got the big job, Taft played golf with such passion—and governed with so little interest—that the game became a metaphor for his detached and disappointing single term in office.

There was another reason Taft never should have played. He was absolutely atrocious at the game. He rarely broke 100, though some accounts (perhaps being overly polite) put his score in the 90s. Most of the press accounts from the time did not discuss his score; instead, the reports respectfully praised his jovial manner, his long ball, and even his short game, though his putter was the weakest club in his bag. "He gets around a hundred mostly," the *Saturday Evening Post* reported in 1909 in one of the only published references to his score. But then the magazine went on to give the President a typically gentle review: Taft "is not much of a distance man, except occasionally, but is consistent and keeps well on a course. When he is playing, he is as earnest about it as a consul asking to be made a Minister." Yet behind the fawning publicity, people snickered behind Taft's ample back at his wobbly and often wild swing. And they found much amusement at the way the gargantuan president stomped around a fairway wearing a wide grin while leaving a wider trail of deep divots.

Most of all, Taft should never have even considered picking up a golf club because his weight ballooned during his single term in the White House to at least 340 pounds, an enormous bulk for a five-foot ten-inch man to have to drag around eighteen holes. Or perhaps he weighed 350, even 360. No one knew for sure. The number, like his golf score, was high enough to be guarded as zealously as any state secret.

Whenever the subject of his weight was raised, the President used self-effacing humor as a shield. Taft told reporters that the Speaker of the House, Thomas B. Reed, who weighed 275 pounds, "used to say that no gentleman could weigh more than two hundred pounds. I have amended that to three hundred."

Shortly after the turn of the century, jumbo-sized men were not expected to participate in athletics, and that list of no-no's included the relatively sedate game of golf. Roosevelt, the nation's beloved oversized legend, was an average-sized man who carried that famous big stick. Here was another way that Taft failed miserably to measure up to his political mentor: On the golf course, Taft was a large man who carried a small stick.

Despite all those reasons to lock the clubs in storage, Taft loved the game and became its most enthusiastic apostle. "Golf is in the interest of good health and good manners," he told a reporter in the Oval Office. "It promotes self-restraint and, as one of its devotees has well said, affords the chance to play the man and act the gentleman."

President Taft was so devoted to the game that during some stretches of his time in the White House, he played almost every afternoon. And he looked and dressed like a serious golfer. He wore tailored trousers, a pleated dress shirt and V-neck vest, accented with a dangling, sparkling watch chain, and spit-shined golf cleats. Beneath his floppy Panama hat, Taft's reddened, jolly face was adorned with a snow-white handlebar mustache that was as impressive as it was expansive. The big numbers on his scorecard, including the usual platoon of "snowmen," the euphemism for an unwanted 8 on a single hole, rarely diminished his beaming expression, his eyes hinting that his booming laugh was just beginning to leap up from his ample belly. His portly face always conveyed a boundless optimism that the next hole or the next round, by golly, would be better than the last.

Taft was introduced to the game by his younger brother, Henry, one of the pioneers of golf in the United States. Henry Taft was among the early members of the St. Andrew's Golf Club, the nation's first golf course, in Yonkers, New York. But Henry Taft's membership was too late to allow him to qualify as one of the club founders, who collectively were known as the Apple Tree Gang. In the summer of 1894, William and Henry Taft were visiting Murray Bay, Quebec, where the family had a summer home. Not far from their house was a new, hillside golf course—a course that was in shoddy shape, but no one complained because there were no alternatives. The course's condition did not matter to Henry, who managed to persuade his older brother to try a round of golf. William Taft was smitten by the game immediately, spending the rest of that summer—and any opportunity he could seize that fall—to sharpen his skills.

Taft, a Republican, was handpicked by Roosevelt to succeed him as president, and what Roosevelt saw in him remains an enduring mystery. One story, perhaps apocryphal, is told about Taft and his wife having dinner with President Roosevelt one evening in the White House in 1908. Roosevelt paused, leaned back in an armchair, closed his eyes, and in a deeply serious voice announced: "I am a seventh son of a seventh daughter, and I have clairvoyant powers. I see a man weighing 350 pounds. There is something hanging over his head. I cannot make out what it is. At one time it looks like the Presidency, then again it looks like the chief justiceship."

"Make it the Presidency," Taft's wife, Helen, said.

"Make it the chief justiceship," William Taft said.

He was eventually persuaded to run for president by his wife, his older brothers, and, most important, President Roosevelt, who was accustomed to getting his way. Taft waffled and wavered, but eventually Roosevelt and Helen browbeat him into running. During the campaign, Taft played golf and spoke frequently about his love of the game. He told a California crowd that golf was "full of moments of self abasement, with only a few moments of self exaltation. And, we Americans, who are not celebrated for our modesty, may find such a game excellent training."

IN 1908, Taft defeated William Jennings Bryan, who lost his third presidential election. Taft became the most reluctant president of the twentieth century and possibly any century. During his long four years in the White House, the big man behaved as if someone had conned him into becoming president.

Even before he took the oath of office, Taft established the tone for the laissez-faire theme of his administration. In the week prior to his inauguration, the capital was thrilled about the occasion. Thousands of people from Taft's native Ohio made the trek to the capital for a week of festivities. Electric lights were strung from lampposts, across Pennsylvania Avenue, from the Capitol to the War Department. A pathway from the White House to the street glistened with thousands of colored glass globes. Taft's broadly grinning face had become his political insignia, and thousands of people wore buttons emblazoned with the words "Smile, Smile, Smile." Bleachers with the capacity to seat 50,000 people lined both sides of Pennsylvania Avenue for the inaugural parade.

"In the midst of all these lavish preparations, Taft, it seemed, was the least interested person in Washington," Taft biographer Charles E. Barker wrote. "Reporters described him as 'holding aloof from all details of the inauguration.' He spent his last two days of freedom on the Chevy Chase links appearing to be more concerned, *The Washington Post* protested, about his golf game than 'in matters of state.' When reporters tried to engage him in discussion about the next day's events, Taft rebuffed them by turning the subject to golf."

To a city filled with people who wanted to celebrate his presidency, Taft sent an unmistakable message: I'd rather be golfing than governing.

Knocking the ball around the Chevy Chase Club that week, Taft projected the image of a confident president-elect who looked forward to the grand challenge that awaited him after taking the oath of office. The problem for Taft was that this cocksure image was wasted on his playing partners, a few members of the White House security detail and a small gallery of golfers, local residents, and well-wishers who watched him tee off the first hole and putt on the 18th green.

Walter J. Travis, the three-time U.S. amateur champion and noted golf-course designer and writer, played several times with Taft during his presidency. Travis played with Taft at Chevy Chase in May 1909, just two months after the inauguration. "Of course what every golfer wants to know is what sort of a game Mr. Taft plays," Travis wrote in the *American Golfer*, a periodical that he also edited. "If the President will pardon me, I do not really think he would have much chance in qualifying in one of our amateur championships, but for all that he plays a very sound game, one free from bad faults of any kind . . . far better than the average 'duffer,' both in style and results. Mr. Taft, in his modest way, some time ago described his own game as being of the bumble-puppy order. This is altogether wrong, and quite misleading." Travis did not offer a definition of the term "bumble-puppy," but it can be assumed that it means something like "many strokes away from playing scratch golf."

Travis continued, "Unlike most golfers who are not in the front ranks he plays every stroke in good form . . . has nothing to 'unlearn'

President Taft demonstrates his wobbly, wild swing off the first tee. Taft resembled a sumo wrestler trying to swat a gnat. Niether his weight nor his golf scores were divulged by White House aides.

or correct and needs only some steady practice to develop a strong game." On the 18th green during that round, Taft "left himself one of those horrible two to three-foot putts that all of us . . . 'even the youngest of us' . . . have missed so many countless times," Travis wrote. "And I fear the presence, for the first time during the match, of the 'gallery' around the home green did not help matters. For, be it known, the President prefers to do his golfing away from the limelight."

Throughout his life, Taft came alive on the golf course. From the first tee to the final hole, the big man beamed and bantered and roared with laughter. His friends and aides observed that the storm clouds (perhaps *that* is what Roosevelt had envisioned hanging over Taft's head) menacing President Taft scattered the moment he approached the first tee. There is good reason to believe that without golf, he would have found almost no pleasure at all during his four long years in the White House, where disappointment, exasperation, and embarrassment lurked around every corner.

When Taft was working, he was rarely happy. And so, early on in his administration, he devoted himself to doing as little work as possible while looking for ways, usually with golf clubs in tow, to have as much fun as possible.

His laugh qualified as the most infectious kind. And he was quick to chuckle at the Fat Man jokes that so amused the nation. Henry F. Pringle, one of his biographers, said the Taft laugh was instantly loved by anyone who heard it. "He laughed uproariously and happily," he wrote. "It became an American wonder, and contributed measurably to his success. It was deep, rumbling, wholesouled, boyish. It was heard in America, Europe and Asia. It oiled the machinery; and carried as much influence as anything he said. . . . When he laughed, even his enemies had to laugh with him. They couldn't help themselves, his humor was so contagious."

There are few pleasures like telling a joke about someone who laughs harder at the punch line than anyone else. Only someone who could laugh as effortlessly at himself as Taft would continue to play bad golf with such unabashed enthusiasm, chuckling at the game's propensity to cut even a 350-pound man down to size.

With Taft, there was so much to poke fun at. The most famous joke about the President had nothing to do with golf, but it was one that he enjoyed retelling, and his enthusiasm for the punch line helped secure its place in the pantheon of presidential humor. From 1900 to 1903, Taft served as the head of a commission organized to end American military rule in the Philippines, which had been ceded to the United States after the Spanish-American War. While there, Taft sent a progress report by cable back to Washington to Secretary of War Elihu Root. Taft described what he had seen during an excursion to a mountain resort on a winding, pockmarked road.

"Stood trip well," Taft wrote. "Rode horseback twenty-five miles to five thousand foot elevation."

By return cable, Root wondered: "How is the horse?"

Most of Taft's friends enjoyed telling jokes about the President's enormous size. Many people were surprised that his friends would treat the President with such disrespect, at least to his face. Chauncey Depew, a senator from New York, stepped up to Taft and placed his hand on his "big frontal development," in the words of one observer.

"What are you going to name it when it comes, Mr. President?" Depew asked.

Taft pounced on the question with gusto. "Well, if it is a boy, I'll call it William; if it's a girl, I'll call it Theodora; but if turns out to be just wind, I'll call it Chauncey."

Even Supreme Court justices could not help needling the President about his weight. Justice David J. Brewer said, "Taft is the politest man in Washington—the other day he gave up his seat in a street car to three ladies."

And the entire capital gossiped about the news that an extralarge bathtub had to be installed at the White House to accommodate the new president. It was closer in size to a small swimming pool than an extralarge bathtub. Guaranteed merriment followed the telling of the story—apparently true—that Taft had gotten stuck, more than once, in the Executive Mansion's old, regular-sized tub. Each time, two workmen were summoned to pry out the President.

As a sad solace to the deep misery that the presidency inflicted, Taft depended as much, or even more, on food than golf. Some biographers observed that while he lived in the White House, he "ate as never before," the bounty of great feasts promising temporary comfort from the pressures of the office. The immense amount of food caused Taft to literally fall asleep while people spoke with him. Senators, statesmen, and supporters who addressed Taft were alarmed to see him doze off or respond to a question with a throaty snore. More than once, the President slumbered while *he* was doing the talking.

"Most of the time," said James Watson, a Republican congressman from Indiana and a friend who did not hesitate to criticize Taft, "he simply did not and could not function in alert fashion. Often when I was talking to him after a meal his head would fall over to his breast and he would go sound asleep for ten or fifteen minutes." When the President awoke from one of those slumbers, Watson told him that he was the "largest audience" he had ever put to sleep. This quip, of course, caused the President to laugh out loud.

Hᴵˢ ᴾᴬˢˢᴵᴼᴺ ꜰᴼᴿ ᴬꜰᴛᴇʀɴᴏᴏɴ ɢᴏʟꜰ was just as pronounced as his taste for rich food. Both became habits. Although he was quick to chuckle or shrug at jokes about his twin obsessions, Taft confided to his wife, Helen, and close friends that he would some-times find the torrent of jokes hurtful or even humiliating. For ex-ample, as his waistline expanded, the President noticed that people snickered and guffawed as he rode a horse on the White House grounds. "Did you notice people laughing?" Helen asked an aide. "He seemed to think he caused amusement."

As his presidency wore on, he found it more difficult to laugh at himself behind closed doors. Taft's private concern about his weight inspired him to play more golf in an attempt to shed the pounds. For a man who was privately tortured at being turned into a waddling punch line, it was something of a vicious circle: Taft played golf to attempt to stop the snickers about his weight, but soon there were as many jokes about his golf.

"Golf is a game that leads you to walk without realizing you are walking," Taft explained. Players walked the course during Taft's era; golf carts would not be invented for another forty years. "When you play a game of 18 holes and walk four or five miles, there is only a pleasant feeling of fatigue when you get through."

That presidential justification did nothing to swat away the golf jibes directed his way. What most alarmed his critics was the simple fact that Taft played a round nearly every day. Almost nothing de-terred him from the golf course; appointments were shuffled or postponed, thunderstorms and lightning rarely caused a round to be shortened or canceled, heads of state were forced to wait or were hurriedly turned away. Taft bragged to friends that golf was essential to his good health, or a necessary part of his pursuit of better health. "My time is being pretty well filled up now," he said, "especially as I insist on taking the whole afternoon for golf."

Those explanations did not satisfy the President's political oppo-nents and most journalists. To them, Taft's golf-heavy calendar had simply proven Roosevelt's famous admonition about the game's po-litical perils.

It bothered Taft that he did not measure up to his glamorous predecessor. The public was endlessly fascinated with Roosevelt during Taft's four years in the White House, and the newspapers were full of stories about Roosevelt's daring exploits in private life. "Theodore Roosevelt Attacked by Two Dozen Hippopotamuses," one headline said. The two locals on the rowboat with the Rough Rider were reported to be frightened by the confrontation, but not Roosevelt, who shot the hippopotamuses single-handedly. Another famous story portrayed Roosevelt rescuing his entire hunting party from a wild rhino. In the Belgian Congo, Roosevelt hunted for a rare white rhinoceros in an amazing, eleven-month hunt, in which he bagged a total of 296 animals. The details were breathlessly reported by the American press: six buffalo, seven hippos, eight elephants, nine lions, eighteen rhinoceroses, fifteen zebras, and twenty-eight gazelles.

Those numbers must have hit Taft in the gut. How else could he have reacted? His numbers—a 102 at Chevy Chase, a 99 at the Town and Country—were rarely reported and never with even the slightest hint of awe. After a Gridiron dinner in the spring of 1910, Taft complained to his military aide, Major Archibald Butt, about the evening's main topic of conversation: Roosevelt. "Nothing shows what a hold Theodore has on the public mind more than the dinner this evening," Taft said. "Even when he is away and in no way interfering in politics, such is the personality of the man that almost the entire evening was wit and humor devoted to him, while the President, with most of the Cabinet present . . . [was] hardly mentioned."

Indeed, it was a rare but harsh slight to be hardly acknowledged when you are the guest of honor at a dinner in downtown Washington, just a few blocks from the White House. Some presidents might have tried to undo such indignities. But it just never occurred to Taft to emulate Roosevelt by trading the golf clubs for an arsenal of hunting rifles. Taft merely accepted the fact that he had the misfortune of succeeding a man who had transformed the presidency. "I don't know much about politics," Taft complained to his closest confidants, somewhat pathetically. "But I am trying to do the best I can with this administration until the time [comes] . . . to turn it over to somebody else." On another occasion, Taft said lamely: "It is a very humdrum, uninteresting administration, and it does not attract the attention or enthusiasm of anybody, but after I am out I think that . . . I can look back with some pleasure in having done something for the benefit of the public weal." Words like those made it obvious to anyone listening that Taft knew he was destined to be a one-term president.

GOLF WAS SUCH AN IMPORTANT PART of Taft's four years in the White House that he dubbed his coterie of fellow players "the Golf Cabinet," an exclusive clique that more than a few ambitious men clamored to join. For example, Secretary of War Jacob M. Dickinson had suggested to one of Taft's most trusted aides that he be invited to play with the President sometime in the spring of 1910. But Dickinson was a lousy golfer who simply wanted the excuse to spend some quality time with Taft. "When I told him the President wanted him, the old war horse looked frightened for the first time and began to make all sorts of excuses," recalled Archie Butt. "He played an awful game, making each hole in anywhere from ten to sixteen, besides paying no heed to the etiquette of the game, but kept walking and talking on the putting greens and driving out of turn, etc."

Afterward, Taft demanded that Dickinson's name be stricken from the Golf Cabinet roster. "The next time you ask a Cabinet officer to play golf with me, be sure that he knows something about the game!" Taft bellowed. "Poor old Mack! I felt more sorry for him than I did for you or me, for he hates to show himself deficient in anything, and even he could see that he knew nothing about the game. However, I'll bet anything he will begin to take some lessons, and the next time he offers to play he will be up on the game, and will, before he quits, play as well as any of us, if he does not become an expert."

Major Butt played frequently with Taft, but complained in his letters that Taft himself "hasn't the slightest idea of the etiquette of the game."

"Of course he thinks I will watch out for him," Butt wrote in 1909. "I had my lesson early this spring when I put a brassie shot right into the fat part of his leg just above the knee. He squealed when I hit him, but said it was his own fault. That did not prevent me from feeling like a cur, especially when the bruised spot covered over six inches in diameter." It knocked him off the links for a spell.

Taft observed that swearing on the golf course has never improved one's game. Grantland Rice observed that yes, President Taft was correct in his observation, but it was an undeniable fact that golf improves one's swearing.

During the summer of 1909, Congress was gridlocked in a heated argument over the Payne-Aldrich tariff bill. The bitter dispute forced Taft to cut his vacation short and return to the capital. He told aides that he was not as angry about the interruption as he would normally be because he had suddenly thought of "all the golf he could play in Washington while the battle raged," noted Judith Icke Anderson, a Taft biographer.

Not long after he returned, Taft vowed that he would no longer waste his time negotiating with Congress on the bill's fine print. Why talk when you can tee off? "They have my last word and now I want to show my scorn for further negotiations by spending the afternoon on the golf links," he vowed. Moments after writing a carefully considered note for Congress, he took a car to Chevy Chase for a late-afternoon round. Taft used golf as a threat, but the warning quickly fizzled. The President's foes on Capitol Hill were only too pleased to watch Taft ludicrously seek refuge on a golf course during a heated national political dispute. And sure enough, Taft was bombarded with criticism for that decision; the editorial writers said that Taft would clearly rather play golf than work out an important agreement with the Congress.

But the catcalls failed to quell Taft's passion for the game, nor did they make him contemplate quitting the game or playing less frequently. In fact, as he neared the end of his term, powerless to stop the squabbling and gridlock in Washington, Taft discovered he was

At the edge of a fairway, President Taft pauses to visit with some children on an unidentified golf course. Chances are good that Taft's ball was stuck in an out-of-bounds thicket, perhaps at the children's feet.

becoming more and more dependent on his escapes to the links. Almost out of necessity, he became stubbornly obsessive about his golf game. It was a reliable escape hatch leading quickly to a much-needed afternoon getaway. One more hour spent on the course at Chevy Chase was one less hour spent in the White House.

The criticism simply inspired Taft to dig in and become more stubborn about the game. He refused to divert his attention to more pressing matters on most afternoons. Taft berated the unfortunate aides who interrupted an iron shot or a long putt to deliver some message about governmental or political matters. Taft would sternly warn them never to do such a thing again. He unleashed a furious tirade at an unknowing State Department official who asked him to meet the president of Chile during his visit to Washington.

"I'll be damned if I will give up my game of golf to see this fellow," Taft snapped.

The nation's satirists and cartoonists lapped up those quotations. In one famous cartoon, Nelson Aldrich, the Rhode Island senator who was the sponsor of the tariff bill, was seen feeding the tariff legislation to a GOP elephant while Taft was visible in the background, far from the action, concentrating on—what else?—the accuracy of his golf shot. Mr. Dooley, a popular and devilishly funny character created by Finley Peter Dunne, quoted Taft as saying, "Golf is th' thing I like best next t' leavin' Washington!"

There were so many jibes that Taft became convinced that he was a national joke. He accepted his aides' advice and promised the public he would become more engaged in the affairs of state and would play fewer rounds of golf. Nothing really changed, of course, except Taft began sneaking off to the country club, telling almost no one in the Executive Mansion where he was going. On several occasions, the White House staff frantically searched for Taft, who was hard to misplace. Eventually, they were relieved to hear that the President had not been kidnapped but instead had merely sneaked off to indulge in his eighteen-hole addiction at Chevy Chase.

At a dinner in April 1910, the President laughed at how he had been defeated by two strokes by Vice President James Sherman, and yet the newspapers had erroneously reported that the President had won the round. "You don't have to play good golf if you have someone to do the official lying," Taft said with a laugh.

"You don't mean to say that the Vice President beat you?" Mrs. Taft asked.

"He did yesterday, my dear," Taft said, "But if I live four years I will give him such a beating that he will not recover from it."

A woman at the table said, "I don't understand."

"My dear," Taft replied, "all I have to do to beat the Vice President is to live."

That competitive nature was seen on the golf course and was felt by Taft's aides when his frequent health problems interfered with his ability to play golf. He also struggled with the gout, a condition he tried to keep a secret, and more than once the swelling of his feet and calves kept him off the course.

In his bid for reelection in 1912, Taft was forced to run against two candidates: Woodrow Wilson, the Democrat, and Theodore Roosevelt, who had become so disgusted with Taft's lack of leadership that he challenged him for the Republican nomination and, when that failed, ran under the banner of the Progressive or "Bull Moose" Party. The last remains of Taft's good humor had disappeared by the fall of 1912, as he angrily read glowing newspaper reviews of Wilson's intelligence and honor and Roosevelt's courage and charisma.

"There is no news of me except that I played golf," Taft groaned. "I seem to have heard that before."

NOT SURPRISINGLY, the voters did not reward Taft with a second term. He was relieved. He left the White House, making room for another golfer, Woodrow Wilson. In retirement, Taft continued to play golf and describe its many wonders to anyone who would listen. In November 1913, Taft was the guest of honor at the twenty-fifth anniversary dinner of the St. Andrew's Golf Club in New York. "The game's virtues include, first of all, self-restraint and call for mental discipline and ethical training," said Taft. "There should be no objections to playing it on the Sabbath day if one attends to his religious duties first. Church in the morning and golf in the afternoon on Sundays is an excellent compromise. It should be indulged in when the opportunity arises, as every man knows who has played the game that it rejuvenates and stretches the span of life."

When the job of chief justice of the United States opened up in 1921, Taft's name was whispered all over the capital. It was the job that Taft had wanted more than the presidency, and President Warren G. Harding seemed prepared to offer him the appointment; it seemed as sure a thing as a six-inch putt. But Taft was not counting on this gimme.

"I'll wait until the golf ball is in the hole," he said. Within a week, the job was his, making him the only man in American history to have the dual honor of serving the country as both president and chief justice.

He was much happier on the court than he was during those long four years at the White House. His happier mood helped him shed more than 100 pounds; it also helped that he frequently played golf and tamed his ravenous appetite. He continued to play the game, and not particularly well, until the age of seventy, when he was forced to quit because of a heart condition. During his final summer at Murray Bay in 1929, Taft sat on a clubhouse porch and glumly watched the golfers hit off the first tee.

Taft died in Washington on March 8, 1930, at the age of seventy-two. Within an hour of Taft's death, President Herbert Hoover issued the customary proclamation declaring that thirty days of mourning would follow. Hoover's private secretary, George Akerson, announced to the press corps the news of Taft's death and details of the funeral arrangements and the President's proclamation. There was a slight delay before Taft's death was publicly announced, however, because Hoover administration officials had to search for Akerson, who could not be located on the White House grounds. They found him on the fairway of a nearby golf course.

Woodrow Wilson

A Hopeless Love Affair

Woodrow Wilson tried golf because he was ordered to play by his doctor, but he quickly discovered that he loved and depended on its charms. Wilson's awkward putting technique explains why he almost never broke 100 and why he once needed approximately fifteen putts to complete a hole.

An ineffectual attempt to put an elusive ball into an obscure hole
with implements ill adapted to the purpose.
—Woodrow Wilson

NOT LONG AFTER MOVING into the White House in March 1913, Woodrow Wilson began to play golf every day except Sunday. Not every other day, not twice a week, but *every day,* from Monday through Saturday, rain or shine, even on a snowbound course with golf balls painted red by Secret Service men.

His personal physician prescribed the game, like a bottle of pills, as a necessary form of exercise for Wilson to battle the anguish of stomach cramps and migraine headaches related to a heart condition that was aggravated by stress. The doctor believed that golf, as well as horseback riding, would help relieve Wilson's mind of the presidency's pressures and worries. Wilson responded to the unorthodox prescription in the same grim way that many people react to a new health-regimen mandate from a doctor. It was a hassle and a chore. One biographer observed that Wilson played his daily round of golf "with the dogged determination of his Presbyterian nature." This was a polite way of saying that as he trudged through each morning's round, usually just after the sun came up, Woodrow Wilson played golf reluctantly, joylessly, and most of all, horribly.

It was not enough for Wilson to play golf because of doctor's orders; his playing partner each day was the doctor who had ordered him to play—Dr. Cary T. Grayson, who also just happened to be one of the President's closest friends. It was his way of making sure Wilson did what he needed to do to stay healthy. Like any good friend, Dr. Grayson worried that Wilson's condition would be exacerbated by an unhealthy diet and the incessant pounding of workday stress. It would turn out that each of Dr. Grayson's concerns, even the ones that seemed most petty, were well founded. Dr. Grayson changed Wilson's diet and advised him to exercise each day.

But taking his medicine with the doctor who prescribed it was also the President's choice. Wilson hated having to play with politicians or business leaders, as Taft had regularly done, because those people wanted to talk politics or current affairs on the links. He did not want, or need, any distractions.

"The fact of the matter is that he did not want business mingled with his recreation," Dr. Grayson explained in his memoirs, "and he soon found that most men whom he invited to play with him insisted on introducing public business into the conversation. He did one thing at a time. When he worked, he worked to the exclusion of everything from his mind except the matter in hand, and he carried the same spirit into his diversions."

Wilson famously said he had "a one-track mind," and when it came to golf, he concentrated on whatever track he was playing.

Despite the usual Washington jockeying for position, there was no "Golf Cabinet" during the Wilson administration. In the first days of his first term, Wilson was satisfied with a one-man Golf Cabinet, and Dr. Grayson was it. Their instant chemistry was likely due to the fact that each man played a sloppy, train-wreck game of lost balls and 4-putts. A triple-digit score goes down much smoother when you play with someone who shares your pain.

"He's terrible," remarked Joseph E. Murphy, the chief of the White House Secret Service detail, about Wilson's golf ability. "So is Grayson."

Colonel Edmund W. Starling, Wilson's personal bodyguard, lamented the chore of having to watch the two men take a total of more than 200 strokes to get around a golf course. Starling said: "A melancholy prospect—following two poor golfers over a windswept course on a winter's morning."

WILSON WAS NOT ATHLETIC. He stood nearly six feet tall, but at 175 pounds, Wilson was less than half the size of his predecessor, William Howard Taft. Wilson did not begin playing golf until he was in his forties, and it showed. His play was hampered by poor vision in his right eye that was the result of a retinal hemorrhage. "My right eye is like a horse's," Wilson said. "I can see straight out with it, but not sideways. As a result, I cannot take a full swing because my nose gets in the way and cuts off my view of the ball." His average score was 115, and he once needed twenty-six strokes to finish the par-4 second hole at the Washington Golf and Country Club. A conservative estimate is that he needed a 15-putt to finish.

Wilson brought to his golf game the same kind of determination he demonstrated as a boy, when he learned to read at the age of ten despite severe dyslexia. A decade later, he graduated from Princeton.

Through sheer will and hard work, Wilson became a scholar. He labored just as hard on his golf game, but he would never enjoy that same kind of success on the links.

No American president played more than Woodrow Wilson did.

By playing every day for long stretches of his first term—and by playing once or twice a week, even while serving as a wartime president during his second term—Wilson played at least 1,200 rounds of golf during his eight years in the White House, though the actual figure may be closer to 1,600, or twice as many rounds as Dwight D. Eisenhower.

Wilson's daily routine was to wake up early, eat a big breakfast, and play ninety minutes or two hours. During the week, he usually played twelve holes before returning, by midmorning, to his desk at the White House. On Saturdays, often in the afternoon, Wilson took three or four hours to play eighteen holes.

Driven in equal parts by his physician's wishes and that dogged determination, Wilson gradually discovered a purist's passion for the game, its simplicity and difficulty as appealing as any of his workday challenges. It did not matter if a chronic slice would force him to toil in the 100-plus vineyards for his entire golf career. It did not matter if everyone knew about his pronounced lack of athletic ability. (One writer quipped that Wilson "was a fidgety player who addressed the ball as if he would reason with it." The same writer added that his wild swing "would bring tears to the eyes of his caddy.")

Perhaps most striking of all, it did not matter to President Wilson if the press chided him for first going to the golf course on weekday mornings. It turns out, though, that the press was far gentler to Wilson than Taft when it came to golf, even though Wilson played more often. It may simply have been that the press knew that when Wilson was at work, he was *working*. With Taft, one never knew. All that mattered to President Wilson was this inexplicable joy that he accidentally discovered when playing the game. By his second term, the impossible, elusive game had suddenly become one of the most important things in his life.

Like Taft, Wilson described golf as the "perfect diversion" from the pressures of the Oval Office. Unlike Taft, Wilson had a no–nonsense, professorial mind; he was obsessive about the details of his work. Golf gave President Wilson a fine excuse to temporarily rest that mind and concentrate on something that was trivial yet fun. "My chief real interest is golf," he wrote in a letter to a friend in 1914. "It seems to put oxygen into my heart."

"While you are playing," he wrote to another friend, "you cannot worry and be preoccupied with affairs. Each stroke requires your whole attention and seems the most important thing in life."

WILSON WAS FAMOUS for being on the golf course at important moments during his two terms in office. In fact, he dubbed himself the "crisis golfer," which meant that crises had a way of finding him on the links.

Wilson's election to his first term as president was only a few hours old when he celebrated by playing a round with Dr. Grayson, on November 6, 1912. At the 18th hole, a few players near the clubhouse spotted Wilson and asked how he had played. Grayson "has me three down, but I don't care," Wilson said. "I am up four states on yesterday's election."

In 1914, the Mexican government refused to apologize for arresting American sailors at Tampico. Wilson stopped his round at the

Town and Country course across the Potomac in Virginia to sign an ultimatum that threatened military action against the Mexicans.

On the morning of May 7, 1915, Wilson hurried off a course in Maryland after hearing the tragic news that 123 Americans had died when a German submarine sank the *Lusitania,* a Cunard cruise liner. Upon returning to the White House, Wilson convened a meeting of his military advisers to discuss the crisis.

In November 1916, one day after the presidential election, the result was still in doubt as the President played a round of golf at Spring Lake. An observer said that Wilson "seemed as calm as ever, and played just as poorly." On one of the fairways, Dr. Grayson rushed up with the good news that California was in Wilson's win column, clinching a second term. Wilson just kept on playing.

A second important person joined President Wilson's Golf Cabinet in 1915. The new recruit was a surprise member—in fact, a woman. Her name was Edith Bolling Galt, an intelligent, attractive forty-three-year-old widow. And within ten months of first meeting and playing a round with the President, she became the First Lady of the United States.

Their love story begins, refreshingly, on a golf course. Or, perhaps it is more precise to say that their love story began because of a shortened round of golf. On a windy, bright Saturday afternoon in March 1915, Wilson and Dr. Grayson played twelve holes at Town and Country. It had rained the night before, and the course was a muddy mess. They had intended to play eighteen holes that day, but the mud, combined with the gusty late-winter winds, brought the round to a premature halt.

The two men took a Pierce-Arrow landaulet, affixed with the presidential seal on the door, from the course back to the White House. They walked through the grand foyer and up a staircase, leaving a trail of mud from their boots on the marble floor. They rounded a corner on the second floor, and a beautiful woman walked "almost into the President's arms," an observer said.

The woman was Edith Galt, a close friend of the President's cousin, Helen Bones. The two women had gone for a walk that day through the capital and had also collected mud on their shoes. Helen Bones persuaded her reluctant friend to join her for a cup of tea at the White House.

After the President and Mrs. Galt literally bumped into each other, Helen made the introduction. "Cousin Woodrow," Helen told the President, "I should like to present Mrs. Norman Galt."

Mrs. Galt was quite disheveled herself; her boots were caked with mud, her hair was a windblown mess, and she had worried earlier that she was in such a state of disarray that she might "be taken for a tramp." And yet, she would later recall, she didn't look *all* bad.

"The President and Dr. Grayson, just returned from golf, with boots as muddy as ours, were rounding the turn of the hall," Mrs. Galt wrote in her memoirs. "We met face to face. We all laughed at our plight, but I would have been less feminine than I must confess to be, had I not been secretly glad that I had worn a smart black tailored suit which Worth had made for me in Paris, and a tricot hat which I thought completed a very good-looking ensemble.

"The two gentlemen, I am sorry to say, were not so well attired. Their golf suits, as I found out later, were made by a cheap tailor the President had known years before and whom he was trying to help by giving an order. They were *not* smart.

"This was the accidental meeting which carried out the old adage of 'turn a corner and meet your fate.'"

It may sound trite, but Woodrow Wilson, the fifty-eight-year-old melancholy widower President, fell in love at first sight, at that very moment, almost completely by surprise and in a sweetly innocent way. The President insisted that the accidental foursome have tea in the Oval Room on the second floor. The ladies freshened up, the men changed out of their golf attire, and they sipped their tea before a crackling fire. It was "an enchanted hour," one biographer said. "Edith Galt, responding happily to the atmosphere, felt as if she were among old friends. She was aware that the President could hardly take his eyes off her."

Wilson had been very lonely since the death of his wife, Ellen Axson Wilson, months earlier of nephritis with complications. Her last words to Dr. Grayson were, "Promise me that you will take good care of my husband." Wilson was so devastated by her death that he remained by her deathbed for two nights after she died.

It seemed obvious to both Helen Bones and Dr. Grayson that the President was falling helplessly in love with Mrs. Galt. A few days later, Mrs. Galt was invited back for a White House dinner, and everyone remarked on how captivated the President was by her charm.

"She's a looker," observed Pat McKenna, the White House door-keeper.

"He's a goner," said Arthur Brooks, Wilson's valet.

Wilson was gone before the spring turned warm. The President quietly changed the routine of his late afternoon automobile rides to include a walk in Rock Creek Park, a few miles from the White House. The walks were always with Mrs. Galt, accompanied, at a safe but respectful distance, by Colonel Starling, the President's personal bodyguard, and a few other security men.

"He talked, gesticulated, laughed, boldly held her hand," Starling observed. "It was hard to believe he was 58-years-old. He had a natural lightness of foot, and walking along the woodland paths he leaped over the smallest obstacles, or skipped around them." Before long, newspapermen heard rumors about the President's sweetheart. To try to keep the relationship a secret, Starling and the other Secret Service men created a code word for Mrs. Galt. They referred to her among themselves as "Grandma," but Starling was quick to add that the security detail intended "no offense to the lady."

The courtship was quick. Before the leaves changed that fall, they were engaged.

Not everyone in Washington approved of Wilson becoming en-gaged so quickly after Ellen's death. A saucy joke made the rounds:

"What did Mrs. Galt do when the President proposed to her?"

"Fell out of bed."

The happy couple ignored the whispers. Exactly one week before Christmas, they were married during a small evening ceremony at the White House. The next morning, the First Couple traveled to The Homestead, a popular resort in Hot Springs, Virginia, for a ten-day holiday honeymoon. That first morning in Hot Springs, Starling overheard someone whistling a tune echoing down a hallway at the resort. He peeked into a sitting room, and saw a familiar figure wearing a top hat, tailcoat, and gray morning trousers. His back was to Starling, hands thrust deeply into his pants pockets, and the man—the President of the United States!—was dancing "a jig," his heels clicking almost ridiculously in midair. "Oh, you beautiful doll!" the President sang. "You great big beautiful doll. . . . "

THE NEW FIRST LADY possessed another quality that Wilson cherished. She played golf, and, according to most accounts, she was a more talented player than the President—or Dr. Grayson—which was not a difficult standard to surpass. At The Homestead, they awoke early each morning in their suite, which overlooked the golf course, and after a quick breakfast, they played a round of golf. Several times over the next few years, Mrs. Wilson would write this entry in her diary: "Played golf with W and Grayson. Beat them both."

Mrs. Wilson played both the best and worst holes of her life during her honeymoon. The worst was a short, uphill, par-4 on a cold, drizzly day. Mrs. Wilson topped the ball on her second shot, driving it deep into the rain-soaked ground. She later recalled that she "flailed away" at the ball, with "mud flying in all directions." It took the First Lady seventeen strokes to extricate the ball from the muck.

It turned out that her best hole was also a par-4, ending with the kind of impossible shot that one had to see to believe. It began as troublesome as most of the First Lady's holes. Mrs. Wilson's drive off the tee failed to carry over a road lined with rail fences on each side. Her ball stopped right in front of the fence, a ridiculously impossible lie. Her caddy, a Secret Service agent named Jarvis, asked her what club she would like.

"A putter," she said.

The agent apparently shook his head hopelessly, and Mrs. Wilson

President Wilson fell almost immediately in love with Edith Bolling Galt, a striking, forty-three-year-old widow. Ten months after being introduced to Wilson inside the White House, she became the First Lady of the United States and the President's favorite golfing partner. She was skilled enough on the links to defeat Wilson and his doctor, Cary Grayson. "Played golf with W and Grayson," the First Lady wrote in her diary. "Beat them both."

had the feeling that if her name were still just plain old Mrs. Galt, the agent would have yelled, "You're crazy!"

With an enormous swing, Mrs. Wilson slapped the ball under the fence. It skittered across the road, rolled fast up the fairway and onto the green toward the hole, where it incredibly dropped into the cup . . . for an eagle.

Mrs. Wilson noted in her 1938 memoirs that there were few "triumphant moments" that she and the President enjoyed more than that eagle, and the shocked expression on Special Agent Jarvis's face.

When they returned to the White House, after the New Year, the new Mrs. Wilson joined her husband and Dr. Grayson on their early morning golf outings. One morning at the Spring Lake Club, the First Lady struggled with her golf game. Usually, Secret Service men caddied for the President and First Lady, but on this day two elderly members asked for the honor of carrying their bags. Mrs. Wilson was playing so poorly that the elderly gentleman who was caddying for her was becoming increasingly impatient with each hole. She observed that the man was becoming "more and more bored. Finally, I thought to placate the old fellow by asking his advice. When I had a very near approach to the green, I asked in my most beguiling way, 'Do you think I can reach the green with the midiron?'"

"'Yes, if you hit it often enough,'" he replied.

The three-person Golf Cabinet convened at several area golf clubs. Their favorites were Kirkside, in Chevy Chase, Maryland, and the Washington Country Club, in Arlington, Virginia.

Early in his first term, Wilson enjoyed playing at another local club, the Town and Country, in Rockville, Maryland. In the spring of 1914, Wilson hit a drive on a par-4 hole toward a green that was not visible from where Wilson was standing. The foursome ahead was still on the green, and Wilson's ball almost skidded by one of the players, Fulton Brylawski, a club member. Brylawski angrily rushed toward the tee box, loudly protesting the breach of golf etiquette. But as he approached the offending foursome, Brylawski realized, belatedly, that his target was the President of the United States. Brylawski was teased the rest of his life by his friends about the incident; they yelled "Fore" at him as he rode the capital's streetcars. He later felt so badly about what had happened that he wrote the President an apology.

Wilson never returned to the Town and Country.

M RS. WILSON MOVED INTO THE STREAM of White House life without disturbing its even flow," Colonel Starling wrote. "She went golfing each morning with the President, and he got a great deal more fun out of the game with her [as his] partner. . . . The President and Mrs. Wilson were inexpert golfers, he averaging about 115 and she about 200." Despite that astronomically high average score, the First Lady managed to occasionally beat the President, leaving one to wonder whether Starling had overestimated her average or underestimated his.

"She used a niblick most of the time, and depended on me to keep her out of trouble," Colonel Starling wrote. "I cheated for her, retrieving the balls she knocked into the woods and dropping them on the edge of the fairway."

One day, Mrs. Wilson whispered to Colonel Starling, "You could beat all of us if you were playing."

"I would rather caddy for you," he replied, "than be the best player in the world."

"She blushed prettily," Starling recalled, "and my day was made. There is not a bit of use in denying it—I was her slave."

Colonel Starling observed that the First Couple's sky-high final scores did not diminish their enthusiasm for the game. "Walking along the fairway between shots," Starling wrote, "the President regaled her with dialect stories and gave impromptu impersonations, one of his best being an interpretation of serious little Dr. Grayson addressing a ball."

On another day, Mrs. Wilson laid her club across her husband's shoulders and bent him forward so that it would not slip off. "Immediately," Grayson observed, "he changed his stride to imitate the lumbering gait of an ape. . . . They both laughed—they laughed at anything and everything in those days. They were completely happy, and the increasing burden of his job rested lightly on the President's shoulders."

The First Couple's happiness brought pleasure to everyone at the White House. "She was a blessing and a delight to President Wilson," observed a White House doorman named Mayes. "He was so lonely before she came. I remember him and Dr. Grayson sitting back to back every evening in the study reading by the light of that little old oil lamp."

The joyful air lasted only for a year. One day in January 1917, Mrs. Wilson saw her husband return from the Oval Office looking shaken and ashen. "What's wrong, Woodrow?" she asked.

The President handed her a yellow piece of paper, an Associated Press dispatch with a Berlin dateline. "Read that," he said.

It said: "The German government has announced that unrestricted submarine warfare will begin around the British Isles tomorrow, Feb. 1."

"What does it mean?" the First Lady asked.

"It means war," Wilson replied.

Within the hour, the official German cable arrived from the State Department, warning that every ship entering the "war zone" would be sunk. But the Germans added that only one American ship a week would be permitted to sail, and only to a port in Great Britain of the Germans' choosing. This enraged America more than anything because Germany was dictating where and how the American ships should sail.

The next morning, as the President waited for his secretary of state, Robert Lansing, he seemed deeply shaken. "I feel as though the world had reversed itself and instead of turning toward the east, we're revolving westward," the President said.

Colonel Edward House, the President's closest adviser, joined them. "We sat listlessly, killing time," House wrote in his memoirs. "The President nervously arranged his books and walked up and down the floor. We had finished the discussion in half an hour and there was nothing more to say."

Mrs. Wilson suggested, "We might play golf. Do you think that would make a bad impression, Colonel?"

"I don't think the American people would feel that the President should do anything trivial at a time like this," House said somberly.

Wilson struggled for weeks with how to handle the crisis, trying to devise ways to avoid war. "I doubt if the Constitution will survive a war," he told Frank Cobb, the editor of the *New York World,* on April 1. "A nation can't put its strength into war and keep its head level. It's never yet been done."

"Perhaps America will be different," Cobb suggested.

The strain on the President was visible to everyone. He had not gotten a good night's sleep in weeks, complaining that he lay awake at night obsessively trying to devise ways to avoid war. Mrs. Wilson was convinced that golf was the only way to alleviate the President's stress, despite Colonel House's warning.

So on the morning of April 2, the First Couple woke before dawn and drove to Kirkside for a round of golf. She risked the criticism. "If people think it's trivial, let them make the most of it," she decided.

That night, President Wilson traveled to Capitol Hill, where, in a level voice but still hinting of emotion, he asked Congress for a declaration of war against Germany. He told the packed chamber that the war would be fought in an attempt "to vindicate the principles of peace and justice in the life of the world . . . to make the world safe for democracy."

"America is privileged to spend her blood and her might for the principles which gave her birth and happiness and the peace which she has treasured," Wilson continued. "God helping her, she can do no other."

Four days later, on April 6, 1917, President Wilson signed the declaration of war. On that day, too, he played a quick nine holes of golf.

M RS. WILSON SAW IT AS HER JOB and her patriotic duty to insure that her husband was fit, felt fine, and was even happily distracted, despite the intense pressures of serving as commander in chief. On the day after his war speech at the Capitol, for example, she had to beg him to play with her before he hunkered down in the Oval Office. He reluctantly agreed to join her. "Only getting my Precious for nine holes," she noted in her diary.

Planning and supervising the war consumed eighteen hours every day. "Before six, the President was at his desk and often he was there at midnight," the First Lady wrote. Dr. Grayson told the First Lady that the President no longer had time to play golf every morning, as it usually consumed at least two hours. But Wilson still needed to exercise, Dr. Grayson said.

"Horseback riding," he suggested. "And you've got to make him think it's your idea." She persuaded her husband to ride horses with her, usually through Rock Creek Park in the capital, on the days when there was not time for golf, and it helped him immensely.

After the war began, security on the links was tightened. World War I created a tradition that has since been used to protect every golfing president: Secret Service men hiding on a golf course, usually out of bounds and out of sight. "They still played golf, of course," Starling wrote, "but now, as they walked along the fairway laughing and joking, they had an unseen audience, of which they were unaware. The woods were full of Secret Service men, who took up their post before the couple arrived and remained until after they left, moving with them as they walked along the course, but always keeping out of sight."

One day, as the President teed off, Edith Wilson recalled that "two little boys who had been following along asked the other, 'Who is them men who don't play?' With much scorn, the other answered, 'Why them's his keepers.' Mr. Wilson said he did not mind muffing his shot."

The war continued to curtail Wilson's golf schedule in unexpected ways, even threatening his pastime of wintertime golf. Dr. Harry Garfield, the head of the government's Commission on Fuel, banned the use of fuel at country clubs during the winter of 1918. Knowing all too well that Wilson depended on his golf game, Dr. Garfield called the White House to offer exemptions to any of the country clubs where the President might play golf.

But Wilson rejected the exemption, sending this message: "I would not for anything have him make any exception with regard to the country clubs at which I play golf during the winter. I would not consent in any case, but as a matter of fact, I never make use of the clubhouses." Unlike Taft, who liked to hang around the clubhouse, Wilson would only enter one if he needed to walk through it to get to the first tee or use the bathroom.

It was likely the stress of the war that put the President in an especially foul mood one humid day in early August 1918 at the Kirkside course. "I was carrying his clubs, since no caddies were available," Starling wrote. "He drove about 50 yards from the tee and I saw as he walked toward the ball that he was in an ugly temper. Generally he asked me what club he should use, but this morning, he said, 'Starling, give me my number two iron.' As he was addressing the ball, a boy at a house on the edge of the course cupped his hands to his mouth and tried to call like an Indian. The President stepped to one side, rested on his club, and said in a disgusted manner, 'That boy must be training to be a Senator. He is always making a noise with his mouth and not saying anything.'

"He then hit the ball and topped it, rolling it ahead 25 yards. Then he asked me for a brassie—he should have been using a number six iron—and got a beautiful shot which landed 100 yards on the other side of the green. This tickled him, and his good humor was restored."

IN THE SPRING OF 1918, at the height of the war, a British tank, the Britannia, was on display at the White House. Wilson took a ride in it, down the driveway to the complex's front gate. Before he climbed out, he inadvertently grabbed a white-hot pipe, severely burning his hand. It needed a large bandage, and for several weeks he could not use the hand. Incredibly, he kept on playing golf, using just his left hand. "Woodrow is becoming the greatest one-arm champion in the world," Mrs. Wilson said.

When the war finally ended, Wilson worked even harder on a peace settlement, campaigning vigorously on behalf of the League of Nations both at home and abroad, where he traveled to Great Britain, France, and Italy.

The foreign trip was the first long stretch during which Wilson failed to keep up with his daily routine of golf and horseback riding. That fact alone worried his wife. In Paris, "other great men could go golfing on weekends," Wilson biographer Gene Smith wrote, "but when they returned, always they saw lights burning in [Wilson's] chambers." The overseas trip exhausted the President. But coming home to try to sell the League of Nations was even worse. In the summer of 1919, Dr. Grayson's fears came true when, at the age of sixty-two, the President suffered from thrombosis and then a severe stroke, which left him unable to serve as president. This fact was kept from the nation, and during his last seventeen months in office, the affairs of state were secretly managed by Mrs. Wilson and Dr. Grayson and other advisers.

President Wilson survived through his last day in office and for three years following. But Mrs. Wilson often wondered whether his health would not have declined so rapidly if he had continued to do what Dr. Grayson had prescribed—if he had kept riding horses, taking walks in Rock Creek Park, and playing a daily round of golf.

CALVIN COOLIDGE

THE WORST OF THEM ALL

Calvin Coolidge poses for a photograph, demonstrating his usual relaxed, carefree demeanor. As president, Coolidge played the game so infrequently—and with so little enthusiasm—that no photographs could be located of him on a golf course.

I did not see the sense in chasing a little white ball around a field.
—Calvin Coolidge

NO ONE DRESSED WITH LESS FLAIR and imagination for a round of golf than Calvin Coolidge. But his sartorial choices were appropriate. No American president played the game with less flair and imagination than Silent Cal.

His game was a disheveled, chaotic mess. He played so infrequently and with so little enthusiasm that some biographies of Coolidge state flatly that he never picked up a golf club. Perhaps they were being technical about it. On the golf course, what Coolidge did bore almost no resemblance to the way the game was intended to be played.

Golf boomed during the Roaring Twenties despite Coolidge's famous ambivalence about his own ineffective game. Americans' infatuation with the game was inspired by the astounding feats of the great amateur Bobby Jones. Its popularity was also fueled by the stock market's astonishing acceleration, which allowed an increasing number of Americans to afford the game's considerable greens fees and other costs. As his tenure in the White House wore on and golf's popularity surged, Coolidge was actually chided by the press for not playing more often, even though his pronounced lack of ability was the source of nationwide merriment.

In 1927, after Coolidge failed to play a round of golf during a vacation in Sioux Falls, South Dakota, the *American Golfer* complained that "it was too bad" that Coolidge was not as smitten by the game as so many of his constituents were. "For Sioux Falls was equipped and ready to lead him to the scenes of activities of this kind that must surely have pleased him, had he been only of the golfing clan," the magazine wrote, almost wistfully.

Coolidge had to know he was the worst White House golfer to date, but at least Taft, Wilson, and Harding enjoyed themselves on the links or, at the very least, savored those moments when the game was enjoyable. Coolidge probably never imagined that nearly a century later, he would still qualify as the least talented American president to swing a club and as the only president to play the game with pure apathy.

Self-awareness, like a smart sense of fashion, had never come naturally to Calvin Coolidge. He was apparently oblivious to the stares and snickers of his playing partners when he stepped on the first tee one bright, crisp morning in the autumn of 1923. Coolidge looked as if a traveling circus had lent him a clown costume to satirize the ridiculous game (and his inability to hit the ball certainly qualified him for the assignment). The president wore cream-colored, high-waist pants that one observer noted "had long since served their usefulness for social functions," and garish, canary-yellow suspenders. He also wore a navy blue dinner jacket, with gold studs. The shoes were even worse: a pair of high-top white sneakers that resembled well-worn slippers. On his head, he wore a white canvas hat. His playing partners were all sharply dressed in the day's golf style: argyle vests with matching socks, pressed cotton trousers and shirts, and spit-shined golf shoes with cleats.

Coolidge peeled off the dinner jacket and handed it to an aide. He paused a moment. His fellow players must have wondered whether he was going to tee off or make a toast. He selected an iron for the first hole, which was believed to be the easiest par-3 in all of Washington. The hole was located at the Friendship estate, a private course owned by Edward B. McLean, the publisher of the *Washington Post*.

It could have been the first hole at St. Andrew's. It really didn't matter. Coolidge's first tee shot dribbled about ten yards, then stopped cold. On his second swing, his club just grazed the top of the ball, and this time the ball rolled an even shorter distance. He kept slapping the ball, again and again. By the time the ball managed to make the journey onto the green, Calvin Coolidge had taken eleven swings. He was on pace to exceed 200 strokes for the round.

And yet none of it mattered to Coolidge. Not once did anyone overhear Coolidge complain, or swear, or scold himself for the sloppy play, or even beseech the golf gods to grant him a single effortless swing. It was bad golf—no, it was horrendous golf—and it was excruciating to watch. But it was played by Coolidge and his friends amid the kind of silence enforced by tennis referees and school librarians.

So why did Coolidge even bother to play? He may have felt duty-bound to try the game after being repeatedly asked to play by other politicians and friends in Washington. After observing him play a few rounds, though, they stopped asking him.

It was understandable that Silent Cal had little to say on the golf course. He had little to say throughout his presidency. In one of the most famous anecdotes told about Coolidge, a woman who sat next to the President at a White House dinner confided to him that she had bet a friend that she would be able to coax more than two words out of the President's mouth. Coolidge stared at her for a very long moment.

"You lose," he said.

COOLIDGE ALWAYS SAW THE BENEFITS of choosing as few words as possible. "I don't recall any candidate for President that ever injured himself very much by not talking," he observed. As his nickname, "Silent Cal," caught on, he told Ethel Barrymore, a correspondent for *Time* magazine: "I think the American public wants a solemn ass as a President. And I think I'll go along with them." He equated his silence as a subtler way of saying no to the many glad-handers who dropped by the Oval Office with some selfish request or urgent need. "You have to stand every day three or four hours of visitors," he grumbled. "Nine-tenths of them want something they ought not to have. If you keep dead-still, they will run down in three or four minutes. If you even cough or smile, they will start up all over again."

Coolidge came to Washington as Warren G. Harding's vice president, a job he accepted specifically because its demands were so few.

"It was my intention when I became Vice President to remain in Washington, avoid speaking and to attend to the work of my office," he wrote in his autobiography. "But the pressure to speak is constant and intolerable. However, I resisted most of it."

Harding died in August 1923, and Coolidge was suddenly elevated to the presidency. A few days after he moved into the White House, a gang of laborers was tearing up a street in front of the Executive Office Building. The job's foreman watched as Coolidge and a senior aide crossed the White House lawn toward the street for an early morning walk. A White House Secret Service agent overheard the foreman exclaim: "What a fine looking man our new President is! So tall and straight! Who's the little fellow with him?"

The foreman was informed that the little fellow was the President.

"Glory be to God!" the foreman said. "Now ain't it a grand country when a wee man like that can get to be the grandest of them all!"

Rather than inflate his confidence, the highest office in the land seemed to swallow the grand wee man. The office of the presidency has transformed the lightest of weights, but it failed to burnish America's view of Coolidge or his own self-image. He despised arrogance and detested conceit, and so he refused to project either one. His awe at living in the White House was obvious. "It was as if he were a small boy whose daydream of being king had suddenly been made real by the stroke of a magic wand," observed Colonel Edmund W. Starling, the chief of the Secret Service and one of Coolidge's closest friends. "He would almost tiptoe around, touching things and half smiling to himself."

The nation sensed, and even appreciated, Coolidge's easy acceptance of his own limitations. On the golf course, Coolidge would never think of taking an extra shot. And that aw-shucks humility was recognized by the American people, who gave him a term in his own right in the 1924 election against John W. Davis.

"It is a great advantage to a President, and a major source of safety to the country, for him to know he is not a great man," Coolidge once said. As president, Coolidge was always lowering the expectations. Sometimes, it worked. But the habit also convinced some Americans that Calvin Coolidge lacked the confidence and grittiness that they had come to expect from presidents, beginning with Theodore Roosevelt. Who wants to have confidence in someone who lacks it in himself, especially a president?

Americans rarely listen carefully to their president. Instead, their eyes do all the work, searching for subtle signs of strength and self-confidence in the chief executive's manner and speech patterns. But in Coolidge's case, there were few discernible signs of strength or self-confidence. He barely exercised, for one thing, and he had few hobbies or outside interests. He did not go hunting or swimming or hiking or horseback riding. He did not play billiards or poker or croquet, nor did he collect stamps. He once said, "All growth depends upon activity. Life is manifest only by action. There is no development, physically or intellectually, without effort, and effort means work." Those words could easily be applied to his golf game, which he would have agreed was nothing more than "a good walk spoiled," as Mark Twain famously called it.

To Coolidge, an early morning walk, preferably without an audience, was sufficient "activity." He especially enjoyed walking up and down F Street, gazing into the shop windows at clothes and antiques. It was something he did almost every morning, rain or shine.

"Guess you wonder why I like to window shop," he told an aide. "It takes me away from my work and rests my mind." Another of his hobbies was riding a mechanical horse that was kept in the White House's personal residence. In fact, Coolidge rode the mechanical horse with far more glee than he ever swung a golf club. When it was first given to him by a friend, an aide dared Coolidge to try it, but he refused. The following morning, he attempted to ride it with no witnesses. He found the machine irresistible. That afternoon, he took aides to his room to show off his prowess. But he insisted on keeping his hat on.

Riding the mechanical horse was much easier for Coolidge than trying to hit a golf ball with any consistency. The only other time Coolidge exercised was on a golf course, and considering that there is no record showing that he ever broke 100, the few rounds that he played may have qualified as his most strenuous exercise. Perhaps that is why he detested the game.

CALVIN COOLIDGE, the thirtieth president and a native Vermonter, had never been much of an athlete, preferring textbooks to playbooks of any kind.

At Amherst College, Coolidge was described as "a shy, slight auburn-haired lad" who was extremely serious about his schoolwork. He did not participate in any extracurricular activities. Sensitive about his bookish image, Coolidge never liked being asked questions about whether he participated in college athletics, just as he did not appreciate being asked about his golf score. "I tended to the education of my head, not my legs," he said of his priorities in college.

Coolidge got his first taste of golf at Amherst, where he played a few rounds. He picked up the game again during his honeymoon in Montreal in 1905. But he played only a few times and then gave it up until 1921, when he played in Washington after becoming Harding's vice president.

By the time Coolidge moved into the White House, golf was a deeply entrenched part of the capital's culture. The *American Golfer* reported that "golf bags in the Senate and House office buildings are as common as briefcases, lame ducks and lobbyists." Coolidge was soon surrounded by golfers: Vice President Charles G. Dawes, Secretary of State Frank Kellogg, and other Cabinet members were devoted hackers.

And so Coolidge took up the game again, fretfully and even fearfully. Perhaps it was the game's expensive fees that frightened him. Coolidge's Yankee upbringing taught him to be almost painfully frugal, a trait that defined him nearly as much as his silence.

One early September evening, Coolidge was out for a walk when a man in a horse-drawn carriage pulled up alongside him. The driver lifted his tattered stovepipe hat.

"Would y'all like to take a ride?" the man asked Coolidge.

The President's eyes sparkled at the prospect, and he told his aide, "Let's take a ride."

"It'll cost you three dollars," the aide said.

"We'll walk," Coolidge said.

If golf carts had been available for rent in the 1920s, Coolidge would have never gone for a ride in one of them, either.

On the rare occasion when he did play, Coolidge played at Chevy Chase Club, where he was made an honorary member in March 1921, shortly after being sworn in as vice president. He was usually accompanied by Freddie McLeod, one of the leading golf professionals who lived in the capital. On one occasion, as McLeod looked on, the President took a fat swing, striking the ground and not the ball, the impact shattering the wooden shaft of his club.

"Freddie, that can be fixed, can't it?" Coolidge asked. He was crestfallen when he learned that a broken club must be replaced at an exorbitant cost.

As for his playing partners, they were often dumbfounded at what to say to the President, his play was so awful.

"You have to dress for golf," Coolidge grumbled during his presidency. "Then you have to drive out to some club. It takes three hours to play a round, then you have to undress, take a shower, dress again and drive back." There were more complaints about the game's costs: "Callers at the White House might wonder why the President wasn't on the job."

During the course of his five and a half years in office, Coolidge played the game less and less frequently as the years passed.

Challenged once about why he even bothered to play a game that he so effortlessly mangled, Coolidge confided that he had found some benefits to the experience. "I think it is a fine method of relaxation for men in business life," he said dutifully. But he quickly added this caveat: "Like everything else which is an outside enterprise, it can undoubtedly be carried to excess."

In 1924, Coolidge and his wife, Grace, attended the opening of the Congressional Country Club in Bethesda, Maryland. The club had built the lavish Presidential Suite, where President and Mrs. Coolidge ate a dinner of grilled steak and French fries. The club had promised that the Presidential Suite "would be kept ever in readiness for occupancy by the President of the United States."

The club also built a secret passage between the Presidential Suite and a nearby room to allow the President to slip away if reporters or other "hangers-on" showed up after a round, the Congressional history says. It is not hard to imagine the escape hatch being built according to the specific instructions of Coolidge, who would appreciate such an option more than most presidents.

But Coolidge never came back. The splendor of a private Presidential Suite at one of the nation's top golf clubs was lost on him. He saw it as just another place to eat supper. In fact, the Presidential Suite would sit unused for six years because Coolidge's successor, Herbert Hoover, was not a golfer. In 1930, the Congressional Country Club rented out the Presidential Suite for $25 a day (there were few curious Coolidge fans willing to pay that rate). Later, the suite was converted into a tournament office.

Coolidge played golf so rarely that the Burning Tree Golf Club history mistakenly claimed that he had never played. The error was corrected in a later club history edition. The following anecdote was included about Coolidge's decision, as vice president in 1921, to visit Burning Tree for his first round of golf in sixteen years: "He jabbed at the ball. He pecked away eleven times before finally reaching the green. The foursome decided that that was enough, and Coolidge's golf remained a honeymoon memory."

When Coolidge left the White House in 1929 to make way for Herbert Hoover, he remembered to pack his mechanical horse for the trip home to Northampton, Massachusetts, where he would spend his final days. In a White House closet, left behind, was a set of barely touched golf clubs.

RONALD REAGAN
THE GOLFING GIPPER

With his wife, Nancy, standing behind him, Ronald Reagan grimaces at an ugly putt at the Annenberg estate during his annual New Year's Eve round of golf on December 31, 1988, his last round as president. Just three weeks later, Reagan left the White House and settled into retirement in California.

I learned a long time ago that if you're going to throw a club in anger,
throw it in front of you so you won't have to go back and pick it up.
—Ronald Reagan

M OMENTS AFTER President Ronald Reagan's ball landed on the famous par-3, 16th green at Augusta National Golf Club on a Saturday afternoon in October 1983, several Secret Service agents informed the President and his playing partners that a terrorist, armed with a .35-caliber pistol, had taken control of the pro shop. The gunman, who was holding seven people hostage, including two White House aides, made two demands: He wanted a bottle of whiskey. And he wanted to speak with the President.

It is not at all surprising that Ronald Reagan reacted this way to the news: We'll play through, thank you. It was Reagan's first opportunity, as president, to play a round at America's most prestigious private golf club, and he'd be damned if he was going to allow the occasion to be spoiled by some hostage-taking nut. The President's foursome included Secretary of State George Shultz, Treasury Secretary Donald Regan and Nicholas Brady, a former Republican senator from New Jersey who was a serious, competitive golfer.

Brady had hit a beautiful drive that stopped less than two feet from the hole, but he never got a chance to tap in his birdie putt. The Secret Service men, armed with Uzis, insisted that Reagan and his golfing entourage get off the course. Without further discussion, the Secret Service agents first hustled the President, then the other three men, into an armored limousine, which whisked them off the fairway to safety.

The idyllic Augusta course was quickly transformed into a hot zone of paramilitary chaos. Low-flying helicopters, filled with men armed with semiautomatic weapons and binoculars, buzzed the course. Members of a negotiating team, carrying bullhorns and wearing grim frowns, shouted instructions into their radios. Dozens of Secret Service agents and sheriff's deputies set up a perimeter surrounding the pro shop. The armed men pointed pistols and sub-machine guns at the pro shop's well-lit windows filled with man-nequins wearing Augusta hats and Augusta shirts and Augusta V-neck sweaters.

Reagan was rushed to the course's Eisenhower Cottage, where he was spending the weekend. Using a car telephone, President Reagan repeatedly and unsuccessfully tried to speak with the gunman. "This is the President of the United States," Reagan said into the phone, according to a transcript of the one-way conversation. "This is Ronald Reagan. I understand you want to talk to me. [Pause] This is the President. If you're hearing me, would you please tell me and we can have that talk that you wanted." The gunman hung up. Reagan redialed the clubhouse at least five additional times; each time, the gunman listened for a moment to the President before hanging up.

The "terrorist" was a forty-five-year-old Augusta man named Charles R. Harris, who was despondent over recently losing a fac-tory job. Harris rammed his blue-and-silver Dodge pickup truck through an iron gate at Augusta and stormed the pro shop, brandish-ing the gun, taking hostages and shouting demands.

Over the next two hours, Harris released each of the seven hostages, one by one. Only one bullet was fired; it punctured a hole in the pro shop floor. Negotiators—and Harris's mother—managed to persuade him to surrender, quietly, as the sun began to set on Augusta.

Doctors and police officials said Harris had been drinking and was depressed not only over the recent loss of his job but also over the death of his father that spring. Friends pronounced themselves baffled at what had motivated Harris to disrupt the President's round at Augusta. "He called me on election night to crow that his man had won," said Johnny O'Bryant, a coworker. "He thought Reagan was just what this country needed." Harris was sentenced to ten years in federal prison and ended up serving three and a half be-fore being paroled in 1987.

Reagan's crisis-shortened round at Augusta was the first and last time he played that famed course while in office. You could have received some fat odds if you'd bet that one of Reagan's few times on a golf course during his presidency would be interrupted by a gun-wielding, hostage-taking, whiskey-guzzling Reagan man.

If the foursome had not been interrupted, Brady had an easy tap-in for a birdie, which would have allowed him and the President to win the hole and the afternoon's wagers against Regan and Shultz. But Brady never got a chance to hit his tap-in.

"Golfers never pay on a match that's not finished," Don Regan said later, somewhat sheepishly. "And anyway, I think Shultz should have paid them—if anyone—because I think I mentioned it later to the President, asked him if I owed him, and he said forget it."

Even after the crisis concluded, the presidential foursome's golf balls remained, untouched, on the 16th green.

IT MIGHT BE A SURPRISE to find Ronald Reagan among the four worst presidential golfers. Although Reagan's handicap as a young man was as low as 12, he played golf only a dozen times during his eight years in the White House, from 1981 to 1989. President Reagan's golf scores were not disclosed to the press, and it was assumed at the time that the secrecy was necessary to keep the public from learning about Reagan's triple-digit embarrassments.

Those assumptions were correct. Several people who played with President Reagan said they cannot recall him ever breaking 100, though if he did, they said his score was in the 90s but enhanced by gimmes on the greens. This level of play places the "Gipper" securely in the company of the twentieth century's early hackers—Taft, Wilson, and Coolidge.

Reagan's poor play did not diminish his geniality on the links or the enjoyment of his playing partners. Few presidents played Reagan's brand of carefree golf. He refused to allow the game's frustrations and perils to anger or annoy him, and even ever-spiraling scores and an increasing number of muffed shots failed to ruffle his good-natured demeanor.

For recreation, Reagan preferred riding horses, chopping wood, and building fences on his California ranch. When Reagan was in Washington, the words "staff time" on the White House schedule were a wink-and-a-nod euphemism for the President's horseback riding time at Quantico or a quiet midafternoon nap.

For Reagan, golf became an annual tradition, practically a holiday obligation, like making New Year's resolutions that were bound to be broken. Just once a year, on New Year's Eve, Reagan dragged out his golf clubs for a round at Sunnylands, the California estate owned by Walter Annenberg, the publishing magnate and former ambassador to Great Britain. Sunnylands was the appropriate name for this 209-acre estate of twelve manmade lakes, rolling hills, and a private nine-hole golf course, cordoned off from the public by a thick wall of tamarisk trees and oleander bushes. Annenberg had built the nine-hole golf course after being forced to wait to tee off at another area country club. The private course insured that Annenberg would never be kept waiting on a golf course.

When Reagan played with Annenberg, he was given "permanent honors"—he was permitted to tee off first, on every hole, regardless of the results on the previous hole. The honor embarrassed Reagan a bit, but Annenberg insisted that it was a "course rule" and not negotiable.

Every New Year's morning, the nation's newspapers published photographs of Reagan preparing to tee off at the Annenberg estate. Throughout the 1980s, Americans woke up each New Year's Day to the image of Reagan preparing to play golf as they prepared to settle down to a marathon of college football bowl games.

On New Year's Eve 1986, reporters posed their annual golf question: What did the President shoot? And as usual, Larry Speakes, the chief White House spokesman, refused to say. But that year, for some reason, he razzed the reporters by reminding them that the White House had managed to keep Reagan's golf scores a zealously guarded secret throughout his presidency.

Members of the White House press corps, of course, were not amused by the needling. And the reports reflected reporters' attempts to give it right back to the White House. Lou Cannon wrote

President Reagan enjoyed golf anecdotes and jokes more than he enjoyed puttering around the links. The Gipper gets an Oval Office putting lesson from golf great Raymond Floyd on June 24, 1986. Earlier that week, Floyd won the United States Open Championship at Shinnecock Hills Golf Club in Southampton, New York.

in the *Washington Post*, "Reagan's golf scores were as closely guarded by the White House as the chronology of the clandestine Iran arms deal put together by Lieutenant Colonel Oliver L. North before he left the National Security Council to take refuge in the Fifth Amendment."

ONE OF REAGAN'S EARLIEST, and fondest, memories of golf was playing in his hometown of Dixon, Illinois, with his father, Jack, and his father's friends. They played schmooze golf. On the links, Jack Reagan preferred telling stories and teasing his pals far more than knocking the ball around. "He was blessed with the re- markable gift of storytelling and used to enjoy making the guys laugh," Ronald Reagan recalled.

Reagan inherited from his father that rare gift to tell fine, and often funny, stories, usually at his own expense. And like his dad, Ronald Reagan spent the rest of his life using the golf course as a stage to deliver wholesome but coy stories with that irresistible tilt of the head.

Reagan played football and competed on the swimming team in high school. He dreamed of becoming a pro athlete. But Reagan's athleticism was recognized not on the gridiron or the golf course. He demonstrated quickness, agility, and endurance from the lifeguard's catbird seat perched above a popular swimming spot in Lowell Park on the Rock River. Over the course of six summers, Reagan rescued a total of seventy-seven people, becoming a local legend prior to heading off to college. Reagan recalled spending "some of the most glorious months of my life" watching over that river. But one summer job was not enough for him. He also worked as a caddy at the local country club, hustling for tips. "I've been playing golf practically since the Stone Age," he recalled. "During my youth, however, I probably spent more time carrying clubs than actually swinging them." Reagan's combined earnings from both summer jobs was $400, enough to pay his first year's tuition at tiny Eureka College in nearby Peoria, Illinois.

At Eureka, Reagan emerged as a campus leader and was a headliner in several plays for the Drama Club. After graduation, he gravitated toward a career in broadcasting, working at WHO in Des Moines, Iowa, where he merged his love of sports and interest in drama as a baseball announcer. Like many broadcasters of the day, he recreated the games from the pitch-by-pitch reports clattering off a telegraph machine. Reagan traveled with the Chicago Cubs to spring training in southern California in 1937, and while there, he took a screen test and was offered an acting job by Warner Brothers.

In those early acting years, golf was Reagan's favorite hobby. It was something to do. Golf was irresistible for a sometime actor with a lot of extra time. "Golf was a relaxing way to spend a weekend afternoon," Reagan said.

In the late 1930s, Reagan first joined Lakeside Country Club, but he resigned after discovering that there were no black or Jewish members. He then joined Hillcrest Country Club in Los Angeles, a club where many entertainers played golf. Reagan and his first wife, Jane Wyman, played golf together, though his second wife, Nancy, was not a golfer. Among his fifty-four film roles, one was as a hacker in a short film entitled *Shoot Yourself Some Golf.* Reagan's character was taught how to swing a club by three-time U.S. Open champion Jimmy Thomson, one of the game's first long-ball hitters off the tee.

His most important role, in 1949, came in another sports movie: *Knute Rockne—All-American.* He played the memorable role of George Gipp, a football star who died while still enrolled at Notre Dame. In the film's most famous scene, Gipp lies on his deathbed and delivers an inspirational request to Coach Rockne, played by Pat O'Brien. "Someday when things are tough," Reagan (as Gipp) says, "maybe you can tell the boys to go in there and win just once for the Gipper." The nickname became a touchstone throughout Reagan's political career; when he ran for reelection in 1984, voters were asked to go out and win one more for the Gipper.

Reagan got his first taste of politics after World War II, as the president of the Screen Actors Guild. He negotiated a new contract with the studios that earned actors better pay and benefits. And he then continued his unique preparation for political life in 1954 when he was hired to be the television host for General Electric Theater. His public-speaking ability was well honed in the job as he addressed audiences in GE factories and Rotary Club meetings across the country.

And it was also as the GE spokesman that Reagan played the best golf of his life, getting his handicap down to 12. As part of the corporate world, he traveled with a set of Tommy Armour clubs and played often with GE executives. But once he entered politics, first as governor in California and then as president, he played so infrequently that his game suffered.

"When I became President," he acknowledged, "my golf game took a dramatic nosedive." Whenever he was asked to reveal his handicap, Reagan delivered a quick reply that was both funny and classic: "Congress."

Several weeks before a planned trip to Augusta National Golf Club in October 1983, President Reagan was joined on the practice tee by Vice President George Bush and Secretary of the Treasury Donald T. Regan. Regan joined the President on the weekend trip to Augusta, but it was cut short when an armed man took hostages in the Augusta clubhouse while the presidential foursome was on the back nine.

REAGAN'S TRIP TO AUGUSTA in October 1983 seemed snake-bitten from the start.

"Our coming to Augusta was supposed to be a secret, but the people lined the streets on that Friday night when we arrived— some secret," recalled George Shultz. "That Friday night, about 2:30 in the morning, our national security adviser, Bud MacFarlane, called down to talk about Grenada. We had been concerned about Grenada for a long time. There were 300 or 400 American students down there in a school. The island had become murderous, and you could see a hostage problem coming. The surrounding countries were very worried about it. They called on us to support them, which we wanted to do. All of the pieces were in place and Bud MacFarlane had called at 2 o'clock in the morning. We woke up the President and gave him that information and briefing and we had a secure phone conversation at the Eisenhower Cottage—that's where the President made his decision to go into Grenada."

Some advisers suggested that the President return to Washington immediately, but Shultz advised against it. "People will want to know why, and they'll figure it out—so we stayed," he said.

The next morning, Shultz woke up early. An avid golfer, Shultz was anxious to get out on the course and start playing.

"When you get invited to play at Augusta, you drop everything," he said. "When you get there you just want to spend every minute playing that course. You want to get up as early as you can and play at least 36 holes. It's Augusta. That's not the Reagan approach. He went out and hit a few balls and putted around. And we didn't start playing until 10 o'clock, played only nine holes, and then we stopped for lunch. A golfer hates that, but we do what the President wants. So all that day, we were on super-alert with Grenada when that hostage situation developed in the clubhouse."

By nightfall, the mood inside the Eisenhower Cottage was somber. The long-awaited Augusta weekend was not turning out as planned.

"That night was a very sober night—we had Grenada on our minds," Shultz recalled. "We had dinner brought over to the Eisenhower Cottage and went to bed. At 2 o'clock that morning, we learned of the blowing up of our marine barracks in Lebanon." The truck bombing of the U.S. Marine Barracks in Beirut killed 241 American servicemen and wounded eighty others.

"And so we woke the President up again to give him that terrible news," Shultz said. "After that, we got in the cars in the middle of the night and came back to Washington. It was raining, and it was a very sober, sad time."

Some commentators accused the Reagan administration of launching the Grenada invasion, which occurred later that week, as a way to divert attention from the marine barracks tragedy. "You can see that is totally false," Shultz said, "one had nothing to do with the other."

Ronald Reagan was photographed, en route to the Geneva summit in 1986, putting down the aisle of Air Force One. Not surprisingly, the administration's two most enthusiastic golfers—Shultz and Donald Regan, then chief of staff, watched, smiling, in the background. Also in 1986, Reagan took putting lessons in the Oval Office from Raymond Floyd, the winner of that year's U.S. Open at Shinnecock Hills Golf Club in Southampton, New York. In another famous photo, Reagan holds the putter like a sword, stands on his tiptoes, and opens his mouth in an exultant shout as Floyd looks on. The putt dropped into the practice hole.

"Ronald Reagan is not particularly known for his golf," Bob Hope said. "He favors other hobbies. We usually spend New Year's together, and last year when I went over to see him he was at the tail end of his press conference and I heard him say, 'And I 1-putted four greens.'"

Reagan remained a sports fan, especially of baseball, during his years in the White House. In 1988, Reagan threw out the first ball at Wrigley Field, and he called one and a half innings of play-by-play for WGN. "In a few months," the President said, "I'll be out of a job, so I thought I'd audition here."

After Reagan left the White House, he set up an office near the top of a skyscraper in Century City, California. Between speaking engagements and travel, he found he had plenty of time to reacquaint himself with golf. But his game had deserted him. "I've had to take some lessons to relearn much of what was automatic in my early years," he said at the time. He was given an honorary membership at the Los Angeles Country Club, where he received regular lessons from the head professional, Ed Oldfield Jr. Reagan worked hard to get his score closer to 90 than 100.

He played with a large contingent of Hollywood friends, including the actor Tom Selleck, and former administration members such as George Shultz.

During those first few years of retirement, Reagan followed the same routine: He ate lunch at the club, then played nine holes of golf. As always, the humor was far more important than the numbers on the scorecard. He tried to play with metal woods, but struggled. With that gleam in his eye, Reagan told a playing partner, Thomas "Tuck" Trainer, "I think I know what I'm going to do with them. I'm going to melt them down and make an ashtray out of them—and, Tuck, I don't smoke."

Reagan managed to hit a few good shots, however. In 1991, Reagan invited his successor, George Bush, to play a round of golf with him at the Sherwood Country Club in Thousand Oaks, California. Bush, who had turned sixty-seven earlier that week, and Reagan, then eighty, played with three longtime Republican financial supporters: Arco chairman Lodwrick Cook, film producer Jerry Weintraub, and billionaire developer David Murdock, who had built the golf course.

The posh golf course, laid out in the foothills of the Santa Monica Mountains, is one of the loveliest in southern California, with lush fairways, perfectly manicured greens, and miniature brass archers that serve as tee markers.

"You got mulligans on this fancy course?" President Bush asked on the first tee with a smile. Good question; it turned out that he needed one. Bush's first shot was a ground ball that traveled fifty yards. But Bush's second shot sailed far down the fairway. Reagan warned the spectators that his game was creaky and maybe a bit long in the tooth, announcing with a grin, "You might as well know my alibi in advance—I'm camera shy." Reagan, however, did not need a mulligan. He hit his tee shot down the left side of the fairway, only 150 yards, but it was playable.

On the 9th hole, Bush just smiled when asked whether he was outplaying the former president. After Reagan turned his back, Bush grinned and shot a gleeful thumbs-up sign at reporters. Bush finally beat his old boss at something.

Reagan did not hit many good shots that day (his score was not reported), but as he continued to play in the 1990s, he was still capable of the terrific golf shot. On the par-3, 185-yard 5th hole at the Los Angeles Country Club's South Course, Reagan deposited his tee shot into a deep sand trap. From the deep trap, Reagan could barely see the top of flag, about fifty feet away. But he swung hard, sending a large spray of sand and his ball toward the flag. The ball bounced once and glided into the cup. Even well into his eighties, Ronald Reagan could still shoot a birdie.

IN A LETTER TO THE AMERICAN PEOPLE on November 5, 1994, Ronald Reagan revealed that he had been diagnosed with Alzheimer's disease. "I now begin the journey that will lead me into the sunset of my life," he wrote.

Nancy Reagan has been there every step of the way, helping her husband endure the debilitating disease with both strength and grace. She tried to keep the former president active. He still went to his office, and he continued to play a weekly round of golf, usually on Saturday. After retreating from public life, golf became more important to Reagan than it ever was in his youth.

Through the mid-1990s, Reagan's playing partners were still awestruck by the man's ability to play a few holes of golf, always with enthusiasm. "Once in a while he gets off a pretty good shot, and he enjoys it, though he used a few expletives when he hit a bad shot," a former British ambassador said after nine holes with Reagan in 1997.

By the spring of 1999, Reagan's degenerative brain disease had worsened. His condition was so bad that he was forced to stop his regular exercise sessions in the basement of his Bel Air home. He stopped regularly going to the office. And he gave up his Saturday round of golf.

It hurts his family to watch Reagan slowly give up each of the things that he used to love. "The long good-bye," his daughter,

Maureen, called it. "It's watching somebody disappear before your eyes, and not being able to do anything about it that's devastating. It hurts."

With each passing year, Reagan's legend has grown. He is an American hero, far bigger than any character he played. In the fall of 2000, his name was repeatedly invoked by Republicans all over the country. They were still trying to win one for the Gipper.

PART THREE

HAIL TO
THE CHEATS

Hole	1	2	3	4	5	6	7	8	9	Out	In	Tot
Distance	410	160	300	520	360	195	396	451	356	3148	3100	6248
Par	4	3	4	5	4	3	4	5	4	36	36	72
Clinton	5	3	4	6	4	4	4	6	5	41	41	82
Nixon	6	4	4	5	5	4	5	5	6	44	43	87
LBJ	7	6	8	7	6	6	8	7	6	61	59	120
Harding	6	4	4	7	6	4	5	6	6	48	47	95
Handicap	5	15	13	4	1	3	7	2	14			

*claimed average scores while president

William J. Clinton   *Lyndon B. Johnson*

Richard Nixon   *W.G. Harding*

O N THEIR SCORECARDS, without a twinge of guilt or a trace of regret, millions of weekend hackers use miniature pencils to write fiction. They cheat because it is the only way to level the playing field and extract a little revenge against the unconquerable game. Does it really matter that some American presidents have also cheated at golf and lied about their scores?

To many American golfers, it *does* matter.

It is not just presidents who have succumbed to the temptation to bend the rules. Eighty-two percent of corporate executives admitted cheating at golf, according to a survey by Starwood Hotels and Resorts in the summer of 2002. Most executives confessed to secretly improving the lie of their ball, refusing to count a missed tap-in putt, taking a mulligan without permission, and allowing playing partners the luxury of cheating on their scorecards, especially if turning the other cheek improves their chances to strike a lucrative business deal.

And because life often imitates golf, it should not have surprised anyone that a crisis of confidence devastated Wall Street that same summer. Eight trillion dollars of accumulated wealth were wiped out, causing millions of investors to flee to the safety of savings accounts and floor safes. The numbers published in some corporations' quarterly reports were as cooked and crooked as the small digits transcribed on the executives' golf scorecards. Several CEOs' signatures, on the bottom of their earnings reports and their scorecards, were decorative ornaments that guaranteed the accuracy of nothing.

Incredibly, the same percentage of golfing executives who confessed to cheating—82 percent—also admitted that they became angry when their playing partners cheated at the game. Apparently in golf, as in business, the executives cheat because they assume their playing partners are going to cheat, too. It is the old businessman's vow: I'll do it to you before you get the chance to do it to me.

Although millions of weekend hackers treat themselves to mulligans, there are millions of other golfers who believe the rules are neither breakable nor bendable. In 1925, the great amateur golfer

Bobby Jones lost the U.S. Open, in a playoff, after he penalized himself a stroke for inadvertently moving the ball no more than a fraction of an inch with his club head. No one had even seen the infraction. For Jones, there was never a moment of doubt that he would penalize himself the stroke.

"There is only one way to play the game," he said. "You might as well praise a man for not robbing a bank."

As criticism engulfed Bill Clinton in the 1990s over the veracity of his golf score, some of his defenders said lying about a golf score is as commonplace as lying about sex. In other words, "everybody does it." That cynical defense was the mantra of Bill Clinton's defenders who tried to dismiss their boss's attempts to conceal his affair with a twenty-one-year-old White House intern.

After playing a round with President Clinton in Arkansas in 1999, Georgia Tech golfer Bryce Molder, who later turned pro, observed: "He shot about a 90. But I think he wrote down an 83 or 84."

Molder later complained that he got into "trouble" for accusing Clinton of cheating during their round at Chenal Valley Country Club in Little Rock, Arkansas—during the same round that Molder shot a 60, no less! All anyone wanted to know was whether Clinton cheated. "Pretty much every weekend golfer pretty much, technically, doesn't go by the rules, so it's kind of hard to say he cheats, because he lets everybody else in the group do it too," Molder said. "It's not exactly cheating, but he doesn't play by the same rules as someone else might."

Clinton first claimed to shoot an 82, then amended it to an 84, with "no mulligans," he said. But Molder remembered it differently: "I'd give him about 90. Hard to tell. Everybody in the group"—except Molder, of course—"was hitting a bunch of shots again. If he counted every shot, he wouldn't have shot better than 92 or 93. But he hit enough good shots that he could get away with saying he shot an 85 or something."

Barbara Bush was furious at the reports that President Clinton was fond of the mulligan. She was especially appalled at the suggestion that Clinton was merely playing the game the way most of his constituents do.

"Everybody does *not* cheat at golf," Mrs. Bush declared during the family's summer vacation in 1997. "We played nineteen holes today. It took that long to get a winner, and nobody cheated. Nobody we play golf with would play with us if we cheated."

Surely, the Bushes would agree with the observation of golf commentator Peter Alliss, who once said: "You can fiddle with your income tax, you can have body odor, you can do anything—but if you cheat at golf, nobody wants you."

Among the members of the presidential cheating foursome, no one endured more suspicion about the legitimacy of his golf score than Bill Clinton. A century from now, Clinton will still likely be remembered among the White House's most polished and prolific golf cheats. But is that reputation deserved?

Bill Clinton

Taking Billigans

No president has suffered through more skepticism about the veracity of his golf score than Bill Clinton, who heard howls of disbelief from millions of American golfers after claiming to break 80 during his presidency. Clinton flashes a mischievous smile at the Farm Neck Golf Club on Martha's Vineyard, one of his favorite courses, where he took his share of mulligans.

My mulligans are way overrated. . . . You know what?
It screws your game up. You'd be amazed at
how many times you don't get a bit of good out of it.
—Bill Clinton

BILL CLINTON STEPS GINGERLY OUT of the back seat of the black Suburban, grips my right hand in a firm handshake, and says, "Great to meet you." Clinton is trimmer than I expected, but he still looks larger in person than on television. He spots my blue-and-white golf cap, emblazoned with the words "Farm Neck Martha's Vineyard," and says with a smile, "I'm gonna play there next week on my birthday."

We are standing side by side in the circular driveway of the Golf Club of Purchase, a posh country club just down the road from his white house in Chappaqua, New York. Leaning against the Suburban, Clinton slips on a pair of black Nike golf cleats to complete his Everyman duffer's uniform: a cranberry Lacoste golf shirt, navy shorts, white ankle socks with the NBA logo, and a wide-brimmed straw hat from the Emirates Golf Club in Dubai.

The President and I (along with a pair of multimillionaire venture capitalists) are preparing to play eighteen holes of golf on a scorching hot Tuesday afternoon in the middle of August 2002. Three years earlier, almost to the day, I portrayed President Clinton as a shameless golf cheat in an article for the *New York Times,* an accusation that infuriated him. And yet, here he is, graciously agreeing to play a round of golf with me for this book. I cannot help but wonder how long it will take for the touchy subject of mulligans to come up.

It takes about two minutes.

As we walk to the practice tee to hit a bucket of balls, I warn Clinton that I will likely rip up this narrow, wetlands golf course. I tell him I had not hit a golf ball for a year until the previous Sunday, when I shot a pathetic 55 over nine holes.

"Don't worry," Clinton says, his blue eyes fixed on mine. "I'll give you a mulligan any time you want it."

As I would soon learn, I was wrong about Bill Clinton and golf.

He does not take mulligans. He takes a type of do-over shot that is less obvious, more devious, and entirely his own invention.

He takes Billigans.

SPEND AN AFTERNOON playing golf with Bill Clinton and you walk away shaking your head with wonder at a lot of things. Armed with a big-headed Nike driver, he crushes the ball off the tee, occasionally exceeding 300 yards. "Pretty good for an old guy," he says.

He talks to himself and the ball, before and after his swing, calling himself "Billy" as he tries to launch the ball straight and far. "Come on, baby," he tells the ball on the green's fringe. "Come to Daddy."

He delivers a running commentary on his own shot-making and offers his playing partners unsolicited lessons to try to improve theirs. "Turn your ass! Turn your ass!" he shouts at me after watching my flawed swing on the tee. "You've got to turn your ass!"

Without much prodding, Clinton launches into a dissertation on the hundreds of clubs he has owned over the years—the beat-up putters that saved the most pars, the custom-made irons that were the most forgiving, the graphite shaft drivers that suddenly cured a stubborn slice.

Before almost every swing, he solicits suggestions from his playing partners, the caddies, even the Secret Service agents. "Am I aimed correctly?" he asks. "Are my feet right? Where's the pin? How fast is the green? Where's the break?"

He is a lot of fun, too. He chatters almost nonstop about golf, blossoming when asked to describe playing with Arnold Palmer or Jack Nicklaus or Greg Norman or Michael Jordan. And he goes out of his way to relax his playing partners, most of whom are bundles of nervousness and worry. He recalls the minutiae of rounds played a decade ago. For a man who said "I don't recall" more than 100 times during his federal grand jury testimony, Clinton demonstrates an uncanny ability to remember everything about golf. He gives moment-by-moment recitations of holes played years ago—the lie of the shot, the yardage of his drive, the break of the putt, the comments of his playing partners. He describes the holes in such rich detail that you'd think he played them that morning.

Most of all, Clinton hates to lose. He is an aggressive competitor. If he blows a putt, he will flash some anger at himself first and still have a bit left over for his caddy who misread the break. A caddy dispensing bad advice might feel compelled to scurry off to a less perilous profession, like bounty hunting.

I ask Clinton why American presidents, for a century, have made golf their most cherished game. "I think one reason is you can play it no matter what condition you are in," he says. "And because of the handicap system, anybody can fairly play anybody else. And I think the third reason is interestingly enough because it's slow and it takes time. Most presidents lead busy, crowded, packed lives. They get to go outside. They don't have time to go out to Wyoming and ride horses every day. They don't have time to walk in the Adirondack Mountains every day. So you are outside, you are in trees, you are in beautiful surroundings. And it takes time."

"One of the reasons I always liked golf is because the rest of my life is going at breakneck speed and everything had to be done fast and this is the place where I had to slow down. And I think the final reason is—you literally can't think about anything else. If you do, you can't hit a shot."

BILL CLINTON LOVES GOLF as much as Ike loved it, as much as Wilson loved it, as much as Kennedy loved it. I ask Clinton if he thinks he played 400 rounds of golf during his eight years as President, a total that would put him behind only Woodrow Wilson and Dwight Eisenhower.

"Sounds about right," he says.

184

Throughout Clinton's presidency, politicians and writers used Clinton's golf playing as a metaphor to describe his character, his truthfulness, his style of politics, even his fitness to serve as president.

On the golf course, Clinton was as easily distracted as he was in the Oval Office, his mind zigzagging from subject to subject. His plodding pace often kept other golfers waiting, just as he had kept visitors and audiences waiting when he was chief executive. And on the golf course, as he did under oath, Clinton was fond of hiding his game's shortcomings in a thicket of rule bending and technicalities. Clinton's liberal use of mulligans presented itself as a perfect metaphor for his presidency.

"President Clinton has developed the mulligan into a fine art," John Omicinski wrote in August 1997 in an article for Gannett News Service that unleashed dozens of Clinton golf-cheating stories through his second term. "Apparently Clinton's zeitgeist tells him that if he thinks he shot 79, then he shot 79. Call it Zen golf." By leaning on a liberal use of do-over shots, Clinton was just fooling himself—"and no one else," Omicinski observed—into believing his game was better than it actually was.

The golf cheating accusations deeply annoyed Clinton. In August 1997, at Farm Neck Golf Club on Martha's Vineyard, reporters challenged his claimed score of 79 on a day when everyone watched him take three shots off the first tee. "Yeah," Clinton said, "and the only reason I took two, three shots out here is because we didn't have time to go to the driving range."

"That's a good excuse!" someone shouted from the crowd.

Clinton insisted that he played all his bad shots during his round of 79. "Ask the guys I played with," he told reporters. He motioned to one of his golfing partners, Vernon Jordan, the Washington super-lawyer. "Ask Jordan. He was there."

Jordan stood on the tee and said nothing.

With the pressure on, Clinton then teed off from the first tee. His ball sailed left, clearing a sand trap before disappearing deep into the woods. "Oh, look what I did," the President muttered. Stepping off the tee, Clinton told himself, "I've been playing good." No mulligan for the President.

His playing partners—Vernon Jordan, Jack Welch, then the chairman of General Electric, and Ben Heineman, another GE executive—powered their tee shots straight and far down the middle of the fairway.

After the round, the President reported that he had shot an unruly 86. "Not a good day," he said. Clinton decided to play another quick nine holes. Again, off the first tee, with a throng of reporters watching, Clinton hooked his tee shot out of bounds. "No!" he shouted. "I did it again!"

He quickly fished another ball out of his pocket, and this drive mimicked the crooked path of the first shot. "Oh no!" the President said.

The local and national press had a field day. On the day when Clinton had sworn his score of 79 was legitimate, he failed to put a single ball in play while the press corps watched.

"At his level," John Omicinski wrote, "Clinton isn't really going to improve much if he continues to re-load on errant shots. In golf, as in life, he's got to learn to take his punishment and learn from his mistakes, rather than covering them up." Omicinski wrote those words less than five months before the world heard the name Monica Lewinsky.

In the never-ending year leading to Clinton's impeachment and trial, the President spent nearly every Monday afternoon playing golf at the Army-Navy Country Club in Arlington, Virginia. "This is just about all the fun I'm allowed right now," he confided to a friend. During the long summer of 1998, as he practiced his chips and putts on the South Lawn and the White House putting green, Clinton developed the Ken Starr shank, named after the independent counsel who was investigating him. "Lots of times," Clinton says, "I'd be feeling bad and distracted, and I'd shank them. I'd start shanking it and I'd kick the grass and couldn't understand why I was shanking them. It would drive me nuts."

But *not* playing drove him the most nuts.

A year later, on a Sunday afternoon in October 1999, Clinton unexpectedly told his staff that he wanted to play golf. He was driven over to the Army-Navy Country Club, where he played a dozen

President Clinton loved the game as much as any president, playing in the ugliest weather conditions, even in the dark, alone, in the pouring rain. With temperatures parked in the mid-thirties, Clinton reacts to a misguided putt on the ninth green of the Black Rock Golf Course in Hagerstown, Maryland, on November 24, 1995. After the round, the President blamed the cold weather for more than one errant shot.

holes of golf alone, in the dark. When the rain started splashing down, he kept right on playing.

It seemed pathetic to nongolfers, but the golf fanatics nodded their heads and understood. A lame duck President's lonely, after dark, rain-soaked golf game was too rich with symbolism for some columnists and commentators to pass up. It presented "the stark image of an increasingly isolated and frustrated President heading towards the end of his second term, his temper rising and his power waning," wrote Ben Macintyre in the *Times* of London.

"He was playing in the pitch dark," one White House correspondent said. "He was swinging and wildly hitting balls everywhere."

On at least one occasion, Clinton played golf when what he really wanted was to be out on the campaign trail, doing what comes naturally to him—patting backs, squeezing shoulders, and amassing votes. On the Saturday before the 2000 presidential election, as his vice president, Al Gore, was preparing to face off against Republican challenger George W. Bush, Bill Clinton was not on the campaign trail, trying to get a Democratic successor elected. Instead, he was playing golf.

He was playing on a course in Maryland near Camp David, and he confided to a friend: "I can't believe I'm out here today. On Tuesday, my legacy is on the line. I should be out there campaigning."

I ask Clinton about that day, and he seems, at first, not to recall it. "Where was I?" he asks.

"At a course in Maryland," I say.

He thinks about it a moment, and it seems that he is uncharacteristically at a loss for words. He looks off in the distance and then says quietly, "It wasn't up to me to decide. If I had been asked, I would have been out there. I think it might have helped. I campaigned in California and in Arkansas. Those are the places where we defeated incumbent Republicans." Clinton does not mention that Al Gore lost Arkansas or that a win in Bill Clinton's home state would have given Gore the presidency. Clinton pauses a moment again, turning over in his mind Gore's decision to keep him on the sidelines down the stretch. "Yeah, I didn't think it made a lot of sense," he says. "It wasn't my call."

Hillary Clinton once speculated that after her husband left the White House, he might try to qualify for the PGA Senior Tour. I ask Clinton about this.

"Sure," he tells me. "One of the things I thought about doing when I got out is taking six months and see if I can get down to scratch, which I think I could if I worked out for six months and trained and everything and then go on the Senior Tour."

Why didn't you go for it? I ask. "I just had too much other public service stuff I wanted to do," he says. "And I had to make money—I had to pay all those legal bills, and had to buy these houses, and fix one of them up, and I was trying to help some other people with their legal bills. I just had a lot of stuff to do. So I decided not to do it. And I realized that given what I wanted to do in my life, I would never be able to muster the concentration necessary to win because golf really is a mind game."

I decided not to do it. The way Clinton sees it, the Senior Tour is just another post-presidential career option to be weighed with the

$150,000 speaking fees, the $12 million book advance and, if he wants it, a $30 million a year contract to host a television talk show. If he did not have "a lot of stuff to do," Clinton is absolutely convinced he would be cashing tournament checks right now on the PGA Senior Tour.

It is impossible not to like the guy.

H E   W A S   T W E L V E   Y E A R S   O L D when he first picked up a golf club. It was the late 1950s, a time in America when golf was identified as an exclusive, blue-blooded Republican game befitting the conservative Eisenhower era. Yet growing up in Hot Springs, Arkansas, Bill Clinton viewed golf as a blue-collar game, played on a nine-hole golf course in the infield of the local racetrack.

"My uncle belonged to a country club that was like three miles out in the country, outside of the town of Hot Springs, in the direction that we lived," Clinton says. "So it was easy for me to get out there. There were lots and lots of woods. I started playing alone, caddying. I never had a lesson. I just sort of taught myself."

As a caddy, Clinton carried clubs for a foursome that included pro golfer Tommy "Thunder" Bolt, who played in a tournament in Hot Springs in 1961. Clinton gave up golf when he turned sixteen, concentrating instead on playing the saxophone in the high school band and playing forward on a church basketball league team. He went on to Georgetown University and then Oxford University as a Rhodes scholar. While in England, he played basketball and even tried rugby, suffering a minor concussion in one match.

He did not return to playing golf until 1975, after graduating from Yale Law School and going home to Arkansas to begin his political career. His first golfing partners were his new brothers-in-law, Hugh and Tony Rodham.

Clinton traces his first use of mulligans to a lawyer friend in Little Rock named Mark Grobmyer, who was fond of taking do-over shots. "He wasn't a particularly good golfer, but he was the most fun ever," Clinton says. "He had a rule that everybody got two off the first tee and another free one off the fairway and another mulligan on the green, on the front and back nine. And I'd play whatever the rules are."

In 1978, at the age of thirty-two, Clinton was elected governor of Arkansas, where he played most often at the Country Club of Little Rock, a placid, picturesque course built in 1902. "The old Little Rock course was only ten minutes from my office to being on the first tee," he says, "and I used to go out there a lot in the summertime. I could get there at 6:30 and still play eighteen holes. That's when I played with a lot of my friends, but I always loved to play alone." He often sprayed tee shots deep into the woods, and struggled with his short game. "Since I wasn't very good," he says, "I was in the woods a lot."

Clinton rarely talked politics on the golf course, preferring to chat exclusively about the game. But he made an exception one afternoon in the fall of 1991 as he was playing a round in Little Rock with Senator David Pryor. On the 18th fairway, Clinton sliced a drive into the rough behind a pine tree. As he stood over the ball, Clinton asked Pryor, "What do I do?"

Pryor offered advice on how Clinton might manage to get his ball past the tree and back on the fairway. "No," Clinton said. "What I want to know is: Should I run for president?"

Clinton needed no prodding, but eleven years later he tells me he had not initially wanted to challenge President Bush, who was "very good to me when I was governor."

"Personally, I didn't really want to run in 1992," he says. "I just got so frustrated because [President Bush's aides] were sitting on his popularity from the Gulf War instead of trying to use it. And I thought the country was in terrible shape and I didn't think those guys who were in really knew what they were doing."

Clinton made another exception to his no-politics rule in the late spring of 1992, during a round of golf in Little Rock with Mark Grobmyer, his lawyer pal. Grobmyer had introduced Clinton to Senator Al Gore of Tennessee, and Grobmyer and Clinton spent nearly the entire round talking about Gore's suitability as a possible running mate. "That's about the only serious thing we've ever talked about on the golf course," Grobmyer recalled.

Golf became an issue for Clinton during the 1992 campaign when he was criticized for playing at the Country Club of Little Rock, which barred membership to blacks. He quickly apologized for the mistake and vowed not to play at the club until it admitted black members. (Clinton's moratorium on play at the club did not last long; the Country Club of Little Rock admitted its first black member in December 1992.)

On November 3, Clinton defeated President George Bush, and the next weekend he treated himself to a round at Chenal Country Club in Little Rock. As he prepared to hit off the first tee, the president-elect was given a glimpse of life as a golfing chief executive. He was furious after seeing several photographers assembled to take his picture as he teed off. "I thought we had an agreement that they weren't going to be up here," he later snapped at the club manager.

Several times during the transition, Clinton played in abominable conditions—fog and rain and darkness. He recalled playing a couple weeks before his inauguration, in wintry conditions, with a friend named Walt Patterson, who served as director of the Department of Human Services in Arkansas. "Patterson was an African-American college football player," Clinton says. "He was about six-foot-five, weighed 285. He was about a 4 or 5 handicap, drove the ball forever. He had huge hands, he had these big grips, and it was like grabbing the club was like milking a cow or something. And he swung on the 18th tee, it was 35 degrees and sleet was coming down, and his club went farther than his ball did. It was funny, funny, funny."

Rough weather never mattered to Clinton. He always played through.

IN THE WEEKS FOLLOWING HIS INAUGURATION, Clinton was pegged more as a jogger than a golfer. Clad in too-short gym shorts, Clinton took two-mile runs around the capital, and people just assumed there was always a pit stop for French fries at McDonald's. Before long, however, Americans discovered that their new president was far more passionate about golf. Clinton dropped one hint about his golf obsession when he said at a 1993 White House reception, "Of all the perks that come with being President of the United States, the best one is being able to play eighteen holes of golf with Arnold Palmer."

Clinton brought his golfing obsession with him to the White House. "We've had rain golf, snow golf, mud golf—every kind of golf," said Sharon Farmer, the director of White House photography. "Other than reading and music, he'd rather be playing golf than anything."

In August 1993, after Clinton's bruising battle with Congress over his first budget, he decided to flee Washington's oppressive heat and take his first vacation as president in Vail, Colorado. For two consecutive days, Clinton played golf with former President Gerald Ford and Jack Nicklaus at the Vail Valley Club. The foursome was completed by the chief executive officer of a Houston energy company—Kenneth Lay of Enron, who was there as Clinton's guest.

At this point in his presidency, all that was known about Clinton's golf game was that he claimed to be an 18 handicap. A few people were already wondering whether the new president was that good.

The President played horribly during his first round with Nicklaus, Lay, and Ford. On the 4th hole, a short, 350-yard par-4, Clinton's performance was telling. (I owe this account to John Aloysius Farrell, an enterprising reporter for the *Boston Globe* who managed to spy on the foursome, disguised as a weekend cyclist.)

On the tee, Clinton reminded his playing partners that the Nicklaus and Ford team had to spot him a stroke because of his higher handicap. Clinton then swung wildly under his ball, popping it up and off the fairway.

"Owwwww," the President yelled. "You idiot!"

"Hit the cart path!" Ford shouted at the ball, trying to help.

Clinton was given a free drop off the cart path with about 170 yards to the hole. He hit a weak 6-iron that deposited the ball in a sand trap. The lie was impossible—uphill, atop a thick dune of sand, close to the bunker's lip. "The gallery groaned as a wave of sand exploded from the bunker: *sans* ball," Farrell wrote. "Clinton swung again, to no apparent improvement. And again. And again.

"Finally, the Presidential Titleist was seen soaring in the air to plop softly on the green. Lying seven, out of whatever friendly action that he and his golf mates had going, the President waved disgustedly at his ball and went off to contemplate his failure, alone, in his golf cart, as nearby aides and Secret Service agents concentrated intently on the ground and sky."

Clinton played better during the second round, but two people who watched him said he also took a bushel of mulligans. After the second round, Clinton told reporters he had shot an 80, but this claim infuriated both Nicklaus and Ford. "Yeah, an 80 with fifty floating mulligans," Nicklaus whispered in Ford's ear.

After the two days of golf, Nicklaus searched for a polite way to describe Clinton's game. "I would say, well, he has a lot of potential," Nicklaus said. "Gerald Ford plays a lot more golf. Ford played very well. Clinton did not play particularly well the first day . . . but he learns very quickly."

Nicklaus was asked a simple question: What was Clinton's score on both days?

"Well, let's see," Nicklaus said. Long pause. "His average for the two days was . . . I don't know how to say it. The first day, I said, 'You can have a traveling mulligan,' and he let it travel about 50 times. If he had kept score, he wouldn't have broken 100. He probably would have been way over. But he doesn't play much golf.

"The second day, he only had two mulligans all day and he shot 80. That's a pretty darn good score."

The rounds with Nicklaus, however, introduced the nation to its mulligan-mad president. Questions about the veracity of Clinton's handicap would stubbornly dog him throughout his two terms in office.

On the golf course in Purchase, I ask Clinton about those two days playing with Nicklaus, to see if he will say anything about the mulligans. "First day I was terrible," he tells me. "I had three hours of sleep. Second day, I played better."

Typical Clinton: Rather than recall the unpleasant mulligan controversy, he dwells on the round's lone highlight. "I outdrove Nicklaus by one foot on one hole only," he tells me. I must look incredulous because the President repeats it: "One foot on one hole. And you would have thought I shot him between the eyes!" he says, laughing. "He was so competitive. So competitive!

"So I was on this par-5 hole, with an eight-foot eagle putt, and I literally just stubbed the putt. And he looked at me and said, 'You didn't think you were worthy of an eagle, did you?'

"And I said, 'No.'

"He said, 'You need to get over that.'"

We all laugh.

"Isn't that a great story?" Bill Clinton asks.

Great story.

IN THE FALL OF 1993, Clinton hosted the members of the Ryder Cup golfing team at the White House. Several members, including Lee Janzen, Payne Stewart, and Corey Pavin, threatened to boycott the event because they were angry with Clinton for his recently passed tax bill, which increased income taxes for the wealthiest Americans.

The President tells me in 2002 that their anger was understandable. "I didn't take it personally at all," he says. "When we passed it, I said the one group this is most unfair to are professional athletes, because they don't get to play very long and so they have to accumulate funds, and income-tax rates are too high. I knew that business people would do much better."

The boycott was averted. At the Rose Garden event, Tom Watson, the team captain, gave the President a lesson on his grip. Before the golfers left, Clinton told them to "bring back" the Ryder Cup to the United States. And the team did, beating the Europeans, 15-13.

Wealthy Democrats and congressmen pined to play golf with the President, who used a presidential round as a bargaining chip on

Capitol Hill and as a gift for generous contributors. Clinton agreed to play golf with several congressmen who sat on the fence on the tax bill in 1993 and on the North American Free Trade Agreement, which led to criticism that the President was trading golf for votes.

In the spring of 1994, David Watkins, the White House director of administration, was caught using a White House helicopter to fly himself and two friends to Camp David and then to the nearby Holly Hills Country Club for a round of golf. Watkins told reporters that he was scouting out a golf course for the President to play. Clinton was so angry about the scandal (and, no doubt, the excuse) that he immediately fired Watkins and ordered him to reimburse the government $13,000 for the cost of the helicopter ride.

That September, *Boston Herald* columnist Gerry Callahan wrote one of the harshest indictments of Clinton's golf game:

> After 10 days of preferred lies, and unlimited mulligans, a TV camera Monday finally peered between the trees and onto the green where the leader of the free world was doing what he does best: cheat. . . . There he was, the President of the United States, the moral leader of the country, lining up a three-foot putt.
>
> The same putt he had just missed.
>
> Twice.
>
> On his third attempt, Bill Clinton found the hole at last, and onto the scorecard went yet another par for the President.
>
> He the man!

Clinton often said that he was the only president to lower his handicap while in office, crediting this feat to the advice given to him by dozens of professional golfers with whom he had the privilege to play. But on at least one occasion, the President half-jokingly claimed to have helped a pro win the U.S. Open.

In June 1995, President Clinton played a round at the Army-Navy Club with Corey Pavin, who earlier that day had played at the Kemper Open. The next day, Pavin went out and shot a 63, only to lose the tournament in a playoff. The following week, Pavin won the U.S. Open.

As a joke, White House press secretary Mike McCurry told reporters that Clinton had helped improve Pavin's game. "I'm not claiming credit, I'm just pointing out facts, right?" McCurry said. "We deal with facts here at the White House Briefing Room, and them's the facts. Corey Pavin played golf with the President of the United States and they gave pointers to each other and the President's pointers must have been pretty good, right?"

A reporter asked, "So Corey took mulligans when nobody was looking?" The press gallery erupted in laughter.

McCurry replied, "The United States Golf Association carefully monitors the taking of mulligans at the U.S. Open, believe you me." McCurry went on to say, "The President, as is his custom, only does the tradition of first tee mulligans, known to every golfer as being a perfectly acceptable, Constitutionally protected rite of golf."

AT A PRESS CONFERENCE on his forty-eighth birthday, August 19, 1994, Bill Clinton was asked this question: If you could have three wishes fulfilled, what would they be?

One wish was about a crime bill he had pending before Congress, another was a plea for greater civility in Washington, and the last wish was directed toward the golf gods. "I still have dreams of breaking 80 on the golf course," he said, "before I'm fifty."

Bill Clinton got his wish, with two months to spare.

It happened at the Coronado Golf Course, nestled along the glistening shoreline of San Diego Bay, on a glorious, sun-blessed day in June 1996. The President shot a 78.

But no one believed him.

Two hours after the feat, Clinton wandered back to the press section of Air Force One, and announced that he had finally broken 80. "I was hot," he said, his white grin lighting up his sunburned face. "I was smoking 'em. I was having a good time."

Then he saw the disbelieving expressions. "Heck, even a blind pig finds an acorn sometimes," he said, quickly adding, "No freebies, no second drives, no nothin'." In other words: *A legitimate 78.* It made the cynics on the plane wonder: Are freebies, and second drives, par for the course? Later, there was some confusion about whether he had shot a 78 or 79, depending on the technical scoring of the final hole. Clinton was apparently uncertain, actually, if it was a 78 or a 79. This was a lifelong dream realized. How could he not know his score?

A few months later, an investigative reporter named Byron York wrote a scathing article about the veracity of Clinton's golf claims for the *American Spectator* magazine. He raised major doubts about Clinton's claim of breaking 80 at Coronado. "If you want to learn about Bill Clinton's character problem, you don't have to subpoena Whitewater documents," York wrote. "Just watch him on the golf course."

York's piece was hailed in the conservative community as a landmark piece of reporting. His piece also captured the attention of aides to the Republican presidential nominee, Bob Dole, who was trailing Clinton by a wide margin in the polls.

For the first time, a president's truthfulness about his golf score was turned into an issue in a presidential campaign. At a campaign rally in New Mexico three weeks before the election, the Republicans challenged Clinton's claim that he had shot an 83 during a recent round in Albuquerque. New Mexico governor Gary E. Johnson told the crowd: "President Clinton says he shot an 83, but nobody believes he shot an 83. The people who support him and who will vote for him—none of them believes he shot an 83. Character does count. Integrity does count."

The governor then introduced Dole, who said, "I don't know whether he shot an 83 or 283 or 483. You'll never really know."

White House aides were outraged by Bob Dole's golf accusation. Joe Lockhart, the deputy press secretary, called the allegations a desperate candidate's last-gasp attempt to get attention. "I think it's safe to assume that the President follows both the spirit and the letter of each and every rule and regulation as set forth by the United States Golf Association," Lockhart said.

Lockhart's hedged, couched wording was typical of spokesmen for the Clinton White House. He said, "I think it's safe to assume."

He did not simply say, "The President follows both the spirit and the letter of each and every rule and regulation as set forth the United States Golf Association."

Lockhart knew the truth, having played a few rounds of golf with Clinton. His denial qualified as a typical Washington, wink-and-a-nod kind of half-truth, the kind of half-truth that certain Clinton administration officials had mastered the art of telling. Millions of Americans were outraged by the White House's truth-twisting. And no one in Washington was more contemptuous of the practice than a bespectacled lawyer named Kenneth W. Starr.

CLINTON CRUISED TO A SECOND TERM, but he did not have much time to enjoy it. In January 1997, he was criticized for selling overnight stays in the Lincoln Bedroom to wealthy Democratic donors for $50,000 apiece.

Much of that first year of his second term was devoted to a campaign finance scandal, though Clinton continued to play golf with donors who wrote big checks to the Democratic Party.

One of Clinton's closest friends is Terry McAuliffe, a gregarious money man who raised more than $300 million for the Democrats over a glittering twenty-year career. After Clinton's term ended in 2001, McAuliffe would go on to become the chairman of the Democratic National Committee.

McAuliffe often insisted that Clinton did not cheat during their competitive rounds. "He is as competitive about golf as he is about life," McAuliffe told me. "He doesn't like to lose, and neither do I. Neither one of us will give the guy a break."

McAuliffe and Clinton play golf together often. When I ask Clinton in Purchase to name his favorite golfing partners, he mentions McAuliffe first. "Every day is a fun day with Terry," he tells me. Clinton mentions several other friends, including Erskine Bowles, who served as White House chief of staff. Oddly, Clinton does not men-

During his two terms in the White House—and after leaving the presidency—one of President Clinton's favorite golfing partners was Terry McAuliffe, a gregarious businessman and fund-raiser who went on to become the chairman of the Democratic National Committee. The two pals enjoy a break late one afternoon on the White House putting green in 2000.

tion the man most people think of as his favorite golfing partner—Vernon Jordan, who helped Monica Lewinsky search for a job in Manhattan.

For McAuliffe and Clinton, golf served as a means to raise enormous sums of money for the Democratic Party and for Clinton himself. Scores of businessmen wrote $50,000 and $100,000 checks to the Democratic Party for the privilege of playing a round of golf with Clinton. Gary Winnick, the chairman of the once high-flying, now bankrupt Global Crossing, was a McAuliffe pal who wanted desperately to play golf with President Clinton. McAuliffe arranged the round. By the back nine, Winnick had agreed to donate $1 million to Clinton's presidential library in Little Rock, Arkansas.

A MONTH AFTER BEING ELECTED to a second term, Bill Clinton played a round of golf with Greg Norman in Sydney, Australia, at the New South Wales Golf Club. "Well, the day I had with Norman was great," Clinton tells me. "I got right out of the car, put on my shoes and duck-hooked the ball out of bounds. And he said, 'Relax, have a good time.' So I hit the ball about 260 miles down the middle of the fairway. We're walking down the fairway and he says, 'Now, we can do this one of two ways. If you want to show me that you are a decent golfer, I'm going to leave you alone and you play your game and we'll do what we do. If you want an eighteen-hole lesson, I'll give it to you. But you'll shoot a lot worse because I'm going to fiddle around with you and change things.' I said, 'I want the eighteen-hole lesson.'

"We get to the last hole—I'll never forget this. The 18th hole is a par-5. I said, 'Greg, just this one time, I'm going to hit my Great Big Bertha.' I had an 8-degree Great Big Bertha, and I drove the ball 295 yards. He said, 'Give me that piece of crap.' So competitive. He took it out of my hands and outflew me by 25 yards. He hit it 320 yards. He said, 'Not a bad stick.'"

Three months later, Clinton and Norman were back together. This time, it was past 1:00 in the morning, and the President and the Shark were swapping golf tales at Norman's palatial oceanside estate in Hobe Sound, Florida. Clinton was in town to play in Norman's two-day Pro-Am golf tournament. At 1:20, the President left the main house to go to a cottage on the estate's grounds to sleep, but he caught his heel on a flight of stairs and fell, despite Norman's attempt to grab him. Clinton tore his right quadriceps tendon, which connects four muscles that go down the front of the thigh to the kneecap, and was rushed to St. Mary's Hospital in West Palm Beach, where he underwent emergency surgery.

Clinton would be on crutches for six weeks. The next day, Clinton told reporters that he and Norman had discussed the damage the fall would do to his golf game. "I told him my handicap was going up by the minute," the President said.

There were all sorts of rumors about that night—that Clinton was drinking, that he was going to the cottage to spend some time with a woman. The White House denied them all.

I ask Clinton about the fall.

"I played golf that day, had a great round of golf. I had run a couple miles, two or three miles. But I didn't stretch. And what happened was it was dark and he had all these white steps and they were lit but it was an optical illusion, and they looked flat but they were going down. I fell only eight feet. Literally my quadriceps shredded, and hung on only by 10 percent. So they cut my knee open as you see here," Clinton says, pointing to two deep scars over his right knee, "and they pulled all these muscles, and they drilled three holes in my knee."

Norman felt absolutely horrible about the accident, seeing the President leave his house on a stretcher. "Oh God," Clinton says, "I felt so awful for him."

MOST AMERICANS NEVER BEGRUDGED Clinton the many hours that he spent playing golf while president. "I think because they know I work hard," he said in an interview with *Golf Digest* in 2000. "If they thought I was not putting in my time, it'd be different."

But millions of golfing Americans did begrudge a president who openly cheated at the game. From the earliest days of his first year in office, Americans assumed that Clinton earned his Arkansas nickname, "Slick Willie," at least partly from the way he behaved on a golf course. He liked to say he gave presidential pardons to his errant shots, a quip that some people found less humorous after Clinton got in trouble over his last-minute pardons, signed hours before leaving the White House on January 20, 2001.

No American president has endured as much criticism for the veracity of his golf score as Bill Clinton did. Every month or two, another story appeared challenging the President's golf score. Mike

Strachura of *Golf Digest* commissioned golfing great Johnny Miller to conduct a critique of Clinton's swing in 1995. "It wasn't smooth and he played badly," Strachura said. "I doubt he got into the clubhouse in under 100 shots." Still, the magazine named Clinton its "Man of the Year" in 1995.

"The President is a so-so golfer, and he's not terribly good at adding up his scorecard," said former U.S. Open women's champion Donna Caponi, who had seen the President play several times. "If he has a chance to break 80 and hits a bad drive on the last hole, he'll drop another ball and have a 'mulligan'—a free shot. And he's not embarrassed at taking a mulligan. But I guess if you are the President, you're allowed to have a few shots that don't have to count. Depending on how many mulligans he takes, he shoots between 80 and 90."

Golf champion Raymond Floyd concurred with that assessment after playing with the President on exclusive Fisher Island, off Miami Beach, in 1997. Clinton took "a lot of mulligans," Floyd said. "But we played in a sixsome on a very casual day. He took some mulligans and a few second putts, but that's the type of round we had."

Because it was a "casual round," Floyd insisted that the President's mulligans did not bother him much. "I take the game a bit more seriously than the average player," he said. "I believe you play the game by the rules. If you shoot an 8, write an 8. That's golf to me."

"Clinton is big and strong, but he can get a little wild," Gerald Ford observed that same year. "I heard he got a 79 last week."

Ford paused, and said with a cough, "Of course, that's with mulligans."

The skepticism caught the attention of Tim Russert, the host of NBC's *Meet the Press.* Clinton was the first and only president to be asked on national television a line of questions that suggested he cheated at golf.

"How many mulligans do you take in the average eighteen holes?" Russert asked.

Clinton seemed surprised by the question. He glared for a moment at Russert and appeared to clench his jaw.

"One now," the President said.

"One mulligan," said Russert, disbelief in his voice.

"Yes."

"And what's your handicap?"

"Twelve, thirteen, something like that," Clinton said. "I'm play-ing—it's better than it was when I became President, mostly because I've gotten to play with a lot of good golfers and they've taught me a lot."

Only a month after that interview, the President appeared, in the eyes of many in the capital, to be developing an obsession with golf. "It's golf, golf, golf—interspersed with politics," Senator John Breaux, a Louisiana Democrat, told the *New York Times*.

B UT EVERYTHING CHANGED for Bill Clinton in January 1998. A sex scandal derailed the exhilarating, legacy-building second term that he had imagined for himself. Even golf was forced to the back burner.

By reading the morning newspaper, Clinton learned that Ken-neth Starr, the independent counsel, was investigating fresh allega-tions that Clinton had lied under oath, in the Paula Jones sexual harassment lawsuit, about the nature of his relationship with a twenty-one-year-old White House intern named Monica Lewinsky.

For eight months, Clinton denied the allegations, putting the country through a terrible ordeal of salacious details about a stained navy blue dress from the Gap, a cigar, and oral sex. Nothing infuri-ated millions of Americans more than the legalistic definitions of sex offered by the President's defenders.

Clinton finally admitted the truth to the grand jury and the American people in August 1998, and the admission confirmed the suspicions of legions of golfers: Clinton *was* a cheater. "Not to be smug, but when I heard about Monica Lewinsky, I thought, Sure, absolutely, no question," Robert Sullivan, an editor at *Life* magazine, wrote in *Sports Illustrated*. "Claiming that something doesn't count because of a technicality—a Biblical technicality, no less—is pre-cisely the type of wacky distinction our Mr. Clinton would make. I said to myself: It's just like with the mulligans."

Sullivan wrote that Clinton's habit of taking mulligans spoke vol-umes about "duplicity, chronic self-delusion, an incapacity for truth-telling. Also, as directly relates to the Lewinsky affair, there's something serious to be said about calling an act something other than what it truly is, so that it vanishes and doesn't count."

Sullivan concluded his piece with a plea: "Mr. President, a golf shot is not a mulligan, it's a golf shot. Count it. Count 'em all. And an assignation with a young woman wherein things transpire that might upset the wife, count that too."

After admitting to the nation, and his wife and daughter, that he indeed did have an "improper relationship" with Miss Lewinsky, the President traveled to Martha's Vineyard for his vacation. There was no golf, no fun. The only time Clinton was seen was when he walked his dog, Buddy. The President truly seemed alone.

There was still a lot more golf to be played, of course, through his final two years in the White House.

Clinton presented the Medal of Freedom to Jimmy Carter and his wife, Rosalynn, at a White House ceremony in August 2000. Carter seized the moment, slyly informing Clinton about some of the things that a golfing ex-president should expect.

"You'll be able to play golf without any telephoto lens focusing on your stroke," Carter, a nongolfer, told Clinton. "But there is a downside: I understand golfing partners don't give as many mulli-gans" to former presidents.

Clinton smiled, but it was a melancholy smile. As much as any of his predecessors, Clinton adored the job, and all its privileges.

I WAS ON A QUEST.
My quest was to play a round of golf with as many living presidents as possible. I wanted to try to judge for myself the way

they conducted themselves over the course of eighteen holes. I invited George W. Bush, Bill Clinton, George H. W. Bush, and Gerald R. Ford to play a round of golf with me.

The current President Bush declined, but that did not surprise me. Too busy overseeing "the war on terrorism."

Ford politely said no, but he granted me an enlightening interview.

The senior George Bush originally said yes in the spring of 2002, but as the weeks went by, I heard nothing, until finally one of his assistants broke the bad news: Bush simply had no time to play with me. He did grant me a short, fun interview. So I cannot complain too much.

But imagine my surprise that day in early August when I receive an e-mail from one of Clinton's aides. In the subject line, three sweet words: *Golf with President.* Yes, the e-mail says, Mr. Clinton has agreed to play with you, next week at Mount Kisco Golf Club. Clinton's office has just one request: They want me to set up the tee time.

I call Mount Kisco Country Club, a pristine, beautiful private course, and I ask for the pro shop, where I try to sound as nonchalant as possible.

"I'd like to set up a tee time for four people—a group that includes former President Bill Clinton," I say.

"Are you a member here?" a man named Trip asks.

"Uh, no," I say.

"Well, *he's* not a member here," Trip sniffs. "Unless he has the permission of a member or a board member to play here, he cannot play here."

I know that Clinton has struggled to join a country club in Westchester County. But this is worse than I imagined—he is not even welcome to play the occasional round at a golf course down the road from his house.

When I call Clinton's office back with the bad news, his scheduler sighs heavily. But he quickly says, "We'll take care of it." I hear the next day that we will play at the Golf Club of Purchase, a private club with a membership of about 170 and an entry fee of $150,000. It is a Jack Nicklaus–designed course, a challenging, narrow wetlands course.

So I play a practice round the weekend before at a beat-up public course in northern Virginia with a friend and fellow hacker, Rich. I shoot a miserable 55, with mulligans, over nine holes. When the round is over, Rich gives me a sympathetic look. "Good luck," he says. He knows it and I know it: It is going to be a long afternoon with the President.

A few days later, I hop in my car for the drive north from my house in Virginia. Before leaving, I put in a call to Donald Trump to ask him about the round of golf he played with Clinton in the spring of 2001 at the Trump International Golf Course in Palm Beach. On the way to New York, he calls me back.

"He's got a lot of golf talent," Trump tells me. "But he really likes those mulligans. If he misses a shot, he wants to take another crack at it. It's like life."

Trump shot a 73 with Clinton, but he cannot recall what the President shot.

Maureen Dowd, the Pulitzer Prize–winning *New York Times* columnist, had told me that Trump had recently built a golf course in Westchester County, in part (he said) because Bill Clinton would need a place to play. The Trump National Golf Club, designed by Jim Fazio, was in Briarcliff Manor, New York, just down the road from Chappaqua. On the phone with me, Trump delivers an instant, three-minute pitch about the golf course and the clubhouse's amenities. He is particularly proud of the man-made waterfall, carved into the hillside on the 13th hole.

When I ask him about his remark about Clinton, he says, "Yeah, the President can't get into Winged Foot or any of the courses up there. I might very well think of asking him to join."

I tell Trump that I am heading to Purchase to play a round with Clinton the following day. Should I tell the President you are thinking of asking him to join your new country club? I ask.

Trump mulls over my rather forward suggestion for no more than a split second. "Not yet," he says. "Let me think more about it. But say hi to the President for me. He's a terrific guy, and he's a lot of fun to play with."

T HE NIGHT BEFORE MY GOLF OUTING with Clinton, I cannot sleep. I lie awake in my hotel room, trying to tame the knots of nervous energy ricocheting around my chest. I fret about my inconsistency off the tee and the appropriateness of my golf wardrobe. Shorts or pants? A striped shirt or a plain one? I invest a good hour wondering whether I should wear my Farm Neck cap or my Masters cap. These trivial worries seem a matter of life or death. As get-rich-quick infomercials drone on and on over the television, I pace the rabbit-warren-sized room, staring past the blinds at the dark parking lot.

I read and reread the story that Rick Reilly wrote for *Sports Illustrated* after playing with Clinton at Congressional in May 1995. I'm searching for Clinton Golfing Eve insomnia tips. In the wee hours prior to his round with the President, Reilly worked on domestic chores. He ironed his shirt three times, and his pants twice, and laid out his socks in his shoes two different ways and then practiced his putting at 3 A.M. So I double-check my clothes in the closet, just to see if they are still pressed, and I look in on my two hats. I draw the line at practicing my putting at 3 A.M. I have my limits. Besides, it's hopeless.

Suddenly, it hits me why I am here: I wrote a newspaper story accusing Bill Clinton of taking too many mulligans. Now he has agreed to play golf with me, knowing the only way I will survive the round is by taking too many mulligans.

This round is Bill Clinton's revenge.

It is one of those thoughts that seem inspired in the middle of the night, only to appear absolutely preposterous by morning light.

I arrive at the Golf Club of Purchase ninety minutes before the tee time. There is more than enough time to snoop around. From the outside, the brick clubhouse, with enormous white columns, looks like Jay Gatsby's West Egg mansion. The club was built in 1998, and it reeks of a freshly minted fortune accumulated from the cashing-in of a few dozen fat telecom IPOs before the NASDAQ imploded. Inside, the clubhouse is a stage-set version of the Yale Club. There are reading rooms (but no books), faux fireplaces large enough to park a Volkswagen, high-backed leather chairs (that appear never to have accommodated a single rear end), and polished, walnut lockers with shiny brass name tags: Michael Douglas in Locker 94; Steven Wynn in 150; Charles R. Schwab in 147; Walter A. Forbes in 113; Gary Winnick in 144; Kenneth Cole in 46; Henry Kravis in 5; and New York mayor Michael R. Bloomberg in 100.

None of those men are there, of course, and for all anyone knows, none of them have ever been there before. The place is that fresh-out-of-the-box pristine. In fact, no one is there except a few dozen employees, standing around, doing nothing. It is noon on a Tuesday in the middle of August, and the famous men are no doubt luxuriating in some faraway, lush place, the Hamptons or Santa Barbara or Jackson Hole or Vail, with not a single thought of Bill Clinton and mulligans.

My partners for the round with Clinton are two rich guys who are not quite as wealthy as a Schwab or Forbes or Bloomberg, but who still have enough cash to play at the Golf Club at Purchase. They are venture capitalists—Michael G. Bronfein, forty-seven, of Sterling Venture Partners in Baltimore, and his close friend Barry Baker, fifty, of Boston Ventures Management in Boston. Barry is a member (Locker 180) and a 7 handicap. Michael is a 13.

Michael is a Democratic fund-raiser and contributor who met Clinton back in 1991 and has played with him twice, at Robert Trent Jones Golf Club in Manassas, Virginia, and at his home course, Caves Valley Golf Club in Baltimore. "He's a good golfer," Michael says of the President. And he vouches for him immediately. "I've never seen him take a mulligan except off the first tee," Michael says. "He does practice while he plays, but he plays the first ball. It's not exactly like he can go to the driving range every week."

We talk about the scorching heat, and the fact that it appears we have the clubhouse, and, presumably, all eighteen holes, to ourselves. "We're in the dog days of August," Michael says. "Why would anyone want to come out here unless you're playing with the President?"

Good point.

It is Barry's fiftieth birthday, and the round with the President is his surprise birthday present. Barry is as gracious, warm, and down-to-earth as Michael. Neither guy acts as if he is worth more than

$100 million, or whatever the number was that day, depending on the market's inclination. There is a hint of a gargantuan fortune socked away, however, when Barry invites me to join him on his flight back to Baltimore that night.

"I've got the big plane today," he says. Oh, the *big* plane. Thanks but no thanks, I tell him. I'm stuck with my car, which I plan on driving back to Virginia.

Clinton arrives shortly before 1 o'clock in a four-car caravan. After we shake hands and he offers me an unlimited supply of mulligans, we walk through the air-conditioned clubhouse and back outside to the practice range, where the heat and humidity assault us with the fury of a blast furnace. The sweat immediately races down my face and back.

Perhaps it is no coincidence that the only non-millionaire in the foursome—me—is dressed like a clown in long, khaki pants (I chose the pants because I figured the President would be wearing pants, too). The other three guys are no dummies; they are wearing shorts. It's 98 degrees in the shade, for God's sake.

"I know quite a bit about presidential golf," Clinton tells me as he grabs his driver and a few other clubs from his beat-up navy blue bag, with tan trim. Emblazoned on the pocket is the presidential seal. He recalls playing in 1997 at a century-old course in Asheville, North Carolina, where Woodrow Wilson had played as president. "Wilson was totally different than what people thought of him," Clinton says. "He was actually a red-blooded rascal who played golf." And Clinton says that Kennedy and FDR were the finest golfers.

On the practice tee, Clinton brandishes a brand-new Nike driver with a head that looks almost twice the size of a Big Bertha head. He explains that last week, he visited the Nike headquarters in Beaverton, Oregon, and Phil Knight, the company's chief executive officer, told Clinton that if he could drive a golf ball into a building at the far end of the corporate driving range, about 340 yards away, he would give him a set of Nike clubs. Tiger Woods had been the only person to nail the building. "I didn't hit it," Clinton says to us on the practice tee, "but I got to about fifteen yards. So they gave me a set anyway."

As we all pound our practice balls, Clinton begins muttering to himself. "There you go, Billy." "That's the way to hit it, Billy." After he duffs the ball, he says, "What are you doing, Bill?" and "Billy! Billy! *Billy!*"

When we are finished, Clinton says to himself, "Pretty good for an old guy."

Michael asks, "When did you get old?"

"A long time ago," Clinton says.

FOR THE WEEKEND HACKER, the hardest shot in golf is the first drive off the first tee. But the hardest shot of a hacker's life is the first drive off the first tee with a president of the United States standing behind you, his hands on his hips, watching and judging you.

Trust me. It's not easy.

This is the moment I was dreading. I am convinced that I am going to swing and miss. Or if I'm lucky, I'll manage to dribble the ball beyond the ladies' tees. Oddly, there are no nerves, partly because Clinton is a master at putting people at ease. He says he will play the match to a 13 handicap, and he teams up with Michael, the 13 handicapper. Because my handicap is 28, I team up with Barry, who has the lowest handicap of seven. One of the venture capitalists sets the stakes: a round of Cokes on the 19th hole.

The first hole is a 422-yard, par-4 hole. Off the championship blue tees, Clinton hits his tee shot about 200 yards. "That's not long," he says, "but I'll take it."

It's my turn. I take a deep breath and a ragged practice swing. Then I smack the ball and it somehow soars far and high and straight. "Nice shot," Clinton said. "I think he's better than a 28, Michael."

For the rest of my life, no golf shot will ever feel as good as that inexplicably perfect tee shot.

The two money guys tee off, launching the balls far down the fairway.

I hit an ugly 2-iron shot, and the President immediately decides to try to turn me into a 10 handicapper. The lesson commences. "You stood up, you scooped it," he tells me. "Take a practice swing, keep your wrist firm. You should get longer clubs—about an inch longer than standard."

On the first green, Clinton sinks a nice eight-foot putt with his Odyssey putter. But for more than half the holes that day, Clinton does not even bother touching his putter. The money guys will give him that many putts, some as long as fifty feet.

Clinton ends up with a 5—a legitimate 5. Barry tells me, "Write down the President wins the hole with a bogey." The venture capitalist guys, perhaps fighting nerves, each get a 6. And the hacker (that's me) ends up with a 7. I was on in three, but I 4-putt the hole. I should have practiced a few carpet putts back at the hotel.

On the second hole—a 159-yard, par-3—Clinton cranks his tee shot far left and only about eighty yards. "Oh God, I came way over it," he says. "Moved my feet and everything else." He frowns. "What's the matter with me?" He takes a second tee shot, without asking, and it also soars left.

We find his first ball lying in a puddle near a sprinkler head. "What's the rule, two clubs?" he asks me. He is on his best behavior, being absolutely meticulous, a stickler for the rule book's fine print. He clearly wants to demonstrate that he plays by the rules.

He takes the drop and chips into the bunker. He then takes a practice shot, then a third. His third practice shot ends up on the green, about 35 feet from the hole.

His partner, Michael, sinks the par putt, and he picks up Clinton's ball. The President does not bother to putt out. "Those are the longest gimme putts we'll get," Clinton says to me, laughing.

Being a stickler for the rules has lasted about five minutes.

In the cart, he explains that when he was president, it often took him four or five holes before he had his first good swing. "I'd be preoccupied," he says.

I am preoccupied right now with staving off embarrassment. On the 3rd hole—a par-5, 486-yard hole—I hit an atrocious drive. It might have rolled fifty yards from the tee box. And Clinton immediately gives me another impromptu lesson. He puts me in a behind-the-back bear hug, demonstrating the proper way to hold the club. "Closer to your crotch," he says, moving my hands that way. "Take the club head back slowly. You've got so much power—stop trying to kill it."

I try again, swinging easily. This time, my drive soars 250 yards.

Clinton powers his drive 280 yards into the left rough. He breaks out an unlit cigar, which he chews, off and on, for the rest of the afternoon. From the rough he hits a beautiful iron shot that lands twenty yards from the green, and his third shot stops just five feet from the cup. And he sinks the putt for a legitimate birdie. It will end up being his best hole of the day.

"Golf's a lot like life," Clinton laughs as we walk off the green. "You get a lot of breaks, both ways. It's a lot better than if you just get simple justice."

On the 4th hole, we all stink. Clinton gets into a rhythm that he will follow for the rest of the afternoon—two or three shots off the tee, two or three shots off the fairway, two or three chips off the edge of the green. Clinton ends up 2-putting the par-4 hole, making a double-bogey. "I won with a double-bogey," Clinton says. "That's pitiful."

Then Clinton makes a startling admission: "I play double-bogey limit golf anyway." In other words, he never counts a stroke above double-bogey.

Three holes earlier, the President was asking me for a ruling on a drop out of a water hazard. Now he admits playing double-bogey limit golf. Some former presidents retain a few privileges on the golf course. Some never have to shoot a triple-bogey.

FIFTH HOLE: SAME PATTERN. Clinton hits a drive into the trees, takes a second practice tee shot. He hits this one short. He hits another tee shot, this one goes long and far. He drives the cart over to the trees, takes a drop, but hits that ball short. He then plays three more practice shots from the fringe and ends up playing the second of his practice shots.

He is on the green in four but picks up without putting. On his scorecard at the end of the day, he takes a 4 on the hole. It's a no-putt 4.

On the 6th hole, Clinton again plays three shots off the tee. On the fairway, he plays his second tee shot from the left bunker on the green side. He is on in two but again does not putt out. His score for the hole is a 4.

It is not until the round is over that I have any sense of what Clinton has done. He cards an 82 for the eighteen holes—a 41 on the front, and a 41 on the back. His scorecard shows eight pars, and one birdie. He plays extremely well on some holes—some 300-yard drives, and some very nice touch shots around the green. But it does not feel like he shot an 82, perhaps because he takes so many swings. Clinton easily hit 200 shots out there during our six-hour round.

These are not conventional mulligans, where a player takes a do-over shot and everyone knows he has discarded his first bad shot, usually off the tee.

This is much more subtle. Clinton practices while he plays. He takes two or three shots off the tee. The second and third shots are practice shots, not to be played. But as soon as he gets out on the fairway, Clinton has two or three balls to choose from. "Which is my first ball?" Clinton asks over and over. "Is this my first ball?" Playing partners become inadvertent co-conspirators, inevitably saying, "No, Mr. President, I think it's this one," pointing to the best placed of the three balls. Of course, sometimes Clinton does not ask and he assumes his second or third tee shot is his first, perhaps inadvertently, perhaps not.

Then if he doesn't like a fairway iron shot, he takes a second practice shot, and a third. And the same routine is followed near the green. "Is this my first shot?" Clinton asks. "Or is it this one? I can't remember."

It is a shell game with golf balls.

The green is something different entirely. On at least half the holes we play, Clinton does not bother taking a single putting stroke.

That's because the match play format sometimes makes it unnecessary for him to putt. If his playing partner makes a putt, Clinton just picks up his ball without finishing the hole. He also picks up his ball if my partner, Barry, the 7 handicapper with a great putting stroke, makes a putt. Both Michael and Barry are terrific putters. But when you pick up, you should not assume you will 1-putt, right? If so, that's a "freebie," as Clinton calls them.

Clinton has always said he prefers playing with at least one player who is better than him. Now I see why.

The President also concedes many putts. After Barry sinks a ten-footer, Clinton points at my eight-foot putt and tells me, "That's good." On the rare occasion that I sink an eight-foot putt, I dance a jig. But what was I going to say? The President of the United States gives you a putt, you take it.

There are moments when I think to myself: He doesn't even realize how sloppy this scoring system is. He's out having fun, but when it's over, he believes his score.

These are not mulligans. They're Billigans.

Playing partners don't just give him gimme putts. They give him gimme fairway shots, and gimme drives, and gimme chip shots. If someone makes a par, Clinton gets a par, too. If everyone makes a triple-bogey, Clinton gets a double-bogey.

Take enough Billigans, and you, too, can break 80.

DURING THE FIRST SIX HOLES of our round, Clinton drives the golf cart with Barry riding shotgun. The next six, it is Michael's turn to ride with the President.

And for the final six holes, I ride with Clinton as he drives, his arm draped on the chair back behind me. He speaks candidly and openly, never shirking a single nettlesome question about his playing practices or his rule bending. When I first jump into the golf cart, he asks me where I was born, where I went to college, and how long I have worked at the *Times*.

When it is my turn to pose a question, I ask him about his mulligan philosophy and why he thinks so many people were so critical of his golf game. Bill Clinton blames it all on the Republicans.

"DeLay attacked me," he says of Congressman Tom DeLay, the deeply partisan House Republican whip. "He said he saw my swing and I couldn't play that well. And I had just shot an 80 in Syracuse on a hard course. And I think I sent him the newspaper article with the pro who went around with me saying, you know, sometimes he hit more than one ball when I was giving him lessons but he always counted his real score."

"You do take a lot of practice balls," I tell him.

I ask the President why Bob Dole tried to make an issue of his honesty on the golf course in the 1996 campaign. "Well, the Republicans did it because it was part of their strategy to deny my legitimacy," he says. "They decided that they would say because [H. Ross] Perot got 19 percent of the vote [in 1992] and nobody could get a majority that even though I had won an overwhelming electoral victory that I was not legitimate. They just decided from the day I was elected to just keep attacking me. They had some friends in the press because I was the designated fall guy in '92, and I didn't fall. So they sort of wanted to keep writing those stories."

He shoots me a sideways glance, a slightly raised eyebrow here that I almost miss. The look says: *Van Natta, you were one of 'em.* But he is too much of a gentleman to say anything about it. Instead, he goes on to discuss Mark Grobmyer, his friend in Arkansas who routinely took the do-over shots. Clinton is absolutely convinced that's how this mulligan criticism got started.

"I just play what the rules are," Clinton says, shaking his head. "It's weird. I just don't understand it."

I just play what the rules are.

Rule 7–2 of the United States Golf Association's *Rules of Golf* says, "A player shall not play a practice stroke . . . during the play of a hole." The penalty for breaking Rule 7–2 is two strokes. Clinton breaks this rule on almost every hole.

It was then I wondered: Has Clinton deluded himself? Is he convinced that he never shaves a single stroke off his game, ever? Have playing partners been so generous for so long that when they insist his third practice tee shot is actually his first ball, he believes them? Didn't he fail to break 90 just a month earlier at the World Celebrity Golf Championship outside Stockholm, where Clinton proclaimed his performance was "terrible" because he had eight 3-putts? Doesn't he *always* fail to break 90 at tournaments where the officials strictly forbid mulligans, not to mention Billigans? Before I get a chance to pursue these questions with him, Clinton climbs out of the cart and looks at one of his golf balls lying about 210 yards from the flag.

"How far have I got?" he asks me. "Forever, right?"

ON THE 15TH HOLE, a stunning par-5, 516-yard hole, Clinton flashes the anger that I had heard about. I had also heard, however, that the anger is quickly forgotten.

Clinton has an almost impossible third shot—he has to hit his ball past a tree and over a deep sand trap to get on the green. "You're 2 here," a caddy tells Clinton.

"I'm in good shape but I don't know what to hit," Clinton says. The caddy hands him the pitching wedge. "What do I do here? So I can play it to the right of this tree, right?"

"Yes," the caddy says.

"Let's see here," Clinton says. He takes a practice swing. "Like that?" he asks.

"Yes," the caddy says. "That's good."

"I gotta miss this tree," he says, "but I've gotta be out of the way of the sand trap. Well, let's see."

He takes a few more practice swings, adjusts his stance. Something is wrong. The caddy steps a few feet closer to the President, and says, "Make sure your club face is open. Turn it a little more."

"Like this? Is this right?" Clinton said. "Am I aimed right?" Clinton looks unconvinced.

"That's perfect," the caddy says. "Now just trust it."

Clinton swings and his ball smacks the tree and ricochets right, farther away from the green, practically behind him.

"Where did it go?" Clinton asks.

"Went right," the caddy says, glumly.

"Because it hit the tree!" Clinton says with anger. "Because I closed the club face!" He drops another ball. "Look at this," he tells the caddy, disgustedly. "Now let's try it with a regular club face and see what happens."

This one also clocks the tree, and the ball zings to the right. "No, that one I didn't try to hit." Clinton stalks in a small semicircle. "That first shot—if I hadn't moved the club face, it would have gone right on the green."

Clinton's face reddens, and he bites his bottom lip. Now I see that he is seething. He shoots an unmistakable look of fury at the caddy, who I don't think notices. "I'm pissed off—I shouldn't have done that," he says to no one in particular. "Twice in a row I listened and I got screwed! Twice!" Then he mutters to himself, "First they told me to aim left . . ."

Clinton stands between two golf balls and asks, "Which one is my first one?" He lines up the closer one to the hole, but the caddy says, "I think that's your second shot."

"Which one is my first one?" Clinton asks again. His first one is about ten yards farther from the green than the second shot.

"Aw, shit, I just feel so mad about that one, I don't know what to do," Clinton says. "I blew two strokes here. I twisted the goddamn club and hit it into the tree."

He hits the chip, but it goes over the green and settles somewhere behind it. He stomps off to the golf cart without finishing the hole. His ball is lying 6; it would take him a minimum of two strokes to get in the hole, for an 8.

On his scorecard, Bill Clinton writes a 6—the angriest, ugliest bogey you've ever seen.

A MOMENT LATER, the anger vanishes as Clinton admires his monster drive off the 16th tee.

Back in the cart, I ask him, "What country clubs do you belong to up here?"

"None," he says. "A guy I went to Georgetown with actually had a place on the back nine at Winged Foot that was a beautiful home. It had three acres, a creek running through it. I loved it. But the house would have had to be totally rebuilt and we simply couldn't afford it. We couldn't afford the house. We sure couldn't afford to rebuild it. I have had to virtually rebuild the house I've got in Chappaqua, outside and inside."

Then he says he was recently offered a membership at "some course" nearby, but he has not been able to accept it or even play there because he has been traveling abroad so much.

I point out that he still often plays at the Army-Navy Country Club in Arlington, Virginia, where he had also played the most rounds as president. "I love that course," he says. "Lucky for me, when Hillary was elected to the Senate, I became a spousal member."

Before the 17th tee, Clinton and I are sitting in the golf cart. He is talking about playing a few years ago with Curtis Strange, and then suddenly, he says, "You know, young people come up to me all the time. They come up to me and ask me advice, they want to go into politics, they want to be president, they want to do this or that. What should they do? I give them advice about college. I always tell them they should study something they are interested in and it challenges them, and it doesn't matter what they study. They can study physics and go into politics.

"And I tell them that they should get to know lots of different kinds of people and listen to them. I always say, you know, you got to understand, there is a lot of difference between wanting to do something and believing you can."

Clinton pauses, and smiles. "I played on a church basketball team when I was in high school. I was heavy. I was about six feet two inches, a little over. One night when I was sixteen, the two best players on the team couldn't play. So I had to play the whole game, and I played, you know, and we played forty-minute games—I scored six-

With author Don Van Natta Jr. riding shotgun in the golf cart, Bill Clinton pauses to tell the story of managing to jump high enough to dunk a basketball, despite being six feet two inches and "heavy," during a game in a high school league.

teen points, led the team. The only time I ever did it. And I got a fast break, and I got a clear run at the basket from half court. Unbelievably, by the skin of my teeth, I dunked the ball. I actually dunked it. I got the hand over the rim and got it in.

"Now I want to do it again, but I don't believe I can."

We all laugh.

"There is a huge difference in life between wanting to do something and believing you can. I try to convince young people all the time—you have to believe you can do the things you want to do. You have to imagine it, you know?"

O N THE PAR-4, 18TH FAIRWAY, Clinton tells everyone he is about to turn fifty-six. He says President Bush sent him a nice note, wishing him a happy birthday. He then asks us our ages. "As long as I can remember, I was always the youngest guy," Clinton says. "Now I'm always the oldest. I should have gotten an age-handicap advantage!"

On the green, the President shows me a chipping technique taught to him by Dave Pelz, the famous golf coach and author. He takes several practice chips off the green, and though he doesn't putt out, he records a par.

"All right, boys—it was fun, wasn't it?" Clinton says, shaking everyone's hand. "It was a great time."

Back in the cart, we drive to the clubhouse and I thank Clinton for agreeing to play with me. It was an easy decision because McAuliffe "loves you," Clinton says. "And I love McAuliffe."

Clinton says that I wrote a story about him a few years back that infuriated him.

I am about to ask him if it was the mulligans story, but he keeps talking. "I can't remember what it was, but I remember complaining about your story to Terry, and he said, 'He's not a chicken-shit reporter. He will only write something if he has evidence that it's true.'

"That's a very nice compliment he paid you," Clinton says.

Back at the clubhouse, Clinton has an 82, Barry has a 79, Michael has an 89, and I have a 96. I probably shot closer to a 110. The Billigans helped me shave about 14 strokes off my game.

"Do you have time for a drink?" Barry says.

"Sure," the President says.

We head to the quiet locker room to clean up, and I realize then that we did not see another golfer on the course. It took five and a half hours to play eighteen holes, and the only people we saw were a few bored, sweaty Secret Service agents whose job it was to follow us around.

In the locker room, Clinton somehow begins talking with me about the economic crisis in Argentina. As he gives a perfectly rounded dissertation on the subject, he shaves, washes up, and takes a leak, still chattering at the urinal about the best way for the United States to help Argentina.

Sitting at the bar in the club room is an elegant, sumptuously dressed woman, around fifty-five years old. She turns, spots Clinton,

Hole	1	2	3	4	5	6	7	8	9	OUT	10	11	12	13	14	15	16	17	18	IN	TOT	HCP	NET
Championship	422	159	486	459	372	160	539	409	335	3341	429	418	518	436	198	516	456	146	418	3535	6876		
Back	401	134	478	447	357	134	508	383	315	3157	395	390	499	374	176	502	435	141	386	3298	6455		
Middle	391	127	472	427	345	122	484	363	310	3041	355	374	462	338	137	491	362	103	356	2978	6019		
Handicap	7	17	11	1	9	15	3	5	13		4	12	14	10	16	8	2	18	6				
The Prez	5	5	4	6	4	4	5	4	4	41	5	5	4	2	3	6	5	3	4	41	82		
Don	7	4	7	6	4	5	6	9	6	51	9	4	5	5	3	7	6	3	5	45	96		
Michael	6	4	6	7	4	3	8	5	4	45	6	4	4	3	7	6	3	5	4	45	90		
Barry	6	3	5	6	4	4	9	4	5	41	5	5	3	3	6	5	2	4		38	79		
Par	4	3	5	4	4	3	5	4	4	36	4	4	5	4	3	5	4	3	4	36	72		
Forward	353	103	428	410	265	109	456	282	287	2693	316	321	426	303	101	409	327	97	329	2628	5321		
Handicap	7	17	11	1	9	15	3	5	13		4	12	14	10	16	8	2	18	6				

THE GOLF CLUB OF PURCHASE

Marker — Rating / Slope
Championship 74.3 138
Back 72.4 135
Middle 70.5 130
Forward 72.9 131

Scorer: _[signature]_ Attest: _[signature]_ Date: 8/13/02

This is Bill Clinton's scorecard for his round of "82" with Barry Baker, Michael Bronfein and Don Van Natta Jr. on Tuesday, August 13, 2002, at the Golf Club of Purchase in Purchase, New York. The names, including "The Prez," were written by Van Natta before the round. By signing the card in the bottom left-hand corner, the former president certified his score's authenticity.

and gives him a withering glare. If Clinton sees it, he ignores it. She is at the bar with two men in their twenties, possibly her sons. Neither man turns around to even glance at Clinton.

The President grabs a chocolate-chip cookie from a tray, then shakes hands with a half-dozen waiters and the female bartender, who whispers to him, "I wish you could run again."

"I would if I could," he says with a laugh.

We sit down at a circular table by the window, overlooking the lush green as the sun sets behind us. Clinton orders a Diet Coke. The rest of us order cold beers.

They arrive in an instant, and we toast a weekday afternoon of golf.

Michael asks Clinton to sign a scorecard for his wife. "When did you meet her?" Clinton asks. Michael says at the age of sixteen when he was in a body cast after being hurt at lacrosse. "She thought, 'This is the only guy whose body can't hurt me,'" Clinton observes.

I ask Clinton who among the golfing presidents he would have liked to have played with. He says he'd like to have played with Kennedy, Wilson, and Reagan. I ask him why he would have loved to play with Kennedy, his political hero. "Just to talk to him," Clinton says, as he munches on fistfuls of peanuts. "And because he was a good golfer. I always like at least one person in my foursome who is better than me."

Then Clinton tells a story. Back in 1996, after Jacqueline Kennedy Onassis's death, her family auctioned off hundreds of Kennedy possessions. Two of the most sought-after items were putters used by the President—a MacGregor putter and a Robot putter.

"Vernon Jordan asked me if I wanted him to get one of the putters," he says, "and I said, 'Yeah,' but I said, 'Vernon, I don't have any money. I can go up to $10,000.'"

The MacGregor putter sold for $65,750, and the Robot putter sold for $63,000. Clinton was disappointed, but then a couple weeks after the auction, a canister arrived in the White House mail with a letter.

The letter was written by a Miami man who had worked as a caddy at a North Palm Beach golf club in Florida in the 1950s. The man talked about trading putters with a player who had played the course in 1957. "Since you love golf," the man wrote in the last sentence of the letter, "and you love President Kennedy, I thought you'd like to have Senator Kennedy's putter."

It is an old MacGregor putter, a gift that Clinton cherishes. "Kennedy apparently had fairly small hands," he says. "I can hardly hold the putter, it's so small, the grip. This wonderful gift was in this little canister."

IT IS GETTING LATE. It's past 7 o'clock, and Michael and Barry stand up and announce they have a plane to catch (they don't say it's *Barry's* plane they have to catch).

"Yeah," Clinton says, "I gotta get home before Hillary starts referring to me as her first husband." Everyone laughs. "That's what happened to me when I bombed in Atlanta in '88," he continues, refer-ring to his speech at the Democratic National Convention that year, which was considered by all to be a dud. "She started going up to total strangers out of the Omni, saying, 'You've met my first hus-band?' That's when I knew I screwed up."

The money men say good-bye, but Clinton isn't going anywhere. I know the Secret Service agents are there, but they're invisible. Clinton is standing as he continues to tell golf stories. He talks more about his favorite clubs, favorite courses, favorite playing partners.

"I loved Palmer—he was such a gentleman," he says. "The great thing about being president is I could go anywhere and play with them and learn from them. Playing with all those pros was wonder-ful. One of my favorite playing partners is Amy Alcott. She won the U.S. Open in 1980 or something. I play with Amy Alcott every chance I get when I go to southern California. She is a joy, but she gets mad when I outdrive her. I say, 'I'm only sixty pounds heavier than you.'"

Clinton cannot help himself. Wearing a big smile, he keeps talking about golf. Finally, I ask him why he loves the game so much.

"I love it—it really is a lot like life," he says. "There is a lot of skill to it, but it's mostly a head game once you reach whatever level you are swinging. If you don't concentrate or get upset or you do all the stuff I did, you make mistakes and you pay for them.

"The other thing I like about it is, to some extent, it's an art, not a science. You do get breaks, both ways. You get some bad breaks, like when I hit the tree. And you get some great breaks—I hit another tree, and it went on the green.

"It's just a lot like life. I love it."

We walk over to the bar, where Clinton talks about the perils of George W. Bush's tax cut between munches of another cookie. The waiting staff and bartender hang on his every word, smiles lighting up their faces. Someone asks him how he liked the course. "First time I played it," he says. "I loved it." As we leave, he snatches another cookie and tells the bartender, "These are great cookies. Thanks."

On the circular driveway, the black Suburban and the Secret Ser-vice agents are waiting. Clinton pauses, and talks about the thrill of playing the famed Ballybunion Golf Club in Ireland, teeing off with 20,000 people watching. "It was amazing," he says. "I love Ireland." And Ireland loves Clinton. At Ballybunion, the Irish built a statue of Clinton holding a driver. It is the only statute of Clinton anywhere in the world.

After September 11, the Irish laid flowers and wreaths at Clinton's feet. "They love that statue," I say.

"Yeah," Clinton says. "The peace meant a lot to them."

The first time the President played the gorgeous links course, he says, the men in the Ballybunion clubhouse laid 20-to-1 odds that he would not be able to break 100. "I had two 7s and a 10," Clinton says, laughing. "But I shot a 95."

Thanks again, Mr. President, I say.

"Thanks, thanks," he says, stepping into the Suburban. "I loved it, I loved it."

H E *is* A TERRIFIC GOLFER, all things considered. Nearly two years after leaving the Oval Office, it is still important to Clinton that the American people recognize that fact. His legacy as president was always more important to him than just about anything. And his reputation as a golfer is also important to him. It is the only reason he agreed to play with a hack like me.

Clinton would have gotten a lot more credit for his golfing talent if he had played the game straight, with no Billigans. But the flaws in his golf game mirror his flawed presidency. If he had played it straight as president, he would have had a much better chance of realizing the promise of all that natural talent and magnetic charm.

Bill Clinton's golf game is as complicated and fascinating as he is. There are not many fifty-six-year-old guys who believe they are only a few practice rounds away from joining the PGA Senior Tour.

You just have to believe you can do the things you want to do. You have to imagine it, you know?

Richard M. Nixon

"Oh, That Didn't Count"

His pants too high and his legs askew, Richard Nixon's golf swing was as herky-jerky as the way he carried himself on the rope line. Often joylessly and always obsessively, Nixon devoted himself to conquering the game that his boss, Dwight D. Eisenhower, loved so much. After resigning from the presidency in disgrace in August 1974, Nixon bragged that he managed to accomplish his lifelong goal of breaking 80. Few believed his boast. It turned out that he needed mulligans and gimmes to pull off the feat.

*By the time you get dressed, drive out there, play eighteen holes
and come home, you've blown seven hours.
There are better things you can do with your time.*
—Richard M. Nixon

R ICHARD M. NIXON was also pardoned by Sam Snead, the golf
champion.

It happened after Snead caught Nixon cheating during a round of
golf at the Greenbrier resort in White Sulphur Springs, West Virginia. There was no need for a cover-up because Snead quietly let
Nixon get away with it.

"He'd landed in some really bad rough no one could shoot out of
unless you had a bazooka," Snead recalled. "I was watching him from
the fairway when he disappeared into the thicket. Hell, I figured he
was going to drop another ball, take his loss like anyone else in that
situation and play on. But hell no—out comes his ball, flyin' high
onto the fairway. Then Nixon comes out of the woods, looking real
pleased with himself. I knew he threw it out, but I didn't say
anything.

"What could I say? He was the President."

In another round with Nixon, Snead realized that not everyone
would generously grant presidential privileges on the green. Snead
was playing with Nixon and Arthur Hill, the gruff chairman of the
board of Greyhound. On the first hole, Nixon had a two-foot putt
to make par and win the hole.

"That's good, isn't it?" the President asked.

"Not for my money it isn't," Hill snapped. "You've got to putt it."

"But Sam usually gives it to me," the President said.

"For my money," Hill told Nixon, "you've got to putt it."

Nixon missed the money putt.

"Do you know that he missed every one of those short takes?"
Snead said. "God, he was red and angry."

L IKE MANY AMBITIOUS YOUNG MEN of his generation, Richard Nixon originally viewed a golf course as an ideal career launching pad. Playing the game held promise as an easy way to curry favor with your boss and perhaps further your career prospects in the process.

But Nixon's boss just happened to be the President of the United States, Dwight D. Eisenhower. And if you were as awkward and uncoordinated as Nixon, and you were trying to score points with a golf-loving boss who did not suffer triple-bogeys gladly, then you might have concluded that playing eighteen holes with the boss would be more likely to endanger your career than to promote it.

Nixon, however, harbored few doubts. Nothing was going to stand in his way, not even utter humiliation.

This was the spring of 1953. The new Eisenhower administration was still finding its footing and so, too, were Nixon and Ike, especially with each other. The two men were searching for something in common, something to talk about. There were not many options because golf and fishing were the only certain paths to the old man's heart.

First they tried trout fishing. It was Ike's idea, though Nixon had never gone fishing before (perhaps Ike had a hunch that Nixon was not golf material). As Nixon later described it, their first—and only—fishing excursion was a "disaster." Eisenhower showed the Vice President how to cast a line, but on his first three attempts, the only thing Nixon caught was a nearby tree limb.

"I caught his shirt on my fourth try," Nixon said. "The lesson ended abruptly. I could see that he was disappointed because he loved fishing and could not understand why others did not like it as well as he did."

Despite his disappointment—or perhaps because of it—Eisenhower became even more committed to finding a patch of common ground with his vice president. The only other option was golf. And so on a perfect September afternoon in 1953, Ike invited Nixon to

Vice President Nixon and President Eisenhower prepare to play their first round of golf together on September 11, 1953, at Cherry Hills Country Club in Denver. Nixon tried mightily to impress the boss, emulating Ike's style of play and choice of hat wear.

play on his team in a match involving some wagering at the Cherry Hills Country Club in Denver.

This, too, had all the makings of a disaster. Nixon had never hit a golf ball until two years before, and he had played only sparingly before becoming vice president. Even so, Nixon told Ike he had a 20 handicap.

On the first tee of a par-4, 352-yard hole, Eisenhower hit a perfect drive of 220 yards. Nixon took a few tentative practice swings as he shot a sweaty, sideways glance at the cameramen.

"Just get up there and hit like you did this morning," Ike snapped at the Vice President. "Quit worrying."

Nixon smashed his drive, rolling his ball right next to the President's. "Great guns!" Ike shouted. "What are you doing? Driving the green?"

"I think I'll go back to the clubhouse," Nixon said, laughing.

He should have. It was his last good shot of the round.

Ike "gambled that I had to be better than my 20 handicap," Nixon recalled. "Eisenhower was a very competitive man. He played to win and hated to lose. If his partner played the wrong cards in bridge or blew a hole in golf, he did not hesitate to show his displeasure." Needless to say, Nixon's horrendous tee shots and jagged putting stroke single-handedly lost at least half the holes for the Ike-Nixon team. When the misery was over, Ike was forced to pay off a bet (something he hated to do as much as anything). He was extremely disappointed in his vice president.

"Look here," Ike told Nixon, "you're young, you're strong and you can do a lot better than that."

Nixon later recalled, "He talked to me like a Dutch uncle."

You can do a lot better than that. Those words seared Nixon's ego and they shamed him into trying to improve his golf game. The President's admonition instantly returned Nixon to his days as a gangly, 150-pound lineman for Whittier College.

Whittier's hard-charging, win-at-all-costs head coach, Wallace "Chief" Newman, made an enormous impact on young Dick Nixon. Newman, an American Indian who stood ramrod-straight, had been an All-American at the University of Southern California, and while he disliked losing, he despised quitting. He had no sons of his own, but he treated each of his players as a surrogate son. Each fall for three years, Nixon tried out for the Whittier football squad. And each autumn, Coach Newman cut him and then encouraged Nixon to try again the following year. During his senior year, Nixon finally made the varsity team, a reward, most likely, for his stubborn persistence.

Nixon rode the bench, playing only sparingly and getting pummeled during scrimmages when teammates treated him like "cannon fodder," in the words of one teammate. "I'd play opposite him in scrimmages," tackle Clint Harris said, "and we couldn't let up or the coach would be on us. So I'd have to knock the little guy for a loop. Oh, my gosh, did he take it."

Besides helping the starters tune up during practice, Nixon found more subtle ways to contribute to the team. He impressed his teammates and coaches with his understanding of football's nuances, and he delivered rousing pep talks at halftime. On the rare occasion when he did manage to get on the field, Nixon was so overeager and nervous that he usually jumped offside.

Coach Newman "could take men who were not too talented in football and make stars out of them, except he couldn't do it with me," Nixon recalled after being elected president. "I got into a few games after they were hopelessly won or hopelessly lost, you know, when they put the substitutes in, and finally the water boy, and then me."

Nixon said years later that above all else, Coach Newman taught him a valuable lesson that he applied to his political career: "You know who a good loser is? It's somebody who hates to lose and who gets up and comes back and fights again." Those words became Nixon's mantra, propelling him to excel at politics despite not being a natural at it. That same determination was devoted to golf.

And now there was a new mantra driving Dick Nixon to buckle down and overcome the long odds. These words were laced with disgust from his boss, the most powerful man in the world: *You can do a lot better than that.*

"I had learned in the Navy that when your superior officer makes a suggestion," Nixon said, "you should take it as a command."

So NIXON PLUNGED HEADFIRST into golf, though it would not be easy. Every one of his professional and personal goals always took a deep commitment to work—not to mention a lot of sweat, some worry, and a dash of paranoia. Golf was no different.

"Nixon was an intense personality, and he was a tough competitor who was very, very determined," said George P. Shultz, who served as Nixon's secretary of labor and secretary of the treasury. "And in golf, I would say, he maximized his potential. He got everything out of himself that he could get. And I think in a lot of ways his political life was the same way—you could see a man who was very determined and worked hard at it but wasn't a natural at schmoozing with people. Golf didn't come naturally to him. And neither did politics."

Nixon asked Max Elbin, the club professional at Burning Tree, to teach him the basics of the game in 1953. But the Vice President was in a big hurry. "I don't want any of that top-drawer stuff," he told Elbin. "I just want to know how to play the game."

Teaching the basics to Nixon was difficult because almost everything he did was wrong. His grip was wrong (he used a baseball grip), and his stance was wrong (he hunched over his putts). After their first forty-five-minute lesson (and Elbin assumed there needed to be at least a half dozen more), Nixon surprised him by saying he wanted to get out on the course immediately to play a few holes.

"I said, 'Mr. Vice President, you aren't ready for that yet,'" Elbin recalled. "He said 'Come on.' Well, we went out to the first tee, and the parking lot is adjacent to the first tee. And he stood there, and he hit three or four balls and they all went in the parking lot. I'm holding my breath—Cadillacs, other cars, just sitting there." They ended up playing two holes, but Nixon felt that was enough practice to take on the game.

Nixon may have felt ready to fit right into the golf world, but the golf world never seemed to be the right fit for Nixon. For starters, Nixon wore his golf pants several inches too high—"Gomer Pyle–high," one writer observed. Another writer said his slacks were pulled up to his armpits. In his first round with Ike, Nixon wore the same exact golf cap as Ike—the same English riding cap style, the same bright white. The problem was that Nixon's hat appeared to be at least two sizes too big for his head (as if he picked a large, cartoon version of Ike's hat to make sure the boss would not miss it). Nixon favored starched Banlon golf shirts, almost always buttoned all the way to the top, even in the stifling heat of a Maryland summer afternoon.

His swing was as stiff as his starched shirts. He looked as if someone had wound him up, but only about a third of the way. After watching the mechanics of Nixon's swing, nearly everyone used the same word to describe it: *herky-jerky*. One satirist observed that

Nixon's swing looked as if he was trying to beat the dust out of a floor rug.

By all accounts, Nixon was not a lifelong golf cheat. He cheated in the beginning, then spent years trying to stop but failed, and finally ended up cheating, at San Clemente, after leaving the presidency in disgrace. Like most people who bend the rules, Nixon embraced the rule bending as the quickest route to a low score and a modicum of golf course respectability.

In those first years, as the Vice President rushed to play a respectable game, he would not hesitate to move his ball to improve his lie or to beseech a playing partner to give him a short, three-foot putt. If he missed a putt, he tried again and again, until the putt "made noise." He often took two, three, even four tee shots until he was satisfied with a drive. Several friends believed he bent the rules because he was frustrated with his inability to quickly master the game.

Sam Snead said Nixon would cheat "when he didn't think nobody could see him." But Snead quickly added, "All hackers do that."

Nixon knew he was a hacker who would never be as good as Ike. Beating Ike, however, was never Nixon's goal. Since his days at Whittier, Nixon had settled for more modest sporting goals. He just wanted to be able to play the game without having to strain to hear the snickers or the whispers.

And he lost a lot of golf balls.

"Nixon was terrible," said Senator George A. Smathers, who played with the Vice President several times during this period. "You wondered whether you were playing golf or out hunting balls."

The club history at Burning Tree is much more diplomatic about Nixon's ability. It observed that Nixon automatically became an honorary member of the club after his inauguration as vice president: "Apparently he had not played golf theretofore—at least his game, such as it was initially, gave every evidence of having been freshly unwrapped."

Patrick J. Buchanan, the future presidential candidate and television commentator, was a caddy at Burning Tree in the mid-1950s. In

1954, at the age of fifteen, Buchanan watched as club pro Max Elbin dragged from the clubhouse "the plaid golf bag we all knew belonged to the Vice President of the United States.

"Soon," Buchanan said, "a car drove up and out stepped Richard M. Nixon, himself."

Nixon was there to play a late-afternoon round with Elbin, Don Sailor, the club's assistant pro, and a retired army general. "Nixon was a hero of mine," Buchanan recalled in his memoir, *Right from the Beginning*:

> He was a famous anti-Communist, the second youngest Vice President in history—and Nixon was known as a fighter. So, the whole time out, I stayed close to the Vice President. When he relieved himself in the bushes (it was, and still is, an all-men's club), I stepped up alongside and did the same, even though we caddies were supposed to go off separately or wait until we got back to the bench area.
>
> What I recall most vividly was the language these great men used—language my father never used—and how sycophantic some were. You did not need to be Ben Hogan to see that the Vice President of the United States was uncoordinated. His swing was not smooth and natural like an athlete's but stiff and jerky. Yet, from the comments his fellow players made, you would have thought we had the young Palmer out here.
>
> "Great shot, Dick, a real beauty," one said, watching at the tee, as the Vice President popped a drive 150 yards down the fairway. "Your game is really improving, Dick," the general interjected smoothly at another point—which made me wonder what it had been like a year ago. When the ball would go dribbling down the fairway like a grounder at Griffith Stadium, or shank off into the woods, you could see the shared pain etched in the faces of the Vice President's partners. "Tough break, Dick," they would say with a grimace. When he lost the ball and we found it deep in the forest, three strokes from civilization, they would call out, "Take one, Dick, and put it on the fairway!"

Even though his language was rough (this was, after all, the Vice President of the United States!), I liked Nixon immensely, and even jabbered with him a bit myself. And he was obviously enjoying himself hugely in that exclusive fraternity. Banging the ball around in that summer sun, he seemed genuinely happy, laughing heartily at the men's jokes and wisecracks. But mainly I stayed close and listened to him.

At one point on a tee, he turned around and blurted out, "Those [expletive deleted] Democrats cut our [expletive deleted] every chance they get."

By 1958, just four years after that round with Buchanan, Nixon bragged that he had managed to get his handicap down to 12. This was an amazing claim, disputed by Elbin, Smathers, and others who played with him. Everyone estimated Nixon's handicap was 20 or even higher. After all, the Vice President hit the ball only 150 or 175 yards off the tee, and his chips and putting strokes were usually awful.

Despite his poor play, some of his playing partners were impressed with Nixon's devotion to golf. "Nixon was deadly serious about the game," said George Shultz. "He wanted to play a good game. He was intense and he worked at it hard. You had to admire him for that."

Nixon played most often at Burning Tree with the attorney general, William Rogers, who would later serve as secretary of state in Nixon's Cabinet. In one of their first rounds together, Nixon and Rogers played the first hole at a slow pace and, just as they were preparing to tee off on the second tee, a fast-moving foursome behind them arrived—a group that included President Eisenhower. Adhering to the club's protocol, Nixon invited Eisenhower's faster-moving group to play through. So Nixon and Rogers watched as Eisenhower and two other golfers hit nice drives off the tee. But the last player smacked the ball into the woods. The foursome, including Ike, searched for the ball. As they hunted for the ball, Ike invited Nixon to tee off, but Nixon refused. Ike insisted that he tee off, but again Nixon said no.

Finally, Eisenhower's partner found his ball and hit a second tee shot into the fairway. For Nixon, those few moments watching Ike's playing partner hunt for the ball demonstrated to him that he was not alone; he, too, had forced Ike to search for his lost balls when they played. This was an important realization for Nixon; after that, he settled down and his game slowly improved.

RICHARD NIXON INTENSIVELY STUDIED golf's nuances and intangibles. Most of all, he was fascinated by the game's momentary shifts from triumph to tragedy, the way it tantalizes you with hope, grants you a perfect iron shot off the fairway or a beautiful fifteen-foot putt for par, and just as quickly takes it all away and breaks your heart. Then through the back nine, you are left only with the searing memory that just an hour before, swinging a golf club seemed effortless.

"He was fascinated by the way golf takes you up and down in a round, beats up your emotions and all," Snead said. "And like a lot of people who play the game, he really wanted to be good."

There are two ways to be better than you really are. One is to break the rules, which Nixon did. The other is to improve your game through sheer will. Nixon tried that, too. He willed himself to be a decent player. Although he was not long off the tee, his tee shots were almost always right down the middle. And he slowly began to improve his short game and putting stroke.

Through gritty determination, Nixon even managed to come within a stroke of winning the club championship, in the middle-range flight, at Burning Tree. Entering the final hole, Nixon was even, but political writer William Lawrence of the *New York Times* sank a par putt on the final hole to clinch it.

In 1960, Nixon ran for the presidency against John F. Kennedy, a man who never had to work hard at golf or at being well liked. It was Nixon, in fact, who had enthusiastically sponsored Kennedy's membership application at Burning Tree several years earlier. Like Kennedy, Nixon was also extremely sensitive about the capital's gleefully told jokes about Ike's love of golf. He did not want those jokes threatening his candidacy, and so he did not play a single time during the campaign, even though he confided to some friends that he pined to play just nine holes. (Unlike Kennedy, who Nixon said indulged in golf like a "secret vice," Nixon did not sneak off to play.) Nixon announced to his campaign aides that he would not give newspapers the chance to publish photographs of him teeing off. Even playing a single round, he said, would be worse than plastering a fat target on his back.

Arnold Palmer was surprised Nixon so quickly abandoned the game he loved. "I think his decision to abandon golf for political purposes revealed something fundamental about the dark side of his character, or maybe his deep social insecurities, that Mr. Nixon never permitted himself to examine," Palmer said. "I do think golf fascinated Richard Nixon, though, and in his heart he wished he could have attacked it with the relish and joy his old boss President Eisenhower had. But, for one reason or another, that wasn't his style."

Nixon lost the 1960 election by one of the narrowest margins in American history and retreated to private law practice. And there was no longer anything keeping him from playing golf, so he played because that is what his partners in a white-shoe law firm did.

Then something approaching a miracle happened. Within months of picking up the clubs again, Dick Nixon shot a hole-in-one.

"I don't remember much about it, except that it was on the third hole at Bel Air on Labor Day, 1961," Nixon recalled nearly thirty years later. "I used a MacGregor six iron and a Spalding Dot ball, and my partner Randolph Scott birdied the hole." His public modesty about the feat may have been a way to minimize golf's growing importance to him, even long after he left office. Privately, Nixon confided that the hole-in-one was "the biggest thrill I had playing golf."

Eisenhower wrote Nixon a congratulatory note. "Dear Dick: You ought to know that I am taking all the credit allowable for *your* hole in one," Ike wrote. "I go around telling people that my game at Burning Tree the other day inspired you. Incidentally, from the publicity in the Easter papers (including editorials) I would venture that a hole in one is roughly equivalent, publicity-wise, to a dozen articles on the Berlin situation. It occurs to me that for eight years we went about our politicking entirely the wrong way."

Nixon replied to Eisenhower, "I imagine that the only people more astonished than I was when the ball rolled in the hole were those who have played with me and know what an erratic golfer I am. Despite the hole in one, I ended up with a 91 and lost three dollars."

That was Nixon. Shoots a hole-in-one, complains about losing three bucks.

It was Sam Snead who had observed that "Nixon wasn't the player Ike was—never scored as low, though he played pretty often. When he was Ike's number two man he couldn't break 100. He was dying to give Ike a game." Nixon was obviously thrilled by the fact that he had achieved something that had eluded Ike despite all those years and all those rounds. Nixon shot his hole-in-one just eight years after learning to play the game.

In November 1962, Nixon lost a bruising campaign for governor of California, which ended with his famous "last press conference," in which he said, "You won't have Nixon to kick around anymore." Nixon then moved to New York City and joined the Baltusrol Golf Club in Springfield, New Jersey. According to the club history, Nixon had a handicap of around 16 and played "pretty respectable golf." (One imagines the writer shaking his head in astonishment as he wrote those words.)

In early 1968, Nixon met at Baltusrol with some of the nation's most prominent Republican leaders to discuss his planned run for the White House. When the press discovered that Nixon was a member of an exclusive club that barred membership to blacks and women, they asked the club president about the policy. "No comment, gentlemen," the club president said. Then reporters pressed Nixon on his membership.

"I'll try to change the club's policy from within," he told reporters. But he was unsuccessful and resigned his membership in August 1968. He remained bitter about the decision for years. Nixon loved Baltusrol, and being forced to quit by reporters just deepened the mistrust and anger he harbored for journalists. Still, there was never any doubt among his aides that Nixon would quit the club. He had very different priorities from Ike, his boss and mentor. For Nixon, politics always came first.

NIXON DID IT. In November 1968, he finally won the presidency, defeating Hubert Humphrey by a margin of just over 500,000 votes. Did he celebrate? Did he savor, even for a single golden hour, the feeling of reaching the summit of American politics? No. The day after his resounding victory, Nixon, his aides, and his family flew on an air force jet to Key Biscayne, Florida. Nixon had rented a three-bedroom bungalow there from Senator George Smathers. That first night in Key Biscayne, Nixon celebrated his triumph by going to bed. He slept soundly for nine consecutive hours; he rarely slept more than four.

His aides worried even before Nixon awakened that they needed to find diversions for the restless president-elect. "What do we do with him?" H. R. Haldeman asked one day during the transition period. "He knows he needs to relax, to come down to Florida. He likes to swim, so he swims for ten minutes. Then that's over. He doesn't paint, he doesn't horseback-ride, he doesn't have a hobby. His best relaxation is talking shop, but he knows he should not be doing that, because that doesn't seem to be relaxing. So what do we do with him?"

Even when Nixon was playing golf or swimming or watching two pro football games at the same time, he had trouble relaxing. If he enjoyed being president, he rarely showed it. There were always challenges to worry about, enemies to obsess over, and fresh plots to hatch. Nixon's presidency, of course, would be undone by his incessant Oval Office chattering, captured on tape, about conspiracies, the goddamn Democrats, the media elites out to get him, the Harvard and Yale mafia who had skated through life, and a host of other fears and insecurities.

That morning after his long, nine-hour sleep, the president-elect immediately embraced the challenge of thinking about Cabinet nominees and the speech he would deliver on Inauguration Day. He was surrounded by pristine golf courses, gleaming yachts, golden beaches. It was America's playground; there was no better place to celebrate. But Richard Nixon refused to be distracted. He went to work.

In fact, he did not think again about golf until his first day as president, when he was confronted, in the Oval Office, with Eisenhower's cleat marks still visible in the floorboards. "I could see immediately that they had been left by Eisenhower's golf cleats," Nixon recalled. "I asked my staff to replace that portion of the floor and carve up the old piece to distribute to some of Eisenhower's old friends as souvenirs." Some pieces were also given as rewards to wealthy Republicans who had opened their checkbooks to put Nixon in the White House.

Nixon was urged by Haldeman and other aides to relax, and he decided to try to find relaxation on a golf course. He played with golf balls emblazoned with the presidential seal and his signature, handing out dozens of the balls to playing partners and club members. "Use it only for putting," Nixon liked to say, always with a slight grin. "I wouldn't want someone to find it all cut up lying in the rough. He might think I hit it there."

He played most often at Burning Tree, which had 550 members during Nixon's presidency. Burning Tree's all-male membership roster never mentioned any member's profession, but one could guess. In 1973–1974, the list, for example, had this entry: NIXON, Richard M., The White House, Washington, D.C. 20500. The club was proud of its informal ambience. Paper place mats were usually used on the heavy wooden tables in the men's grill room, but one Sunday morning, a red tablecloth was laid out for a visit by Nixon. The men were eating their breakfast when a prominent judge burst in, spotted the red tablecloth and said, "Who's the son-of-a-bitch that rates a tablecloth in this place?"

Nixon stood up, smiling, and said, "I guess it's me."

He played other area courses, including Congressional. The press enjoyed ridiculing the new President's sky-high pants, his awkward

President Nixon owned an awkward golf swing and was usually uptight around guests at the White House. Even the wisecracking Bob Hope fails to put the President at ease during a visit on the White House lawn in September 1969.

swing, and his stiff manner on the links. "Not since Calvin Coolidge have we had a more awkward uncoordinated locker-room character in the White House than Richard Nixon," wrote James Reston in the *New York Times* in September 1969.

Nixon's obsessive love of secrecy extended to his scores tallied on the golf course and at the White House bowling alley. A joke, one that did not amuse the President, went this way:

"I scored 128 today," Nixon announces.

"Your golf game is getting better," Henry Kissinger tells Nixon.

"I was *bowling*, Henry," Nixon snaps.

Several photographs—and one in particular that showed him grimacing almost painfully through an ugly swing—were even more hurtful to Nixon's feelings. He assumed the editors were publishing

the most unflattering photos, but of course they were all unflattering. In a September 1969 memorandum to aide H. R. Haldeman,
Nixon declared:

> With the winter months coming on, I will be playing golf in Wash-
> ington rarely, if at all. When I do play in Washington, I will be playing
> only at Burning Tree. Burning Tree is very proud of the fact that for
> over 50 years they have never allowed a photograph to be taken on
> the course. . . . This, incidentally, will also be my policy whenever I
> play in the future. . . . Where clubs do allow photographs, I will not
> play there.

The memo made it official. Nixon attempted to stuff his golf
game back into the closet, but it was as impossible as stuffing a genie
back in the bottle. A decade after Nixon snidely criticized Kennedy
for hiding that "secret vice," Nixon had realized that Kennedy had it
right after all. The less the public knows about a president's golf
game, the better it is for the president.

AROUND THE TIME he became president, Nixon stopped cheating at golf, at least occasionally. Sometimes he even refused the
gimme putts that players routinely lavish on chief executives. At
Burning Tree, club pro Max Elbin recalled, Nixon snapped at an opponent who tried to concede him a short putt on the second green.
"No," Nixon said. "Don't give me the putt. Let me putt it out. I said
I was going to learn to play this game."

The Reverend Billy Graham, who visited Nixon frequently in the
White House, praised many things about the new president, and he
included on that list Nixon's "integrity in counting his golf score."

Nixon even permitted himself the luxury of playing golf on several foreign trips, including a visit to Japan where he was wowed by
the hospitality. "The girl caddies on Japan's immaculately groomed

courses may not understand much English, but they are all great diplomats," Nixon said. "Whenever you hit a ball, whether it goes into the bunker or out of bounds, they always say, 'Good shot, good shot.' There is no better balm for a bruised ego."

At Lakeside Country Club in Burbank, California, Nixon played a memorable round organized by Bob Hope. The star-studded foursome included two celebrities who had been handpicked by Nixon: Jimmy Stewart and Fred MacMurray.

"The entourage landed at my house in the helicopter," Bob Hope recalled in Lakeside's club history. "Gee, first the security guys came and the neighbors all looked out and they thought it was a delivery from Chicken Delight. Then about an hour later, here comes the President."

Nixon was in high spirits that afternoon. "He kissed everybody on this golf course; he kissed the children who took pictures," Bob Hope said. "And I said, 'Mr. President, you are already elected, you know.'"

Back in the Lakeside clubhouse after the eighteen-hole round, the foursome bumped into the comedian George Gobel.

Gobel explained to Nixon that he was going to use the President as an excuse to come home a little late that evening, maybe have a few cocktails in the clubhouse bar with the boys. Gobel told the President, "I'm gonna call Alice and tell her I'll be a little late. . . . And she'll say, 'Well what's so new about that. That's par for the course, isn't it?' And I'll say, 'But you don't understand, I'm having a drink with the President of the United States.' And she'll say, 'Oh, sure, sure, he's a very nice man, but don't get drunk with him and louse up our evening.'"

Nixon laughed out loud. He told Gobel, "Well, I must be getting home, too, but I don't want you to get in any trouble, George. Why don't you just call Alice and I'll talk to her?"

"Sure, that'd be a good idea," said Gobel, laughing. "That should shake her up pretty good."

"Well," Nixon said, "get her on the phone."

The President told Mrs. Gobel how he almost shot a hole-in-one. This was not true, but as Nixon said it he winked at Gobel, who later said it was the first time that a president had winked at him.

Nixon carried on the ruse, telling Mrs. Gobel, "The ball was a brand new ball and it's got my name on it. So I wrapped it up and put it back in the box and gave it to George to bring home with you." She thanked him and they hung up.

As the President was preparing to leave the clubhouse, Gobel joked to his friends, "Gee, I wish he hadn't told Alice about the ball. I was gonna give it to a broad in New York."

Gobel said it when he thought the President was out of earshot. But before he left, Nixon tapped him on the shoulder and whispered, "George, don't worry. Here's another golf ball for that broad in New York."

SOMETIMES, GOLF WAS A POLITICAL ICEBREAKER. During the 1972 election campaign, there was a falling out between the Democratic Party and George Meany, the president of the AFL–CIO and the nation's leading labor voice. The Democrats practically expelled Meany from their nominating convention because they were so furious about his pronounced lack of enthusiasm for their presidential nominee, George McGovern.

Nixon watched this falling out and knew it was an opportunity to be seized.

"Nixon wanted to have a meeting with Meany," recalled George Shultz, then the secretary of labor, who was recruited to reach out to Meany. "I went to George about it and he said, 'It's not a good idea for me and it's not a good idea for him for me to go over to the White House.' So I arranged a golf game."

Meany loved Burning Tree as much as Nixon did. And so Shultz put together a foursome that included Meany, the President, and William Rogers. "We all showed up at the first tee at the same time and had a game, and played eighteen holes," said Shultz, who recalled that Nixon shot in the high 80s during that round. "And then we went and sat on a little patio that looks out on the 18th green and talked for quite a long time. And those two guys loved to talk about politics, how politics work, and it was really fun and interesting to watch them share stories and gossip. They had a great time together." Those eighteen holes at Burning Tree went a long way. The AFL–CIO endorsed Nixon for president in 1972.

IN FEBRUARY 1973, Arnold Palmer received an unexpected summons for him and Bob Hope to fly to San Clemente (Nixon's California home) for a "mini-summit" meeting with the President. "It's not every day that the son of a small-town golf professional gets invited to sit in on a Presidential meeting, with Cabinet officers and other senior advisers present," Palmer wrote in his book *A Golfer's Life*. Palmer was startled when Nixon asked him for his advice on what to do about Vietnam. He drew on a golf metaphor, telling the President, "Go for the green." This pleased Nixon very much.

During his second term, Nixon was reluctant to play golf because of the Vietnam War. "It may have been the seriousness of the times that helped color his decision to abandon golf," Palmer said. "After all, with thousands of young American men and women dying in Vietnam and the college campuses of this country exploding with antiwar demonstrations, it probably wouldn't have sat well with the parents of those young people to know the commander in chief had taken the afternoon off to beat the ball around Congressional or Burning Tree."

Early in Nixon's second term, a group of Republican money men created a nonprofit group called the Golfing Friends of the President. The Golfing Friends paid for the construction of a private, three-hole golf course for Nixon at San Clemente. But Nixon never had a chance to enjoy it. After his reelection in 1972, the most he did was hit a few practice shots. Nixon was absorbed with trying to manage the Watergate crisis as it spiraled beyond his control and consumed his presidency. He rarely played golf during his second term.

After resigning and leaving office in disgrace in 1974, Nixon nearly died from phlebitis. But as he slowly regained his strength following an operation, golf took on new meaning for him.

"Golf was my lifesaver," he said.

Nixon started playing almost every day with Colonel Jack Brennan, his chief of staff. Nixon said the first time he played a round during his post-presidency, he was so "out of practice and physically weak, I shot 125. I almost quit on the spot."

But Nixon endured, playing almost always with Colonel Brennan, a near-scratch golfer with the patience of a saint. To help improve Nixon's golf game, Brennan knew that he needed to fix up San Clemente's three-hole course, which had become overgrown through lack of care. Brennan hired a group of volunteers who restored the course in exchange for regular cases of beer. Nixon's wife, Pat, had refused to water the course after learning that it would cost $100 monthly, but Brennan quietly turned on the sprinklers at 1:00 A.M. each night, several hours after Pat went to bed.

Nixon played often on the course, and he also practiced at Camp Pendleton, where his wild drives could be seen only by the few military players who had access to the course.

Through patience and hard work, Brennan managed to lower Nixon's score below 100. But they had a lot of work to do before they would approach Nixon's goal of breaking 80.

The disgraced former president felt so good about his game that his first lengthy public appearance after his resignation, on October 9, 1975, was at La Costa Golf Club in Carlsbad, California. Nixon was the guest of Teamsters president Frank E. Fitzsimmons, who was a prime suspect in the disappearance and presumed murder of his predecessor, Jimmy Hoffa, just ten weeks earlier. The tournament was also attended by other top Teamsters officials, some of whom would later be indicted for crimes ranging from murder to securities fraud. One playing partner, Allen Dorfman, a convicted felon, would later be executed gangland-style, following a 1982 bribery conviction.

Nixon was offered a tournament cap by Fitzsimmons on the first tee, but he rejected it. "I don't wear hats," he said, perhaps remembering the unflattering photographs taken of his oversized Eisenhower cap. Nixon handed Fitzsimmons a box of six presidential golf balls with his signature and said, "Give these to the poorest golfers in the tournament. Somebody might want one."

A group of reporters congregated near the first tee. When one asked Nixon how he was feeling, he seemed to blanch. After a moment's hesitation, Nixon said, "I'm just fine. And I'm going to play good golf today, too."

Nixon teed off first. His first drive went right. He teed up another, without asking permission. That one zipped far left, also off the fairway. He hit a third tee shot, watched it, and then stepped aside for Fitzsimmons to hit. Fitzsimmons also hit several shots until he liked one. Then Nixon stepped back up to the tee again. "Those others were for practice," he said. "This is for real." This shot seemed to be the straightest and, climbing into his golf cart, Nixon went to look for it.

He shot a 92 in a five-hour round that raised money for the Little City for Retarded Children of Palatine, Illinois. "It looked like the old Nixon," said Robert Dachman, the charity's executive director. "He walked like a typical golfer—when he made a good shot he walked proudly and when he made a bad shot he kind of hunched over." Nixon even paid his own entry fee.

Afterward, Fitzsimmons gave Nixon a small trophy. "This is nice," the former president said. "Where is the union bug on it?" Fitzsimmons did not laugh.

The *New York Times* was not impressed with Nixon playing golf to help needy children. In an indignant editorial, the newspaper criticized Nixon's coming-out golf outing, saying it was outrageous that the former president spent a chummy afternoon with Fitzsimmons and his "mobster associates." The harshness of the criticism shocked Nixon, driving him into a deep funk. He did not make another public appearance for three months.

But he continued to play golf, and he gambled on the game and even began cheating again. He often took several putts, even from tap-in distances. If he missed, he would say, "Oh, that didn't count."

Even when it took Nixon three attempts to sink a three-foot putt, the stroke did not count until the ball hit the bottom of the cup.

STILL, NIXON WAS DETERMINED TO BREAK 80. In San Cle-mente in the autumn of 1978, Nixon claimed to have shot a le-gitimate 79. It is a safe assumption that he managed that score with the help of mulligans or gimmes, or both. "Breaking 80 was an even greater thrill than getting a hole-in-one," Nixon said. "I must admit it was on a relatively easy course in San Clemente, but for me it was like climbing Mount Everest. I knew I could never get better, and so the competitive challenge was gone."

So Nixon quit. That was it. He never hit a golf ball again. In his mind, he went out on top, with a 79, and he had the scorecard framed, though he never said whether the score was attested to by his playing partners.

"It was a hard decision, because I enjoyed the game," Nixon said of his retirement from the links. "It combines physical exercise, stim-ulating competition and warm companionship. From the time Eisenhower gave me that lecture about improving my game, I tried to follow his advice."

It took Nixon twenty-five years to meet Ike's challenge, but he did it. Persistence pays.

When Nixon published an account of his triumphant, valedictory 79 in his 1990 memoirs, *In the Arena,* the claim angered and amused some readers, who figured that Tricky Dick was just telling another lie. The humor columnist, Lewis Grizzard, wrote a nationally syndi-cated column that was incredulous about Nixon's golf claims. "Hold it. Hold it. Hold it," Grizzard wrote. "Richard Milhous Nixon broke 80? The same man who triple-bogeyed the Presidency?

"Do you know how difficult it is for even a fairly competent golfer to break 90? On even the easiest of golf courses? Damn hard. And Richard Nixon, then in his 60s, broke that incredibly tough barrier?

"Who was keeping score? [G. Gordon] Liddy?"

THE GOLF-CHEATING ACCUSATIONS infuriated the ex-president as much as the drumbeat of criticism about Watergate that resonated throughout his post-presidential years, several friends said. But he kept quiet.

Nixon wrote in *In the Arena*, "Sometimes I am asked, 'Was it fun being President?' This trivializes a very profound question. . . . Being President is hard work. A President can enjoy great victories or suffer disappointing defeats. Successful Presidents are those who can take each in stride, recognizing that both are inevitable parts of the job.

"Recreation is a means to an end, not the end itself. You don't want to be President so that you can have fun. You want to have fun so that you can be a better President. The same is true in many other fields. Writing is not much fun, either. But when you create a book, an article, or a speech, it gives you far more enjoyment than making a birdie in golf."

Nixon's successors did not necessarily see the job in the same way. At Nixon's funeral in April 1994, Bill Clinton, Gerald Ford, and George Bush shared a moment together and the conversation turned almost immediately to their favorite game, the game that each of them enjoyed far more than the late president.

"I envy you," Clinton told Bush, "having all the time in the world to play golf."

"There's no doubt about it," Bush said. "Golf is a lot better for your health than governing."

"That's true," Ford said, smiling, "unless you happen to be a spectator when I'm playing."

LYNDON B. JOHNSON

PRESIDENT MULLIGAN

Lyndon Baines Johnson did not care much for golf—and his scorecard showed it—but he still managed to look like a golfer. LBJ routinely took 300 or even 400 swings a round, but he rarely computed his score and he never worried about lowering his score.

One lesson you'd better learn if you want to be in politics is that
you never get out on a golf course and beat the President.
—Lyndon B. Johnson

L YNDON BAINES JOHNSON played golf the way he played politics: By his own rules, at his own pace, and damn the torpedoes.

On the fairways and greens, Johnson flattered, cajoled, needled,
scolded, belittled, and sweet-talked the golf ball the same way he did
a recalcitrant senator. If a shot did not go where he wanted it to go
(and, almost always, it did not), the big man showed no flash of anger
or pang of disappointment. He simply fished another ball out of his
pocket and hit it. No permission was sought, ever. Like the legisla-
tive process he had mastered, Johnson's golf game was the ugliest
sort of sausage making. Golfers familiar with the fine print in the
United States Golf Association's *Rules of Golf* were horrified to see
LBJ routinely take 300 swings per round. As poorly as he played the
game, LBJ's big loping swing managed to produce the occasional
monster drive or the rare beautifully arced 7-iron shot that ended up
within spitting distance of the hole.

One sun-kissed morning at the Seven Lakes Country Club in
Palm Springs, California, in February 1968, Johnson played the most
famous round of his presidency with Dwight D. Eisenhower, a man
who had devoted several thousand hours of his presidency to golf.
Eisenhower revered the game; he cherished its rules and traditions.
LBJ did not.

Eisenhower watched with a mixture of horror and pity as Johnson took one drive, and then a second, followed by a third, all from
the first tee, all before the old general was permitted to hit his own
drive. Ike was flabbergasted. As the more senior of the two, Eisenhower insisted on laying down the rules: no mulligans, no gimmes.

This assured Eisenhower a breeze to victory at Seven Lakes that
day. Eisenhower beat LBJ on every hole leading into the final one.

But on the par-4 18th, President Johnson miraculously strung together two flawless shots. With his ball sitting on the green, only twelve feet separating it from an improbable birdie, Johnson lined up the putt, stroked the ball, and . . .

The moment was captured by an Associated Press photographer in a picture published in newspapers across the country. The headline in the *New York Times* was typical: "The President Messes Up a Putt."

As Johnson gazes at his ball rolling hopelessly past the hole, he is—incredibly—*smiling*. He is grinning one of those wide mock grins as if to say: *So I blew the damn thing. So what?*

Ike stands next to him, grimacing, a reflexive reaction from a man who had spent a lifetime furrowing his brow at thousands of his own blown putts.

Johnson made a par to Eisenhower's bogey, allowing LBJ to win the only hole played in front of the press. It was clear to observers that Eisenhower did not appreciate the gesture; there was no way there would be a rematch. LBJ smirked like the wily pool hustler who saves his best strokes for the moment when the stakes are highest.

OF ALL THE PRESIDENTS, Lyndon Johnson was the most adept at shrugging off golf's agonizing frustrations. He was immune to the game's ability to break your heart. His playing partners watched him with something close to awe: Here was a man who never felt tortured or cheated or robbed or humiliated or even slightly aggrieved on a golf course. LBJ played so poorly it was almost comical, but he did not show even a hint of disappointment or regret about his undisciplined game.

Johnson cared less about the game than any golfing president, with the possible exception of Calvin Coolidge. LBJ viewed golf as a silly game, fraught with potential political consequences. He believed his two predecessors had devoted too much time, trying in vain, to master the game—all those long afternoons, whole weekends. *Hell, in Ike's case, two terms!*

Among the presidential golf cheaters, LBJ was unique. He shattered the game's rules, with gleeful alacrity and without apology, but not because he was trying to pretend that his score was something it wasn't. His motive was simple: He took a few mulligans on every hole because he wanted to feel what it was like to hit a few good shots every time he walked onto a golf course. And if his usual chaotic round took 300 or 400 swings to find a fistful of respectable shots, well, he was the President of the United States, and he was going to do as he damn well pleased.

There is no evidence that Johnson ever broke 100. Most of the time, LBJ did not even bother to keep score. If he had, he would have needed an adding machine to tally his strokes. He routinely hit five, six, seven balls from the same spot until he was satisfied with a shot. Johnson's standard was simple: If I can see it, I will play it.

"He wasn't really a golfer," said Jack Valenti, a Johnson aide who went on to serve as president of the Motion Picture Association of America. "Johnson's game reminded me of the story about this gorilla that they trained to play golf. The gorilla got on the tee and hit the ball 400 yards, and then he got on the green and hit the ball another 400 yards. That was Johnson. No finesse. He just banged away at the ball."

In the spring of 1964, when the country's sadness over the assassination of President Kennedy was still fresh, LBJ was working eighteen hours a day, seven days a week. His frenzied pace was the target of gentle teasing in the press. Valenti, an enthusiastic golfer, suggested to Johnson that he take up golf, a game that he had last played regularly a decade before, until a heart attack sidelined him in 1955.

In his first round as president, played with Valenti, LBJ was clearly rusty. The President used an awkward baseball grip swing. He swung so hard off the tee that he looked as if he was trying to pulverize the ball. He regularly needed four or five putts to finish a hole. "He never took a lesson, and you could tell," Valenti said. "And he couldn't care less what his score was. Every now and then he'd hit a good shot, and he'd flash this big smile at you. And when he'd hack one out, he'd act like it never happened."

For Johnson, golf was a hard sell.

"Well, he didn't seem to think too much of my idea," Valenti recalled. "And I said, 'Let's call Senator So-and-So. Let's go to the head of this important committee and the chairman of that important committee and get them to play with you.' His face brightened up on that. He said, 'That's a helluva idea. This can be a new forum for me to browbeat these guys.'" Which is exactly what the President did.

Although he did not play often, LBJ used the golf course as just another smoke-choked backroom to iron out the kinks of a political deal. It was one of the places where he pushed hardest for passage of the Civil Rights Act of 1964. "He used the golf course the way he used the presidential yacht, the *Sequoia,* or dinners or anything else—to talk business and get things done," said Valenti. "He'd be out there trying to twist their arms into voting for something he wanted. Of course, I'm sure that just frustrated the hell out of them because they just wanted to play golf and get away. The President didn't let them get away."

One headline over an Associated Press dispatch reads, "Golf Bug Bites on Johnson." The report said that Johnson enjoyed playing golf because he harbored "a zest for walking" when it was actually a zest for politicking.

"The President is no hotshot on the links," the story went on to say. "Friends say he shows lots of promise, however. One explained that Mr. Johnson 'has superb reflexes and coordination, which is what it takes.'" Of course, the story also reported that Johnson's form was often faulty. When Johnson swung, he looked like he was chopping wood; the swing was untamed and often wild—"like he was killing a rattlesnake," one eyewitness said.

James R. Jones, LBJ's chief of staff from 1965 to 1969, said the President's "protruding stomach" often impeded his tee shots. And the big man simply had no touch around the greens. "He was often long on putts," Jones said, "by a considerable degree."

The bad play never mattered. "He took lots of mulligans and

While a Secret Service man tends to the flag, President Johnson appears to manage to make a long-distance putt. It is not known whether this was his first, second, third, or thirteenth attempt at sinking the putt.

there were Secret Service agents in the woods," Jones said. "Balls would fly in and end up in the fairway. Sometimes he'd take eight shots and say, 'I'll take the third or the fifth.'"

But Johnson, in his inimitable way, did not care what anyone thought.

"I don't have a handicap," Johnson liked to say. "I'm *all* handicap."

E VEN AS A BOY, Lyndon Johnson cared about one thing—poli-tics. Growing up in the rough Texas hill country, Johnson and his friends played baseball and football. On the baseball diamond,

Johnson always insisted that he pitch, and he was awarded that privilege because he was one of the few boys in the dirt-poor town who owned a baseball.

"He was a terrible pitcher," LBJ biographer Robert A. Caro wrote. "He would take his ball and go home if he couldn't pitch." Even then, LBJ made the rules.

As a young boy, Johnson learned this lesson from his father: "Have an objective at all times." His father's booming voice woke up young Lyndon at five o'clock every morning with this admonition: "Get up, Lyndon! Every other boy in town has got a head start on you!"

Throughout his life, LBJ was always in motion. George Reedy, one of LBJ's press secretaries, observed that the President "knew of no innocent form of relaxation. . . . The only sanctified activity was hard work to achieve clearly defined goals; the only recreation was frenetic activity that made one forget the problems of the day; and the only true happiness was the oblivion he could find in Scotch or in sleep. . . . He did understand dimly that other people had some interests outside of their direct work but he thought of such interests as weakness and, if they included classical music or drama, mere snobbery practiced by 'the Eastern establishment.'

"In a very important sense," Reedy observed, "LBJ was a man who had been deprived of the normal joys of life. He knew how to struggle; he knew how to outfox political opponents; he knew how to make money; he knew how to swagger. But he did not now how to live. He had been programmed for business and for business only and outside of his programming, he was lost."

And so when he came to Washington as a freshman congressman in 1937, Johnson took up golf because that's what other congressmen did and that's what he needed to do to fit in. From the beginning, he did not play the game because he enjoyed it. He played it because it was a means to an end, a place to broker a deal. His wife, Lady Bird, said he used the golf rounds "to explain ideas" to other politicians and "for discussions in a relaxed setting."

Two decades later, as the powerful majority leader of the U.S. Senate, Johnson kept careful track of the score. He remembered slights, and he could recite from memory the accounts receivables and the accounts payable in the Favor Bank. But on the golf course, he rarely counted his strokes. He did not care what he or his playing partners shot—most of the time, anyway.

One of his most frequent playing partners in those early years was Eugene Worley, also a young congressman from Texas. Once, on the first tee at the Army-Navy Country Club, Johnson began complaining that he had not played in so long. "All that he was doing," Worley said, "was leading me up to spot him a stroke a hole.

"We didn't have much money. We were playing, I think for a quarter—a quarter Nassau. So he talked me into the stroke a hole, and sure enough we finish the 17th hole and I'm 50 cents down.

"I said, 'Lyndon, I ought to play you double or nothing on the 18th and still give you a stroke on the hole.' I was trying to get my money back.

"He said, 'Aw, no.'

"I said, 'Well, why not? What can you lose? You're playing with my money.'

"He said, 'Hell, I didn't work 17 holes just to give it all back to you on one hole.' And he didn't."

Johnson may not have cared much about golf, but he cared a lot about winning.

JOHNSON GAVE UP THE GAME after suffering a heart attack in 1955, but he did play a quick nine holes in November 1960 with John F. Kennedy in Palm Beach, Florida, after he had been elected vice president. The game was kept relatively quiet, and there is no indication of how well—or, more likely, poorly—Johnson played. Valenti said he was almost certain LBJ played his usual round of hundreds of strokes to Kennedy's 80.

During the height of the presidential campaign, Johnson had been asked what he thought of President Eisenhower's obsession with golf. His off-the-cuff response about Ike contradicted the Democratic Party playbook's stock answer on the subject. "I'm glad he does play," Johnson said. "I want him to have all the rest that he can get." A Republican member of Augusta National Golf Club could not have said it any better.

Some strategists barked at LBJ for that remark, and he wisely refrained from further sympathetic remarks about Ike's passion. In October, during a visit to Georgia, Johnson declared that "for eight long years the South has been used [by Republicans] only as a golf course to tee off from"—a more pointed reference to nearby Augusta National.

After Kennedy's assassination in November 1963, the press hunted for a hobby of Johnson's to write about, and it was not easy finding one. The Associated Press reported on November 29, 1963, that Johnson "has no daily routine of relaxation, but at the end of a day he likes to sit and talk." The story mentioned Kennedy's swimming and boating, Ike's golf games, and Truman's fondness for taking long strolls. But all the reporter could find out was that Johnson liked to talk after hours as much as he did during his workday.

Johnson searched for ways to unwind. He liked spending time with his pet beagles, Him and Her. He tried waterskiing at his ranch in Texas, as well as bowling. But he viewed every hobby as an annoyance and a distraction from his only true love, politics.

George Reedy observed that Johnson would not even pretend to be interested in the baseball games that he attended as president. "He went only when a game was to be attended by a large number of fellow politicians with whom he could transact some business," Reedy observed. "On such days, I sat at home praying that television cameras would not catch him with his back turned to the field in deep conversation about a tax bill or an upcoming election while a triple play was in process or when a cleanup hitter had just knocked a home run with the bases loaded."

During his first few months in office, President Johnson viewed golf with suspicion, just as Kennedy had. LBJ was convinced that the game was a potential political liability to be avoided, at all costs. After seeing a photograph of Secretary of Commerce John Connor playing golf in the newspaper, LBJ ordered him to stop making high-profile visits to the courses on weekends. LBJ snapped that he did not want an "Ike golf image" for the Johnson administration.

He had only started playing because Jack Valenti convinced him to try to play a few rounds as a way to lobby politicians in a pristine setting.

But from 1965 through 1967, as American casualties in the Vietnam War mounted, as did public criticism, Johnson stopped playing golf. If the American people observed LBJ playing golf while American troops were fighting and dying in Vietnam, they would "eat me alive," he told aides. Giving up golf intensified LBJ's sense that he was cooped up in the White House, like a caged peacock, unable to lobby politicians in a less formal setting. One evening, he drank a beer and confided to an aide that the "Temperance Union would be on my ass" if they knew he was drinking beer.

"I can't play golf because they'll think I'm frivolous," he lamented. "I can't do this, I can't do that."

Just as Washington began to shrug off yet another long, humid summer in 1967, Lyndon Johnson announced at a White House dinner that he had decided to give up alcohol and return to his golf game. As the President saw it, he was going to trade one vice for another.

"This is alarming, if true, for in the present state of the world and the Presidency it really should be the other way around," observed James Reston of the *New York Times*. Golf, according to Reston, was a form of self-torment, invented by the Scots (along with whiskey) to make people suffer. "To substitute golf for 'whiskey's old prophetic aid' is a puzzle and could be a calamity," Reston argued. "And to do it as an escape from agony is the worst miscalculation since the start of the Vietnam War. Golf is not an escape from anything. It is itself an agony."

Earlier that year, Clark Clifford, a senior aide to Johnson, had suggested that the President reacquaint himself with his golf clubs to try, temporarily, to escape the war's anguish. But Reston pointed out that Clifford "was a good player" who could find pleasure on a golf course. "Even Ike, who had two terms on the golf course, was tormented to the end by a disobedient putter, and Mr. Johnson is indescribably worse. He is, in fact, a spectacular dub," Reston wrote. "The traps and hazards and insoluble problems of golf he does not need. He gets enough of them in his regular work." After reading those words, the President laughed and declared that Scotty Reston would have slandered him if what he had written was not true.

On a Sunday morning in 1967, LBJ attended a new church in Washington, D.C. "Sunday morning, I went into the President's bedroom to get him moving, and he asked if I'd checked out the preacher," recalled James R. Jones, his chief of staff. "I hadn't. But I said, 'The Secret Service is handling the details. And, yes, he is very distinguished and fine.' Well, the minister gave one of the first public anti-Vietnam speeches. It was in *The New York Times* and in *The Washington Post* the next day."

As the minister continued his rousing anti-Vietnam tirade, LBJ sat in the pew and smoldered with anger. "The President looked at me—I just shrank to nothing," Jones said. It did not end at the church. Jones and LBJ had eighteen holes to play.

"Afterward he had a tight smile and he chewed on me for eighteen holes," Jones said. "He reminded me on every hole how much I'd screwed it up. It was the worst round of my life."

L BJ ONLY PLAYED SIX OR SEVEN TIMES while he was President. Among the millions of documents, photographs, and records at the Lyndon Baines Johnson Presidential Library in Austin, Texas, there are only a few passing references to golf. One entry, on March 3, 1968, includes these comments: "Played 18 holes, but Congressman [J. J.] Pickle [a Texas Democrat] said later that in essence, the President played three-to-four times that much, because he would hit several balls each hole until he was satisfied with a particular shot."

On March 31, 1968, Johnson announced that he would neither seek nor accept another term as president. The announcement seemed to lift a burden from him, and he indulged in a few rounds of golf later that year.

In May, Johnson greeted eighteen professional athletes at the White House and gave them a brief tour of the grounds. Johnson stumbled on the old Eisenhower putting green that had become overgrown for lack of maintenance. Someone handed the President a putter and a golf ball. LBJ tried to sink a putt from about six feet away. Each of his three attempts missed, but one putt came within an inch.

Not long after that, LBJ took his first announced vacation in his four and a half years in office. It was a shocking development. "Johnson Takes a Whole Day Off," one headline said. He took a one-day golf excursion to Puerto Rico; Johnson was preparing for retirement and was working hard at enjoying the game.

In the days before he left the White House, Johnson told aides that he planned to play golf after returning to his Texas ranch. What else was there to do, after all? He spent most of the first two years in retirement writing his memoirs and working on the construction of his presidential library in nearby Austin. And he played a few rounds of golf, trying hard to enjoy it. After the third or fourth round, LBJ wondered: What is the point? Why devote four or five hours of time to playing eighteen holes if there are no bills to push, no allies to make, no deals to cut?

The former president could not think of a single good reason to play the damn game. So he quit.

WARREN G. HARDING

A BET ON EVERY SWING

Few presidents loved the game as much as Warren G. Harding. Despite Prohibition, Harding enjoyed sipping cocktails while he played golf as president. With a crowd looking on, the President prepares to tee off on the first hole at the Chevy Chase Club.

I may not know everything about being President.
But I do know that a lot of decisions can be made on golf courses.
—Warren G. Harding

BEFORE TEEING OFF ON THE FIRST HOLE, President Warren G. Harding instructed his playing partners to disregard the fact that he happened to be the most powerful man in America. Deference was forbidden by any member of a Harding foursome. He expected—no, demanded—that his playing partners treat him no more favorably than they treated any one else. Harding refused to let anyone grant him a three-foot putt; he always insisted on taking the trouble to try to sink it (and he usually did, as his strength was his short game). If his tee shot soared into a creek or the woods, he hunted for the ball himself and declined the assistance offered by Secret Service agents. If his ball was stuck in a clump of crabgrass or a patch of soggy turf, he rejected his opponents' offers to let him pick up the ball to improve the lie. Instead, he tried to hack it out.

"Forget that I am President of the United States," Harding often told his fellow players. "I'm Warren Harding, playing with some friends, and I'm going to beat hell out of them."

When he did beat hell out of them, Harding took their money. The President placed a wager on every swing, which might explain his respect for the game's official rules. If he was given a break on a shot, at least one bet would have to be called off, a result guaranteed to depress the wager-crazy president. "He played as if his life depended on every shot," observed Colonel Edmund W. Starling, the chief of the White House's Secret Service detail. "And he made so many bets that sometimes he was betting against himself."

Harding's wagers of choice were a series of $6 Nassaus: a $6 bet on the front nine, another $6 bet on the back nine, and $6 to the winner of the match. But this was hardly enough action for the President. He devised a series of side bets, including wagers with his partner for the round's low score, the front nine, and back nine. And he would make bets on individual holes and even individual shots. "I had to keep accounts," Colonel Starling said, "and it was a job for a Philadelphia lawyer."

If Harding refused even a harmless gift on the green, why has he earned the indignity of a place in the foursome of White House golf cheaters? The answer is simple: Harding broke the law of the land on the golf course.

Not long after taking the oath of office in which he swore to preserve, protect, and defend the Constitution, Harding openly violated its Eighteenth Amendment, which prohibited the use of alcohol. Both on the golf course and inside the White House, Harding thumbed his nose at Prohibition. It must have been quite an extraordinary thing to see: President Harding defiantly flouting the United States Constitution while meticulously enforcing the fine print of the United States Golf Association rule book.

At the Chevy Chase Club, Harding would pause every few holes for a shot of whiskey from a bottle stashed inside his golf bag. It did not take long for the on-course imbibing to set off such an enormous scandal that Harding agreed to stop sipping whiskey while playing at Chevy Chase. Instead, he retreated to a private golf club where every four or five holes, black-jacketed butlers served Scotch-and-sodas from silver trays to the thirsty players. The private course was part of the Friendship estate owned by Edward B. McLean, the publisher of the *Washington Post,* who enjoyed mixing alcohol and wagering nearly as much as the President did.

Seventeen-year-old Shirley Povich, who would grow up to become a legendary sports writer and editor at the *Washington Post,* caddied for Harding in the fall of 1922. Povich had been given the assignment by McLean, for whom he had caddied the previous summer in Maine.

"I showed up at the first tee, and McLean was glad to see me," Povich recalled seventy-five years later. "He turned to the man standing with him and said, 'Mr. President, this is Shirley Povich, the best caddy in America,' which was untrue. 'He's going to caddie for you today.'" Shortly after the introductions were made, Povich recalled that he was surprised to see butlers arrive to serve the afternoon's first round of drinks. And—to hell with Prohibition!—President Harding took a glass and a gulp. Imagine that.

Although Harding "labored to break 100" that day (and most days), Povich recalled that the man seemed totally comfortable and relaxed on the private course; the Scotch-and-sodas, deserve some credit for that. The Friendship estate became "a kind of sanctuary" for the President, one friend said. It was blessedly far removed from the judgments of the public and, just as important, the First Lady. "Harding seemed to feel freer at Friendship than anywhere else," another biographer observed.

Once the on-the-course cocktails ceased to be served at Chevy Chase, Harding continued to play there and resorted to a more secretive way to consume alcohol. After each round, the President was served drinks behind the closed doors of the club's presidential cottage, which Taft had frequently used but Wilson had refused to visit. Colonel Starling said Harding kept a few bottles of Scotch and bourbon locked in a bottom desk drawer in the cottage's study. Only Colonel Starling was trusted with the key. Harding turned the club's own cottage into a presidential speakeasy, right under the noses of the club's leaders, who proclaimed themselves very embarrassed and appalled by the President's on-course imbibing. The President and his pals enjoyed the secret sips at Chevy Chase even more than the ones they had taken on the fairway's edge. "While the players drank highballs," Starling said, "I calculated the results of the bets and announced the winners. The President took a single drink, and when this was finished and the bets were settled he would say to me, 'Telephone the Duchess and say I am on my way home.'"

"The Duchess" was the President's slightly disrespectful moniker for the First Lady, Florence Harding. She was a dour, domineering, and determined woman who many assumed held a lopsided amount of power in their marriage and his presidency. She was wise and perceptive, and she was well aware that Harding's good looks and charm attracted the ladies and led him to indulge in more than one extramarital affair. One of his mistresses was Nan Britton, a beautiful blond who was thirty years younger than Harding and worked in Washington, D.C., allowing her to be close to the President. (Britton would later publish a best-selling book about her affair with Harding, naming him as the father of her illegitimate daughter.) Harding was linked to another woman named Carrie Phillips, who was paid hush money by the Republican Party after she tried to blackmail Harding with the threat to go public with details of their affair. And there were other affairs as well.

Suspicions about the President's extracurricular activities led Florence Harding to place severe restrictions on Harding's recreational hours. The golf course and the poker table were the only two places where Harding was able to escape from his wife's steely gaze. And if he had had his way, the President would have played either golf or poker (or both) every day. He managed to play poker and golf at least twice a week, and sometimes more often when he could get away with it, meeting with his old pals from Ohio at a townhouse on H Street for a regular, high-stakes card game. It was not enough for Harding to have a Golf Cabinet; he also had a Poker Cabinet. Ambitious men who wanted to curry favor with Harding aspired to join both cabinets, but each was composed almost entirely of Harding's cronies from Ohio.

As he did with golf, the President wanted his wife to know when he was heading home after an evening of poker, but the alert seemed more obligatory than affectionate. "Exactly at eleven forty-five," Starling recalled, "he would say, 'All right, boys, we will wind up now. Starling, telephone the Duchess that I am on my way home.'"

Harding also hosted raucous poker parties inside the White House. On those occasions, Florence mixed the drinks for the players and kept her disapproving eyes fixed on the President, who smoked cigars and (when his wife wasn't looking) quickly slipped a pinch of chewing tobacco into his cheek. The Duchess was there to keep the stakes within reason. On a night when she was not present, Harding gambled away a set of White House china that dated back to the Benjamin Harrison administration of the 1890s—and he lost it on a single hand. But the President did not always lose. On another night, Harding won a pearl stickpin estimated to be worth $5,000, also on a single hand, though some critics wondered whether it was a bribe disguised as a winning wager.

Alice Roosevelt Longworth, the daughter of Theodore Roosevelt and the wife of the influential Ohio congressman Nicholas Longworth, attended one of the President's poker games while her husband played. She was astonished to see the way the President and his rowdy pals were behaving inside "the people's house."

"No rumor could have exceeded the reality," Mrs. Longworth complained. "The study was filled with [the President's] cronies . . . the air heavy with tobacco smoke, trays with bottles containing every imaginable brand of whisky stood about, cards and poker chips ready at hand—a general atmosphere of waistcoat unbuttoned, feet on the desk, and spittoons alongside."

When he heard later about Mrs. Longworth's criticism, Harding just laughed and assumed she was upset because her husband had left the White House with considerably less cash in his pocket than he had before the first hand was dealt.

WARREN HARDING, the twenty-ninth president, was elected in 1920 with more than 16 million votes, a record number boosted considerably because women were granted the right to vote for the first time. It was assumed by male political strategists that women would vote for Harding because he was handsome, a dubious assumption at best. The more likely reason, for men and women alike, was that Harding's call for "a return to normalcy" was eagerly welcomed by Americans weary of the stresses of World War I and the bitter fight over the League of Nations.

One writer described Harding as "a handsome man, genial, gentle with a warm, resonant, rich voice, a courteous, considerate manner, a man who moved with ease and suppleness, a man with great presence, with a high forehead and distinguished gray hair, and a face that wrinkled into reassuring, paternal smile lines with gratifying frequency; he was calm and contained, solid, forthright, honest, almost noble in bearing, the one man in the group—everyone agreed—who looked like a President."

Harding, of course, did not often *behave* the way a president was expected to behave. He acted more like a frat boy cavorting through the last week of his final semester, though the public was only privy to some of his after-hours shenanigans. The best example of the lengths Harding went to place a bet: In June 1921, not long after Harding's inauguration, a high-stakes poker game was held in the surgeon general's suite at the Willard Hotel, a few blocks from the White House. Among the guests were some deep-pocketed financiers and army officers. Only a few hands into the evening, the suite's doors were suddenly thrown open. The players were surprised to see the President standing in the doorway wearing an expression that was a cross between panic and despair.

"You fellows can't sneak off and have a party without me," Harding protested, quickly stepping inside, peeling off his coat and digging into his pocket for his billfold. "I'm here for the evening."

The President spent a long, satisfying night of losing most of his billfold's contents. When it was over, he ordered the men to give him advance notice next time.

Although Harding was described by Colonel Starling as a "one drink man," he served liquor to guests in the private residence of the White House. This was widely known around the capital. The President believed that what he did in the privacy of his own home was no one's business, especially not that of the local police department.

"Still, such 'sneaking around' by the President to break the law was a fit subject for gossip," Colonel Starling observed, "and when added to smoking, poker playing and gambling, raised in some minds the specter of low-life carousels." At the theater, President Harding could not have been more different from his regal predecessor, Woodrow Wilson. Inside the president's box, Harding shielded his mouth with his program and from behind it called to a pal in the audience, "Hey John, how do you like the girls?"

To most observers, Harding possessed limited intellectual and cultural curiosity. He read no books and preferred burlesque shows to serious theater. He rarely listened to classical or popular music. Poker and golf, both lubricated liberally with alcohol, filled nearly all the hours of the President's spare time. Of the two games, golf was his favorite. "Love" was not too strong a word to describe his affection for the game, one of his friends said. In 1921, Harding presented the U.S. Open trophy to Jim Barnes at the Columbia Country Club in Chevy Chase, Maryland. When the President handed the trophy to Barnes, he said, "I'd give anything to be in your shoes today."

Harding refused to let anything stand in the way of his golf game. He vowed to play through a driving thunderstorm, even a snow-storm, and he often made good on that promise. He was so smitten with the game that he refused to let one of the most important acts of his time in office spoil that afternoon's golf outing.

It happened on July 2, 1921, just a few weeks after he handed the trophy to Jim Barnes. Harding was on a golfing weekend in New Jersey with several pals when a messenger from Congress arrived seeking the President's signature on a joint congressional resolution that would proclaim an end to the long war with Germany, Austria, and Hungary. It took one hour and forty-five minutes to find Harding on a local golf course and then coax him off it. When he arrived at a nearby private home for the solemn signing ceremony, he was wearing a sporty, all-white Palm Beach golf suit, including removable gold studs, a red-and-green bow tie, and grass stains faintly visible on the cuffs. Quietly, yet carefully, the President read the resolution and then signed it. With Harding's signature, World War I was officially over. The historic moment was lost on the impatient President.

He laid down his pen, jumped from his chair, and said, "That's all." Without uttering another word, Harding darted from the house and returned to the golf course. The war may have finally ended, but there were still a few bets to settle.

HARDING'S OBSESSION WITH GOLF started the way it begins for most players: The first time he played a round of eighteen holes, he managed somehow to hit a single beautiful golf shot. And like so many lucky first-time golfers, Harding would never forget that inexplicably fortunate swing, the seductive *thwap!* of the club head smacking the ball and then its magnificent trajectory as it soared toward the flag with the precision of a homing pigeon. For the rest of his life, Warren Harding would savor the effortless beauty of that first perfect golf shot.

It happened in 1917 as Harding, who was then a U.S. senator from Ohio, and a few fellow senators visited Secretary of War John W. Weeks at his New England home for a briefing. The other senators were golfers who decided to play at a nearby course. As a lark, Harding, the only nongolfer on the trip, decided to come along.

Harding "idly picked up a club and then, like many dubs, he made a remarkable shot," recalled Senator Frederick Hale of Maine. "After that, there was no stopping him. We could not head him off even if we had wished to. He insisted on playing right away."

Harding was hooked. He joined a boisterous, bantering group of a dozen U.S. senators, who needled each other gleefully during regular, rowdy rounds at Chevy Chase (setting the tone for many such days to come there for the future president). Unlike some of his fellow players, Harding did not mind that his golfing ability showed no sign of improving. He loved the camaraderie, the joking, and, of course, the wagering. "Nobody is more companionable on the links than he," said Senator Jonathan Bourne Jr. of Oregon. "He's a true lover of the ancient sport. If there does not happen to be a caddy about, he will pick up his bag and carry it cheerfully."

Harding was enjoying himself so much in the Senate that he harbored no interest in seeking the presidency. In Washington, it is safely assumed that every member of the Senate who looks in the mirror sees the reflection of a would-be president. Harding was perhaps the only senator who looked in the mirror and saw a man whose ambition was limited to winning golf Nassaus and poker pots.

Despite his reluctance to step into the national political arena, a group of ambitious admirers recruited Harding for greater things. And, like William Howard Taft, Harding reluctantly agreed to run for president, but it was clear to some that his heart was just not in it. At the Republican Party convention in Chicago in 1920, Harding won his party's nomination. The following day, he rushed back to Washington to play a round at Chevy Chase. For the first time, the new nominee had a large gallery of newspapermen and photographers watching his every move.

Remarkably, Harding's nerves were rattled only on the first tee. The camera shutters clicked as Harding lined up his first shot, and the noise intensified as he followed through a shot that careened out of bounds. "It is not conducive to good golf to hear camera shutters going and photographers shifting plates," Harding said later. "I made a miserable drive off the first tee and didn't do much with my [next shots]. But as I approached the green, I was a few feet off it in the rough. I told the men I was going to hole out from there, and I took my putter and did it! I didn't think for a minute I could do it."

The unlikely shot bolstered Harding's confidence. As reporters followed him around the course, Harding carded the first five holes this way: 5, 5, 5, 3, and 5. After those first five holes, as reporters scribbled the nominee's feats in their notebooks, Harding was only 3 over par, a remarkable score for a triple-digit golfer. Some players would choke at this point; others would let out a primal whoop of celebration, then self-destruct. Harding did neither. As he played the round of his life, he remained relaxed and nonchalant with just the slightest trace of cockiness. He continued to make improbable shots and ended the round with another flourish. On the 18th, he chipped the ball in from off the green—the same incredible shot that he had pulled off on the first green. That final shot gave him a lifetime-best score of 92, but Harding acted as if it was nothing more than a routine afternoon on the links.

In the clubhouse, a Washington politician used a golf metaphor to describe the upcoming homestretch of the presidential campaign. "Well, I see you got over the first nine pretty well at Chicago," the politician told Harding. "I hope you will be as successful in the last nine of the campaign and election."

"Oh," Harding replied, still brimming with confidence from his dream round, "I'm always better on the last nine."

The reporters bought it all. They were impressed by the presidential candidate who could hit the target with pithy quotes *and* the golf ball. Their fawning reports about Harding's golfing prowess and confidence on the links lavished the candidate with a surprisingly strong post-convention bounce. The momentum would carry him through the fall months in his campaign against James M. Cox, the Democratic governor of Ohio (and his young running mate, Franklin Delano Roosevelt).

Harding's unlikely good play that day led some golf historians to credit him with being a far better player than he actually was. One golf-course history in Washington placed Harding's regular score in the low 80s, which is only off by about 20 strokes. By most credible estimates, Harding's average score was 101, and he was thrilled on the rare occasion when he shot in the mid-90s and the rarer occasion when he finished in the low 90s. "He loves to golf," said George B. Christian, who served as the President's secretary. "And if he can get into the low nineties, he's tickled to death."

The golf-outing momentum, however, continued through the fall and helped catapult Harding to an impressive election triumph that November. To celebrate his election, Harding went on a monthlong vacation that included a visit to the Panama Canal Zone, where the president-elect played golf at a beautiful course not far from the canal.

On the bright, frosty morning of his inauguration on March 4, 1921, most of the nation seemed desperate for a change. Woodrow Wilson's incapacity down the stretch had exhausted and even infuriated many Americans. And in the capital on that historic day, thousands of Americans embraced Harding as an uncomplicated man who would have their best interests at heart.

"We have had Wilson eight years, and I have not understood him," a woman at the inaugural said. "I understand Harding already."

ONE OF THE PERKS OF BEING PRESIDENT is that you can choose your golf partners. Harding was one of the first presidents to exercise this presidential privilege, playing with writers,

With two caddies standing behind him, President Harding surveys a shot with an iron off the fairway. As usual, Harding was nattily dressed; in fact, he was one of the best-dressed presidential golfers.

celebrities, and two of his era's finest players, Walter Hagen and Gene Sarazen. (After being impressed by Sarazen's driver, Harding asked for it—he didn't want to borrow it, he wanted to keep it. Sarazen handed it over, laughing, "What can you say when the President asks for your club?" In return, Harding gave Sarazen a special silver police badge to help get him out of speeding tickets.)

Edmund Starling observed that it was impossible to guess who would show up in the White House foyer, golf clubs in tow, for a round with the President. An early Harding golf partner was Will Rogers, though he would not become a regular. Rogers put on a vaudeville skit that featured the President dominating a Cabinet meeting with mindless golf chatter. Harding was not amused, and Rogers was summarily banned from the Golf Cabinet.

Ring Lardner, the wry sportswriter and short story author, played several memorable rounds with Harding, having been introduced by an old friend of the President's, Grantland Rice, a popular sportswriter, author, and golf fanatic. On their first afternoon playing together at Chevy Chase in April 1921, Lardner crushed a screaming drive that sliced a branch off a tree that fell and landed hard on the President, who was momentarily shaken but unhurt. Lardner did not apologize, but instead announced drolly that he was just trying to make a president out of Vice President Coolidge.

Harding laughed out loud at the joke, and the two men got along fabulously well from that moment on. As they walked from the final green to the President's cottage for some post-round refreshments, Lardner told Harding that he had a modest request: he wanted to be appointed the ambassador to Greece.

The President asked why. Lardner's long, dark face grew longer and darker as he said solemnly, "My wife doesn't like Great Neck."

Grantland Rice chronicled their round for the *American Golfer* in an article entitled "The President's Golf Game," which the periodical published on its cover on April 23, 1921. The foursome that day included President Harding, Lardner, Rice, and Undersecretary of State Henry Fletcher. In the picture that accompanied Rice's article, the four men are wearing smart golf outfits and expectant expressions. Only Lardner is not smiling; he appears to be almost awed to be rubbing shoulders with the President. (The caption of the photo reads, "All made up for the drama.") Rice wrote that he was most impressed with the fact that the President refused to stop playing as the rain fell harder and harder through the back nine. "President Harding, from the start, proved to be a sportsman who belongs among the elect," Rice wrote. "Thoroughly human in every way, he has dignity without pretense and the love of a keen, hard contest that calls for a battle to the finish."

Harding's favorite part of any golf outing was the settling of the bets. After one round with Secretary of State Charles Evans Hughes, Speaker of the House Frederick H. Gillett, and Charles G. Dawes, the director of the budget, President Harding asked Starling to announce the wagering damage.

Starling announced, "Mr. Dawes owes the Secretary of State thirty-three dollars."

"Fine," Harding said. "Charlie, fork over the money."

Dawes pulled out his billfold and counted out the money. With a bow, he offered the cash to Hughes.

"I cannot accept this," Hughes exclaimed to the President, his face reddening with embarrassment. "I have never gambled in my life."

"Take it!" the President shouted. "You won it!"

HE WAS MODEST ABOUT HIS SKILLS, and there was much to be modest about. The *New York Times* observed, "The fact that President Harding does not blow his own horn is one of the characteristics which have commended him to steady-going Americans . . . if his fellow countrymen do not like the way in which he sinks himself in his work, remains modest and unpretentious, and faces applause or blame with an equable temper, so much the worse for them."

The enthusiasm and determination that Harding demonstrated on the golf course were rarely on display while he was working in the Oval Office. He struggled to resolve a host of problems during his first term, and he viewed each defeat as further evidence that he was miscast in the role of president.

Upon returning from Chevy Chase one afternoon in 1922 with Judge John Barton Payne, Harding told him, "Judge, I don't think I'm big enough for the Presidency." He told the newspaper columnist David Lawrence that he was nothing more than a small-town man from Marion, Ohio. Harding said he would probably be most remembered for his career as a newspaper publisher, buying the nearly bankrupt *Marion Star* and resuscitating it. "Often times, as I sit here," he said, pointing at his desk in the Oval Office, "I don't seem to grasp that I am President."

Harding was that rare chief executive who willingly agreed to suggestions that were not always in his best political or personal interest. "Warren," his father once told him, "it's lucky you were not born a girl because you can't say no."

He felt most insecure about his lack of knowledge of world affairs. He confessed to a senior aide that he did not "know anything about this European stuff. You and Jud get together and he can tell me later; he handles these matters for me."

The legendary newspaper editor William Allen White found the

President "almost unbelievably ill-informed." He was so eager to please, make friends, have everyone like him, that he often could not make up his mind for fear of offending one camp or the other. "I can't make a damn thing out of this tax problem," he once complained to an aide. "I listen to one side and they seem right, and then—God!—I talk to the other side and they seem just as right, and here I am where I started. I know somewhere there is a book that will give me the truth, but, hell, I couldn't read the book. I know somewhere there is an economist who knows the truth, but I don't know where to find him and haven't the sense to know him and trust him when I find him. God! What a job!"

At night, the President sought comfort in the letters he received from ordinary citizens, reading as many as possible and replying, by hand, to thousands of Americans, many of whom were undoubtedly flabbergasted to receive a handwritten reply from their president. One biographer chided Harding for wasting so much of his time responding "to the juvenile or crackpot letters that should have been handled by some third assistant secretary, if at all."

Because Harding was so identified with golf, some of these letters contained advice to improve his game. Jay E. House, a reporter at the *Philadelphia Ledger,* sent the President some golf tips. In a letter back to House, the President thanked him and called his advice invaluable. "A great many people tell me what to do, but so few of them tell me precisely how to do it," Harding wrote. "You have told me how to reduce my golf scores. Now that is real and very valuable advice!"

In a note to Henry P. Fletcher, the American ambassador in Brussels who had given the President two neckties, Harding thanked his friend for being "so sympathetic concerning golf and 'things.'" The "things" were presumably poker playing and whiskey sipping. "My golf is miserably bad," Harding wrote, "and at other sports they kick me around with no more consideration than is given a Prohibition enforcement officer in the down-town wards in the big cities. I think some of these days my golf will come back. I have a challenge out to play under ninety at Chevy Chase before the year is done. I am going to win it or make a bonfire of all the golf sticks I possess."

Harding's eagerness to delegate important responsibilities to his

Cabinet members was rooted in a deep insecurity that there were vast subjects that he knew nothing about. But the delegating of important matters and Harding's own law-breaking with gambling and drinking set the tone for what became one of the most scandal-plagued administrations in American. history. He temporarily forgot the pressures of governing when he spent time with his golf pals and poker cronies. The President always assumed they would be honest and keep his best interests, but of course they did not.

In early 1923, friends noticed that the President's golf game had suddenly deteriorated. Even the President's rain-or-shine enthusiasm for the game diminished. At the end of nine holes, he'd seem exhausted. His playing partners assumed he was worried about the corruption scandals that had begun to engulf his administration. That was one of the President's problems. The other was that his heart was giving out on him.

"You're working too hard," Starling told the President. "You need a vacation. Why don't you confine your game to nine holes until you rest up?"

Harding roared, "Hell, if I can't play eighteen holes, I won't play at all!"

Later that spring, Harding was playing golf at Chevy Chase when a retired army officer drew Colonel Starling aside and handed him a letter from "a friend out West." The officer asked Starling to deliver the letter to the President.

Starling said the letter contained information that "a scandal was brewing over some leases of naval oil lands, a scandal which might reach the President and involve the whole administration."

As Starling rode back to the White House after the round of golf, he decided to deliver the letter to Harding. "I waited until he was upstairs in his room and the others had dispersed," Starling wrote. "Then I followed him and knocked at the door. He asked me to come in. I stepped inside and handed him the letter.

"He read it, his face turning ashen as his eyes scanned the lines. When he had finished he stood with his hands hanging by his sides. 'I am glad you brought it to me,' he said. His voice was flat and far away. 'It is something that I should know.'"

The President pressed on, traveling to Alaska and California in July. It was there, however, that he was clearly in a state of fear about what had occurred in his administration, and his health badly deteriorated. According to William Allen White, President Harding "kept asking Secretary [of Commerce] Hoover and the more trusted reporters who surrounded him what a President should do whose friends had betrayed him." Harding died suddenly in San Francisco on August 2, 1923, of a heart attack, but some people said the cause of death was a broken heart.

The President's death stunned the nation. There was a great outpouring of grief as Harding's body, placed on a special train, made the cross-country trip from California to Washington. Thousands of people lined the railroad tracks, their hats placed over their hearts, and watched sadly and respectfully as the train glided by. "It is believed to be the most remarkable demonstration in American history of affection, respect and reverence for the dead," a reporter for the *New York Times* wrote. After lying in state in the Capitol, Harding's body was returned to Marion, Ohio, for the funeral and burial.

Many Americans viewed Warren Harding as a victim of his administration's corruption. They forgave his carousing, his affection for golf, and poker, and alcohol—in fact, those vices helped make President Harding an Everyman whom most Americans could understand and embrace, as the woman at his inauguration had observed. But Americans also viewed Harding as a tragic figure who was double-crossed by his friends, and they concluded that the betrayal contributed mightily to his sudden death. Several years later, President Herbert Hoover eulogized Harding in a way that summarized most Americans' feelings about him.

"Here was a man whose soul was seared by a great disillusionment," Hoover said. "Harding had the dim realization that he had been betrayed by a few of the men whom he had trusted, by men whom he believed were his trusted friends. It was later proved in the courts of the land that these men had betrayed not only the friendship and the trust of their staunch and loyal friend but that they had betrayed their country. That was the tragedy of Warren Harding."

PART FOUR

41 AND 43

HOLE	1	2	3	4	5	6	7	8	9	OUT	IN	TOT
DISTANCE	410	160	300	520	360	195	396	451	356	3148	3100	6248
PAR	4	3	4	5	4	3	4	5	4	36	36	72
Dad	5	4	4	5	6	4	5	6	5	44	44	88
Son	4	4	5	6	5	2	5	6	6	43	44	87
					1	3	7	2	14			
HANDICAP	5	15	13	4								

*average scores while president

I T WAS THE SATURDAY EVENING before the final day of the Ryder Cup championship in 1999. The Americans trailed the Europeans, 10-6, facing an almost certain third straight defeat despite a home course advantage at the Brookline Country Club in Massachusetts. Team captain Ben Crenshaw needed some last-minute words of inspiration, and he knew where to find them.

"I called my old friend, George W. Bush," he said.

Bush, then the governor of Texas and a candidate for president, was presented with a choice: He could attend a debate sponsored by the California Republican Party and argue about tax reform with Steve Forbes, or he could fly to Massachusetts to say a few uplifting words to an American team that was a good bet to go down to a humbling defeat.

For Bush, the choice was an easy one. Without hesitation, he hopped on a plane bound for Boston. "He went where he was needed the most," Crenshaw told me.

Bush made a surprise appearance at the Americans' Saturday evening team meeting, reaching for the story of the Alamo to inspire the golfers. He read a few lines from a famous 1836 letter, from Colonel William Barret Travis to the American people: "I have sustained a continual bombardment and a cannonade for 24 hours and have not lost a man," wrote Travis, the commander. "Our flag still proudly waves from the wall. I shall never surrender nor retreat. . . . Victory or Death."

The millionaire golfers were moved by the story.

David Duval stood up immediately after Bush spoke, and said: "Let's go out and kill 'em."

Bush's Alamo story seemed more authentic than some contrived "win one for the Gipper" speech. The Texas governor had delivered a raw admonition to a badly trailing American team: Win one for the Alamo, win one for America.

"It was impressive," said Phil Mickelson. "They were holding off a couple thousand troops, but [Travis] was going to fight to the end. It shows what a number of Americans have done for this country. We might not be soldiers who fight in wars, but this is something of its own, and we need to fight as if it were."

And the next day, with Bush's message still echoing down the fairways and off the greens, the Americans staged the most remarkable comeback in Ryder Cup history, defeating the Europeans, 14 $^1/_2$ to 13 $^1/_2$. Bush, accompanied by his father, watched it in person, wide grins lighting up their faces.

The Bushes had finally managed to help move a Ryder Cup team to victory. Just two years earlier, George H. W. Bush had tried to rally a badly trailing American team. But they lost.

"It was a great speech, great words," Crenshaw said. "And believe me, the first line of it—'We were besieged by the enemy'—we were at the time, and against some pretty insurmountable odds. But darned if we didn't pull it off."

Before being elected president—before many Americans knew who he was—George W. Bush demonstrated that he should never be underestimated, particularly in the inspiration department. Skipping a debate, even one that he was likely to have "won" in the eyes of some spin doctors, was a brilliant move. Instead, he gave a speech that inspired a team of Americans to go out and bring the Ryder Cup back home.

Darned if he didn't pull it off. Those words would be said about George W. Bush, again and again.

George H.W. Bush and George W. Bush

Father and Son
in Wedge City

George W. Bush and his father, George H.W. Bush, wear golf caps signifying their places in the pantheon of American presidents. The two men wore the caps on George W. Bush's fifty-fifth birthday, on July 6, 2001, as they played a quick round at the Cape Arundel Golf Club in Kennebunkport, Maine.

DAD: *Oh, shhhh . . . shanked it.*
SON: *Wedge City.*
—Actual exchange between George H.W. Bush and George W. Bush
at Cape Arundel Golf Club, August 1989

THEY WERE ALWAYS IN A HURRY, always rushing as if they were late for something that promised more excitement, like a game of horseshoes or an afternoon nap.

For the better part of a century at the tiny Cape Arundel Golf Club in Kennebunkport, Maine, a procession of Bushes has stepped hastily onto the first tee and just as hastily off of it. Through five generations, the Bush family (and their forebears, the Walkers) rarely took practice swings before blasting drives down that same first fairway. And in the past half-century, a Bush right foot slammed hard on the golf cart's gas pedal before the last tee shot stopped rolling.

It was always a race around the course between the Bushes and their golf balls. The golf balls always won, but never by much.

Through the years, dozens of golfing Bushes have played Cape Arundel. In the 1960s, Senator Prescott Bush of Connecticut teed off with his son, Congressman George Bush of Texas, who later became vice president and ultimately president. There were rounds played by President George Bush and First Lady Barbara Bush. And, of course, President George Bush teed off with his sons, President George W. Bush and Governor Jeb Bush of Florida. There were two other golfing Bush sons, Neil and Marvin, and a brood of golfing Bush cousins and golfing Bush grandchildren.

When a Bush foursome arrives on the first tee at Cape Arundel, you need a scorecard and a little pencil to keep everyone's names and titles straight.

"That's part of why they love coming here—the longstanding history," said Ken Raynor, the Cape Arundel club professional and a Bush family friend for more than twenty-five years.

Raynor noted that the elder President Bush "can remember when he spent time with his dad as a teenager, and now he is watching his grandchildren coming out and playing on the same course. The family has shared so many wonderful times here. It's what makes this such a special place."

Cape Arundel is less than a five-minute drive from the family's eleven-acre compound, Walkers Point. The club offers little in the way of amenities except its understated Maine beauty, which is a lot. The small clubhouse does not boast a restaurant or lounge or even a snack bar. It is "typical Kennebunkport—unpretentious, slightly quaint and functional," wrote George A. Douglas in a locally published book, *Our Little Golf Club in Maine*. Inside that clubhouse, there are no fewer than seven pictures of the former president. A photograph of Barbara Bush hangs in the ladies' locker room. It may just be the capital of the preppy golf universe. There was one Cape Arundel foursome, including two Bushes, of course, whose names were Bucky, Poppy, Jebby, and Hap.

Although the modest golf club's first tee had witnessed just about every kind of dignitary—a president, senators, governors, foreign leaders, PGA Tour professionals—another first occurred not long after the sun came up on July 6, 2001: A President Bush teed off with another President Bush.

When they arrived on the first tee, George H. W. Bush and George W. Bush tried to chase away any lingering confusion about their identities with some unmistakable fashion accessories. Dad wore a black golf cap emblazoned with a light blue "41"—the number signifying his place in history as the forty-first president, and the nickname that everyone, even his wife, had started calling him. And 41's son, who just happened to be the current president of the United States, wore a black cap that said "43."

Everyone who was gathered on the first tee ignored this obvious, odd thing—these historical digits emblazoned on matching golf caps atop the two Bushes' heads. The silence was too much for 43.

"Nobody is commenting on the birthday hat," the current president finally said. "President 41 gave me the 43 hat." It was George W. Bush's fifty-fifth birthday, and before leaving home that morning, 41 had slipped on his cap and handed the "43" cap to his son. The caps had been shipped to Maine by a Texas friend of the family, Gary Laughlin.

Ken Raynor was eager to see if anything would change on the golf course now that the oldest son had become the president. As long as anyone could remember, the father established the rules for each day's match, determining the wagers and the strokes on the first tee. Negotiating and bickering were forbidden. Waste of time.

"We wondered what it would be like, whether there would be a different dynamic now that 43 was the president and 41 was the former president," Raynor said. "Forty-one is used to being the boss. But 43 *is* the President. It was fun to watch. Of course, nothing changed."

In other words, 41 still set the rules. He still teed off first. And he refused to relinquish the cart-driving privileges.

"Dad always gets the respect of the son, regardless of what the son is," Raynor explained. "The son might be president of the United States, but the President's dad was still making the rules on the first tee, just like always. It gave me a sense of the respect and admiration 43 has for his dad. It really shines on the golf course.

"Whether you are president or not, Dad always wins out," Raynor said. "Dad always comes first."

Before hitting his drive, 43 established one rule, a "no mulligans" rule. A reporter asked the President whether he intended to shoot his age. "On the front nine," 43 said. "Thanks for your optimism."

Dad and son hit their tee shots—both went straight, though not very far. And they rocketed down the par-4, 340-yard first hole. Precisely two hours and fifteen minutes later, father and son materialized on the 18th green, accompanied by Raynor and by 43's brother-in-law, Bobby Koch.

"Well," 43 announced, "we're having a lot of fun out here."

"Easy for you to say," said the old man, grimacing.

A woman preparing to tee off on the nearby first hole noticed the convoy of reporters, Secret Service agents, White House aides, and other hangers-on scurrying around the fast-moving Bushes. "Cripes," she said, "we got all this crap again?"

A YEAR LATER, almost to the day, I asked 41 about this matter of rule-making on the first tee. He chose not to dwell on my question. Then again, he doesn't dwell on *any* question. Forty-one claimed not to notice that Ken Raynor and a few others were watching carefully that morning to see whether anything had changed between the ex-president and the new president.

"Regarding wagers, I do try to give out the strokes," 41 told me. "Someone has to do it and there is no point standing around on the first tee arguing. I throw out a suggestion and if the other three players don't like it they can appeal to the Ranking Committee. That's me."

Some things do change. For years, 41 was a better player than his son and more devoted to the game. Forty-three loved it too, but did not play nearly as often or nearly as well as Dad.

Sometime in the past decade, however, George W. surpassed Dad. Forty-three's handicap is around 15, and his strength is off the tee, where he blasts 250-yard drives. Since leaving office, 41's game has gone in the tank. His handicap has skyrocketed past 22. "I slice off the tee, losing distance in the process," Bush explained in an article that was published in 1999 in *Chicken Soup for the Golfer's Soul*. "My long irons sting my hands. The ball is seldom airborne. Nor can I chip. Putting? Forget it."

He told me, "Forty-three is better than I am. It has not always been that way. I have no distance now and he has a lot. If he played he'd play to a 15, and could be better. The lowest I ever had was 11 and that was back in the '50s. The President surpassed me when I was in my mid-sixties, I think."

Forty-one's putting was always pitiful. A big problem: most ex-presidents just don't get the gimmes, though 41 claims he got few even when he was living in the White House. "My greatest fear is when they say, now that I am no longer president, 'George, would you mind holing that out?'" 41 said. "I'm talking two-footer here."

There have been other humiliations. In his most recent rounds with his son, 41 has been teeing off from the gold tees at Cape Arundel, forward of both the white and blue tees.

"I now play from the 'forward tees,'" he grumbled, "and I am getting a little tired of my sons saying, 'Don't trip on your skirt when you hit the next one, Betsy.' Nasty comments like that as I stride to the forward tees. Not, please note, the ladies' tees."

THEY HAVE THEIR OWN PECULIAR GOLF LINGO, nearly all of it invented by 41.

"Wedge City" is a sand trap.

"On the dance floor" is a ball on the green.

"A power outage" is a weak putt left far short of the cup.

"Vic Damone" is a satisfying triumph, but it's unclear why.

"Arnold Farmer" is a suffering hacker.

"Mr. Smooth" is 41's half-joking moniker for himself.

The Bush brand of game is "speed golf," or "aerobic golf," or "power golf," or—41's favorite label—"cart polo."

A curse word, by either Bush, almost never punctuates one of their many muffed shots. Instead, there are a lot of exasperated "Gollies," and disgusted "Oh, golly darns" and outraged "Oh, golly jeez." It is bad golf, rated G.

"We're not good," said George Herbert Walker Bush, "but we're fast."

"We like to bang away," George Walker Bush said. "My father's measure of success is not how low you score, but how fast you play. His goal is to always finish eighteen holes in less than three hours."

Another term for their style of play is "ready golf," meaning when you reach your ball, you should be prepared to hit, immediately, regardless of whether your playing partners might be standing in the way. "If no one is ahead of you, you don't wait for your honor," Raynor explained. "Talk about pressure—you've got your sights on the green, and between you and the flagstick is the President of the United States, right in harm's way. He has no concern for his own safety in that situation. But it doesn't matter. You are expected to hit and then move."

The family record for eighteen holes played by a foursome: one hour, forty-two minutes. A Clinton foursome never completed *six holes* in that length of time.

"My dad used to complain about slow players, players who wouldn't let you play through," the elder Bush explained. "With me, it isn't a race to finish fast. It is just that the game should not be drawn out and other players should not be inconvenienced by some high handicap guy like me plumb-bobbing his putts and taking five practice swings on every shot."

Forty-one always seemed to be in a hurry during his four-year term, and it may have cost him four more years. During a presidential debate with challengers Bill Clinton and Ross Perot in October 1992, President Bush glanced, twice, at his wristwatch. The image was caught by the television cameras and even the still photographers, and it immediately communicated the crushing image of a president who was just marking time. That quick, impatient glance has become an infamous no-no in politics. A few weeks later, American voters made arrangements for George Bush to play beat-the-clock at home, rather than on their time.

Like his father, George W. Bush has demonstrated an impulse for self-destructive impatience. Even worse, 43 has sounded brusque and even callous when there was golf to be played. On Cape Arundel's first tee early one morning in August 2002, Bush paused a moment to condemn an overnight suicide bombing of a bus in Israel that killed nine people. Holding his big-headed driver in front of him in his gloved left hand, Bush declared, "I call upon all nations to do everything they can to stop these terrorist killers. Thank you. Now watch this drive."

Without hesitation, the President turned his attention from the Middle East to his golf game. He looped his first ball into the rough. Bush fished out another ball from his pocket and granted himself a mulligan—something that 41, Ken Raynor, and others have insisted the President never does. Bush's second shot went straight down the middle of the fairway, and he let slip a loud sigh of relief.

*On the first tee at Cape Arundel Golf Club in
Kennebunkport, Maine, on August 4, 2002, President
Bush declares that he is "distressed to hear about the latest
suicide bombers in Israel." He went on say, "I call upon
all nations to do everything they can to stop these terrorist killers."
A split second later, Bush said, "Thank you. Now watch this drive."*

"Hard this early in the morning to loosen up," he said.

It seemed harshly insensitive that Bush challenged the nations of the world to "do everything they can to stop these terrorist killers," and then, a split-second later, asked a few golf course stragglers to watch him do everything he could to hit a solid drive down the middle of the fairway.

Now watch this drive. Republican strategists heard it and winced. The President's remark brought rushing back a raft of bad memories of his father's long, grim August in Kennebunkport in 1990. Every day, it seemed, 41 spoke with reporters about Iraq's invasion of Kuwait while sitting in his golf cart. "It looks horrible," complained a senior Bush adviser of the image of Bush golfing and cruising around in his cigarette boat, while the United States prepared for war. "The President doesn't even seem to be having fun racing around the golf course. It's almost as though he's on some driven mission."

One morning that August, the rain splashed down in heavy globs, and George H. W. Bush played golf anyway in a determined, unhappy way. The course was flooded. After his ball landed in a pool of water that had collected in a sand trap, Bush asked Ken Raynor if he should play it or count it as a water hazard and take a penalty stroke. He took the penalty stroke.

He went out fishing on his boat, in the rain, with the same grim determination. The fish were not biting.

On the evening news, Americans heard President Saddam Hussein of Iraq warn the United States, through his spokesman, that war could mean the deaths of "tens of thousands of men, women and children," on both sides. They then saw images of their determined president playing golf and going fishing. This angered many commentators and jangled the nerves of Bush's senior aides. One glum aide worried aloud that the volatile crisis had the potential to "send this whole Presidency down the tubes."

On another morning, Bush deflected all questions. He was asked whether he had watched an interview with Vice President Dan Quayle on the ABC news program *Prime Time Live* the night before. "Didn't see it," he said. "I'm on vacation." He was then asked what he thought about the new prime minister of Poland. The President shook his head and said under his breath, "Oh, Lord."

One morning on the first tee, the elder Bush snapped at a reporter who asked if he was staying in close contact with the Situation Room about the plight of Americans still in Iraq. "I just don't like taking questions on serious matters on my vacation," the President snapped. "So I hope you'll understand if I, when I'm recreating, will recreate. And when we're working, which I'm trying to do up here also, I'll work hard."

Members of the White House press corps were surprised that Bush, who was usually so easygoing on vacations, had suddenly found no time for light banter on the first tee. "Mr. Smooth has turned into Mr. Mean," a White House reporter said.

The President's son, George W. Bush, who was then an oil company executive in Texas, was preparing to tee off as the reporters kept firing questions at his father about Iraq. "Hey! Hey!" Junior shouted. "Can't you wait until we finish hitting, at least?"

Back then, George W. was usually identified by the press as "the President's principal golfing partner" or simply "the President's eldest son." Actually, George W. was his father's protector and was well

During George H. W. Bush's one-term presidency, his son, George W. Bush, then a Midland, Texas, oilman, served as his father's frequent golfing partner and protector. More than once, "Junior," as his dad called him, lost his patience with reporters' nagging questions before the two men teed off.

known among the press gallery for a quick-trigger, volcanic temper that erupted whenever he perceived reporters to be stepping over some imaginary line with their questions, which was almost always.

But ten years later, as governor of Texas, George W. Bush forged an entirely different relationship with the press. During his run for the White House in 2000, Bush was touchy-feely with many of the beat reporters aboard his campaign plane, lavishing them with affection and tart nicknames, and never losing his temper with any of them. By contrast, his opponent, Al Gore, rarely spoke with reporters on his campaign plane, and his press coverage suffered in comparison.

Eleven years after one President Bush sat in a golf cart fielding questions about preparations for a war with Iraq, another President Bush sat in a golf cart fielding questions about preparations for a war with Iraq. Even odder, the first President Bush, the one who did not finish the wartime job against Saddam Hussein, sat next to the second President Bush, saying nothing as his son sidestepped questions about whether the United States would, or should, finish the job against Saddam Hussein.

Unlike the outcry about 41's golf during perilous times in 1990, almost no one complained about 43's golf during the summer of 2002. And the son was playing almost as much as his dad did. What changed? For one thing, the nation was already fighting the war against terrorism. But something else was different. The nation's attitude toward golf had changed. The game is much more in the mainstream of America, thanks to Tiger Woods, mostly. Most Americans did not begrudge this President Bush the right to talk about terrorist threats and a possible war with Iraq while on vacation in a golf shirt and khakis on the 18th green.

GOLF HAS RUN THROUGH THE BUSH FAMILY'S BLOODLINES for nearly a century.

Forty-one's maternal grandfather, George Herbert Walker, was a single-digit-handicap golfer who served as president of the United States Golf Association in 1920. He founded the Walker Cup, the trophy that is awarded to the winning team in the biennial matches between top American and British amateur golfers. "My grandfather was good," 41 told me, "but I never played with him." Not surprisingly, George Walker was fond of a quick round, too. Speed golf runs in the family.

Forty-one's father, Senator Prescott Bush, was also a talented golfer, the best ever to play in the family. "Sometimes scratch," 41 said, "sometimes 2 or 3. Once in a while we'd play with him. After the war I played with him quite a bit on vacations, mainly here in Maine, once in a while in Florida." Prescott Bush also served as the president of the United States Golf Association, in 1935.

Eight times, Prescott Bush won the Cape Arundel Golf Club championship. For years, he held the course record of 66, his name emblazoned on a plaque in the clubhouse.

"I never felt 'driven' by my family's golf heritage," 41 insisted. But he has found the rich family golf heritage daunting, at times. In the past, 41 attributed his frequent feelings of intimidation and fear when playing the game to his earliest memories on a golf course. He recalled watching his father walk up a fairway, usually in the lead of the latest tournament he was playing. "I did not start playing golf until my high school years, and then, sparingly," he said.

Golf was not his favorite sport. That was baseball. Bush played for Yale, a national baseball powerhouse that participated in the first College World Series, in 1947, in Kalamazoo, Michigan. The Elis lost to the University of California. The following year, Yale reached the national championship series again, but lost to the University of Southern California.

At Yale, Bush played every game at first base for three years, and he was elected team captain in his senior year. He was outstanding with the glove, fielding .990 on 190 chances, but he batted only .264, with one home run and 28 RBIs, tagging him with a "good field, no hit" label that nagged him through his years in the White House. A half century later, Bush still recalled one game against North Carolina State when he had a single, double, and triple. He played so well that day that some professional scouts were interested in him, but Yale coach Ethan Allen set them straight about his modest hitting talent.

The games did not end there for 41. On January 2, 1989, two and a half weeks before his inauguration, Maureen Dowd of the *New York Times* wrote, "George Bush has taken some time out since the election for sedentary activities like picking a Cabinet and preparing a plan to govern. But mostly he has kept up a grueling schedule of shooting, casting, jogging, putting, pitching, lobbing, boating, diving and body surfing."

No wonder he has no time to hit the golf ball.

"He thinks that competition, whether it's in the political spectrum or athletically, teaches you some pretty good lessons," Marvin Bush said back in 1989. "You learn how to lose and how to be part of a team. You learn that life isn't a straight shot north."

He learned that lesson most painfully on the greens. His putts were never a straight shot north. He struggles mightily on the greens, and his inability to sink putts has worsened as he has gotten older. He has learned to live with the 3-putts and the 4-putts. "Putting and dancing are two of the things I hate the most," he said. "Putting, I can practice all day and still get it up in the neck—can't bring the club through. It's terrible. Your friends laugh at you. They won't give you a six-inch putt because they know you're apt to stab it into the dirt and it's really been a humiliating experience."

Forty-one has feared mocking laughter and spasms of humiliation for years on the golf course. Perhaps that is why he tries to get off the course so quickly. In recent years, 41 established a "no laughing rule," about the same time he started hitting from the ladies' tees—ahem, the "forward tees."

The old man's son, the President, respects this rule, at least when reporters are present. One morning in early August 2002, 41 showed up with 43 at the first tee at 6:10 A.M. The pool reporters were surprised to see that 41 had large, red lesions and splotches covering most of his face. He had undergone two weeks of topical treatment for keratoses caused by years of sun exposure. Forty-one teed off from the forward tees. The tee shot was not very far and not very straight, but the President yelled, "Let's hear it!"

"Good shot, sir," a reporter squeaked.

"Make the old boy feel better," 43 said, as 41 slammed hard on the gas pedal and the golf cart zipped away.

EACH OF HIS FIRST TWO SUMMERS AS PRESIDENT, George W. Bush returned to Kennebunkport over the July Fourth weekend to celebrate his birthday, spend time with his extended family, play some golf, and catch some fish with Dad.

As long as anyone can remember, it is a Bush family tradition at Walkers Point for the sons to greet Mom and Dad in their bedroom, first thing in the morning. The children are met with even more enthusiasm if they arrive carrying hot cups of coffee. And so at 6:00

one morning, President Bush came in, said good morning, and sat down to have a cup of coffee with Mom and Dad. But he made the mistake of propping his feet up on a coffee table.

Mom, the former first lady, ordered her son to get his feet off the table and return them to the floor.

"For God's sake, Barbara," 41 told his wife. "He's the President of the United States."

"I don't care," Mom shot right back. "I don't want his feet on my table."

Some things never change.

On that occasion, and many others, 41 rushed to his son's defense. But 43 often defended his dad from criticism in the press as well, especially during the first Bush administration.

As is the case with many fathers and sons, 41 and 43 have an extremely complicated relationship. But theirs is made even more difficult because they are only the second father and son to have served as president, joining John Adams and John Quincy Adams in that select club. (In the weeks after his son became the president-elect, 41 called him "Quincy.") Should 41 give 43 advice on how to handle Iraq? Does 43 ever tell 41 to mind his own business? It is hard to imagine that their relationship did not undergo presidential strain, though neither man wanted to talk about it.

George W. Bush has always tried to live up to his father's example. But it was never easy. Forty-three followed his dad to Andover, Yale, and then into the oil business. But 43 did not enjoy the glittering success that came so easily to 41. Whereas 41 was a fighter pilot in World War II, 43 took an easier route, signing up to serve as a pilot in the Texas Air National Guard and thus avoiding combat in Vietnam.

Forty-three spent his twenties and thirties drinking a lot of beer, struggling to succeed in the oil business, and leaning, more than once, on his dad for door openings and shortcuts. The challenge of living up to his father's example and high standards seemed to weigh on him.

At the age of twenty-six, George W. came to his parents' home in Washington late one night, drunk, after a night of carousing with his teenage brother, Marvin. He crashed his car into a neighbor's garbage can, dragging it down the street and causing a loud clatter in the neighborhood. The elder Bush confronted his drunk son.

"You wanna go *mano a mano* right here?" George W. slurred at his incredulous father.

"My dad was not happy," said George W.'s sister, Dorothy, who watched the episode unfold. "My dad did not think that was attractive or funny or nice."

In July 1986, on the morning after he turned forty years old, George W. woke up with an awful hangover. He had spent the night before drinking with friends in the bar at the Broadmoor Hotel in Colorado Springs. Bush went for his usual early morning run but felt even worse afterward. He decided to quit drinking, cold turkey. He had tried to quit before at the urging of his wife, Laura, and other friends. He knew that some friends whispered that he had a drinking problem. His decision to stop drinking coincided with his father's preparation to make a run for the presidency in 1988. Surely Vice President Bush's eldest son did not want to do anything to jeopardize his father's chances of making it to the White House.

Although George W. was no longer drinking alcohol, he still possessed a volcanic temper. Several golf playing partners said they had seen flashes of it on the course, but the bursts of anger never lasted long and they were almost always directed at himself.

In Kennebunkport in August 1989, Maureen Dowd, then the White House correspondent for the *New York Times,* recalled how she suddenly appeared on George W.'s radar screen, and not exactly in a good way. Just the sight of Dowd on the first tee unnerved 41, and 43 sent more than one complaining note to his press secretary, Marlin Fitzwater, about Maureen Dowd staring at him while he was trying to hit the ball straight.

That summer, President Bush synchronized his tee time with the sunrise. There was a fringe benefit to the early tee time: It meant a 6:00 A.M. wake-up call for the press, and Bush was always a bit mischievous about eluding his posse, whether it was the Secret Service or the press pool. On more than one occasion, the President managed to elude Maureen Dowd, forcing her to speed around the winding Maine roadways to catch him before he hit that quick first tee shot and raced away.

"After a couple weeks of this cat-and-mouse game during the Bush vacation in Maine, I thought it would be fun to tweak the President, who was a sweet guy with a great sense of humor, and get a little friendly revenge," Dowd recalled. "I dressed in an old Dole for President '88 T-shirt and a Jesse Jackson for President '88 cap. I knew he'd get a kick out of that, although the messages cancel each other out.

"But when the golf cart swung by my spot on the 9th hole, the President and his son, Junior, as he was called by his White House pals in those days, were in the cart and only Junior was looking my way. I'd never met Junior or seen him around the White House much. But he was renowned as the head of the Bush loyalty squad, vetting everyone to see how loyal they were to his dad.

"His father, whom I'd hoped to amuse, did not see me in my rival regalia. He was busy driving the cart fast to the next quick golf hole. But the son got a load of my getup, and didn't find it amusing. He gave me a real glare. Later, a message came through a third party that Junior was not amused. I would feel his wrath.

"I comforted myself with the assurance that Junior, a Midland businessman who was not considered a political comer compared to brother Jeb, the designated dynasty heir, wasn't going to be around to wreak revenge on me.

"I was wrong.

"But he showed mercy. When I brought up this incident with George W. the day he announced his 2000 presidential race at Kennebunkport, sitting on the back porch overlooking the ocean, he smiled his most charming smile and asked, 'Are you still holding that against me?'"

A S 41 MOVED UP THE LADDER IN WASHINGTON, 43's view of his father evolved and, as the years passed, his respect deepened.

"When his father went off to be the ambassador [to the United Nations], that didn't seem to impress George very much," said Doug Hannah, a friend of 43 from Houston, in an interview with *Frontline* on PBS. "When he came back and was head of the Republican Party, I don't know that he was impressed by that. I think he was impressed when his father was the head of the CIA. And I know he was impressed when his father was tapped to be the vice president. That brings with it an aura of impressiveness, for sure."

But Hannah said "their lives changed," both in obvious and imperceptible ways, after George Bush was elected vice president in 1980. "They couldn't just walk out to the golf course and play golf anymore," Hannah said. "They couldn't just walk out and play tennis anymore, without an entourage of people carrying submachine guns and little black pouches around. It was a change. I remember saying to George, I could not live like this. It would be a very tough way to live. Because I'd walk into the showers in our country club and there would be Secret Service agents standing there. I mean, it was just insane."

The Secret Service protection and the press scrutiny intensified after George Bush was elected president in 1988. After nine holes one morning at the Cape Arundel Golf Club in August 1989, 41's first summer as president, George W. was asked for the score, and he said his father had 42 and his younger brother Jeb had 35. A naive reporter asked if these were good scores. George W. scowled at the reporter and snapped, "This ain't bowling."

On another morning, the President was asked a question about an upcoming drug summit in Colombia. "Hey, listen—vacation," Bush said. "I never take questions on the golf course. It gets you in real trouble—very serious trouble. I can't do it. It violates all kinds of rules."

Moments later, Bush, who swears he upholds the rules, then teed off, three times, off the first tee.

Forty-one's biggest problem on the links was his horrendous putting. He tried everything—one-handed putts, cross-handed putts, left-handed putts. The problem became so bad that Bush installed on the South Lawn of the White House a 1,500-square-foot, nine-hole artificial turf practice green. The President and the First Lady practiced on that green, but not often. "He is allergic to practice," Raynor told me. "He breaks out in hives if he has to practice."

Raynor urged 41 to try using a forty-eight-inch Pole-Kat putter. The first time Bush used it, it was like a magic wand. His game was transformed. "He ran in a twenty-footer and got a big smile on his face," Raynor said at the time. "He sank putts from all over the place for the rest of the day. He was delirious."

I asked Raynor years later if the Pro-Kat still works that kind of magic for 41. "Nah," he said. "Nowadays, I spend most of my time reading his putts."

THE BUSHES "ALWAYS PLAY BY THE RULES," Raynor says. "They were born with the rules," he said. "Forty-one's father was a USGA president. The United States Golf Association has always been in the air of the household for years and years."

Paul Marchand, a Houston club pro and old friend of the Bushes, recalled taking a photograph with the President at the White House in May 2002. "The President says through his teeth, 'Smile and remember all the times I beat you on the golf course.'

"I said, 'That's funny, because you never did beat me.'"

But the President bragged a little, saying that he had recently shot a 76 at Cape Arundel. "It was legit," Marchand said. "One thing I can assure you about the Bushes is that it is right to the letter. No embellishments. They have a lot of fun, but there are no gimmes, no mulligans. What you shot is what you shot. The integrity of the game is always upheld."

Others told me the same thing. The professional golfer Ben Crenshaw, a close friend of the family, said both 41 and 43 only take mulligans off the first tee, and only rarely.

I asked 41 about this. "Integrity and honor—playing by the rules—is essential in golf," he said. "I am a member of Jack Nicklaus's Captain's Club—we meet before his Muirfield tournament. At the dinner I attended, both Nicklaus and Palmer talked a lot about the game's etiquette, about playing by the rules all the time, and about speed of play and decorum on the course. I grew up learning these principles from my grandfather and father alike. One who cheats in golf is really looked down upon by those who really love the game."

The implication of that last sentence is not very subtle. There is no doubt that the "one" he is talking about is Bill Clinton. Several Bush family friends told me that 41 thinks Clinton's behavior— both on the golf course and off—inflicted lasting damage to the presidency.

But 41 and 43 have been seen taking mulligans, often, off the first tee. And they have also given each other gimme putts, some playing partners have reported.

Dan Jenkins, the funny and famous golf writer, played a round with 41 in 1990 for *Golf Digest*. President Bush told Jenkins, "My problem with golf is I have to deal with a humiliation factor."

Jenkins wrote: "There were ways around that, I said. White tees only, roll it over everywhere, mulligans were free.

"'Can't take a mulligan,' he said. 'Too much pride.'

"I said, 'Mr. President, let me tell you something. I've been around the game a long time. Par doesn't give a damn about pride. I've seen par wring pride's neck.'"

During their round at Holly Hills Country Club near Camp David, President Bush ended up shooting a two-mulligan 86 to Dan Jenkins's three-mulligan 78.

A S PRESIDENT, 41 HAD A CHOICE. He could play with his usual playing partners, National Security Adviser Brent Scowcroft, Secretary of State James Baker, or Treasury Secretary Nicholas Brady. (There were whispers that the way Brent Scowcroft edged out James Baker as the favorite adviser to the senior Bush was by playing golf, constantly, with the President. Bush once gave Scowcroft a chalk ball that exploded on impact, a practical joke that amused everyone on the first tee very much.)

Of course, the President could also play with Vice President Dan Quayle, a near-scratch golfer whom critics called the golf professional of the Bush administration. "He's so darned good," Bush said.

Quayle had won the Congressional golf championship while serving as a U.S. senator from Indiana. He was also the two-time winner of the club championship at his home course, the Fort Wayne Country Club. "Dan Quayle would rather play golf than have sex any day," his wife, Marilyn, said famously. He played once or twice a week as vice president, but it was less than he had played as a senator, and consequently, his handicap rose from a 3 to a 6.

Golf inevitably got in the way of Quayle's official duties. In 1991, during an official visit to Singapore, where tardiness is viewed as a character flaw, Quayle kept Prime Minister Lee Kuan Yew waiting nearly five minutes before their meeting at Mr. Lee's home. Quayle was on the golf course.

As he waited for Quayle to arrive, Lee frowned at his watch and sighed heavily. After the Vice President finally showed up, the prime minister said, "I hear you had some golf," and each word was soaked in sarcasm. Reporters noticed that the back of Quayle's hair was still wet from his quick shower in the clubhouse before darting over to the prime minister's home.

Former president Richard Nixon was disheartened by the country-club image projected by Bush and Quayle. "The average guy is not on the golf course, the tennis court or a speedboat because he doesn't have one," Nixon told an associate in 1991, according to the *Los Angeles Times.* Nixon had also talked directly with Quayle, telling him to "stop bringing his golf clubs with him as he travels around the world." But Nixon's advice was not heeded.

If Quayle was too daunting a golf partner for the President, he could choose instead to play a round with his wife, Barbara. But this too became fraught with difficulties.

In the summer of 1991, during a White House lunch with a few women reporters, Barbara Bush confided that she had begun to take golf lessons. It was at her husband's suggestion, so they could play together in Kennebunkport that summer.

That August, Mrs. Bush played with a friend at Cape Arundel—separately from her husband. But the President was there, gleefully finding a way to sabotage his wife's wobbly confidence. He told reporters to watch his wife as she putted on the 18th green. "We'll make her nervous," he said, laughing. He was asked why he had not joined his wife for the round. "We're going down life's path hand-in-hand for many years, but golf—we go our separate ways."

Barbara Bush was obviously unnerved by the network television cameras and blew her short putt. And she said, quietly but loud enough for the reporters to hear: "That's so mean." She also said that members of the press were "lucky" not to be married to the President.

Eventually the President was pressed into playing a round with his wife, though it was clear he was not too happy about the prospect. "When?" the First Lady said, rolling her eyes. "Just like he's going to garden with me one day."

But Bush went out and played a round with Barbara, Ken Raynor, and George W.

Afterward, the President was asked how the First Lady played.

"She stunk," he said. "Absolutely a disaster."

Barbara Bush was asked if she intended to play another round with her husband.

"Never again," she said.

AFTER BUSH LOST THE 1992 PRESIDENTIAL ELECTION to Bill Clinton, he tried playing the Pro-Am circuit, but something stopped him: fear. "Ever since I hit a guy with a Titleist off a 7-wood shot in the Doug Sanders tournament," Bush said, "I've been gun-shy about these events."

In an interview with George Plimpton, Bush described how it

happened. "I was looking down this funnel of spectators," he said. "An unforgiving funnel. I told them, 'Please step back. I'm not a good golfer.' And they moved an inch. Actually, this was my second shot, my tee shot having zoomed over their heads. I would have thought they'd have headed for the hills. But they didn't. They moved back an inch. So I took this 7-wood—Callaway 7—and hooked the shot for some reason. I usually slice. And zap! I could literally hear the ball hitting this guy. I rushed up. He was smiling. I said, 'Oh, my gosh, I feel so badly.' He was holding a baby in his arms! But it wasn't the baby I'd hit, thank goodness; it was him. So I sent him a care package—some Presidential golf balls left over and a couple of things. I got back the nicest letter. 'I'm a longtime supporter. Nothing gave me more pleasure than seeing you out there.'"

In 1997, Paul Marchand, the pro at Shadow Hawk Country Club in Houston, and CBS sportscaster Jim Nantz, a close Bush family friend, played a round with former president Bush and George W. Bush (who was then the governor of Texas) after a soaking rain at the Houston Country Club. They were the only ones left on the rain-slickened course.

"Both father and son are going to keep their date if they are scheduled to play golf," said Marchand, an old friend of the Bush family. "The weather has to be mighty bad to cancel a planned golf date. That day Jim broke with the tradition of determining the importance of a key shot in advance and dedicated a shot to the former President before hitting it. The former President got a kick out of that and dedicated a shot himself. On the last hole, the former President had a short iron approach shot and he dedicated it to Barbara Bush and proceeded to put it up by the pin—the best shot of the day. Since that round it comes up from time to time and most always former President Bush dedicates his shot to Mrs. Bush. It may sound a bit curious during a golf round to do such a thing but believe me it brings a smile to our faces when it occurs and it has become a tradition. It is part of the running commentary that can accompany any shot and makes the day fun."

Mrs. Bush may stink at golf, but she can bring good luck.

GEORGE W. BUSH WAS PROPELLED to the White House by his family. His father's Rolodex of Republican moneymen and contributors helped enormously, as did his mother's "Christmas card list" of tens of thousands of friends and supporters. But, of course, Dad bestowed upon his eldest son both his first and last name. Nothing is more valuable in Texas politics.

Bush was elected governor of Texas in 1994. His parents had always assumed that Jeb, George W.'s younger brother, who ran for governor of Florida that same year, was destined for even greater things. But George W. was used to being underestimated. It was almost as if he welcomed it because he could use it to his advantage. And when he won his race while Jeb lost his (Jeb would have to wait four years to make it to the statehouse), his family took notice.

"George is sneaky smart," said his friend, Doug Hannah. "And I think part of his strength is, if you choose to think he's not very smart, so be it. He's not going to worry about whether you think he's smart or not. But he's plenty smart. And it could be an absolute ally if you're smarter than your opponents think you are."

Nothing blunt was ever said about George W. Bush's motivation to run for president. Many people assumed that he was running to avenge his father's defeat to Bill Clinton in 1992. He rarely spoke about the hurt he felt seeing his dad lose after only a single term. "In retrospect, those were such strong emotions for me, to see a good man get whipped," he said in December 1999.

There were other hints. Forty-three often said he wanted to "restore dignity" to the Oval Office. After the impeachment scandal, everyone in the country knew what he meant.

Al Gore underestimated Bush, too. The consensus among political observers was that Bush won the debates against the Democratic nominee, and after thirty-six days of counting, recounting, and court cases, Bush carried the decisive electoral votes of Florida by a margin of just 537 votes of nearly 6 million cast. Actually, he won by one vote, the last vote, when the U.S. Supreme Court decided, in a 5–4 decision, to award the 2000 presidential election to George W. Bush.

FORTY-THREE INHERITED a strong competitive drive and a passion for sports, including golf, from his father.

Although golf is one of his favorite sports, 43's favorite athletic activity is running. He began when he was twenty-five, at a time when he was "out of shape" and drinking too much beer. He pushed hard over the years, and in 1993 he ran his first marathon as Mom and Dad watched and cheered him on at mile marker nineteen.

Barbara sniffed that elderly women were beating him, while his father yelled, "We're so proud of you, son!"

George W. Bush is perhaps the best-conditioned president ever. *Runner's World* magazine declared him to be the "Fastest President." Bush runs five or six days a week, doing three miles in less than twenty minutes. Since the September 11 terrorist attacks against the World Trade Center and the Pentagon, he has even improved his running time. "It's interesting that my times have become faster right after the war began," Bush told the magazine. "I guess that's part of the stress relief I get from it. For me, the psychological benefit is enormous. You tend to forget everything that's going on in your mind, and just concentrate on the time, distance or the sweat. It helps me to clear my mind." Given a choice between playing golf and going for a hard, three-mile run, George W. Bush would choose running, every time.

During the summer of 2001, 43 played a few rounds of golf with his dad in Kennebunkport, and a few rounds with friends near his ranch in Crawford, Texas. He usually shot in the mid to high 80s, his playing partners said.

The terrorist attacks kept 43 off the golf course for nearly nine months. He missed playing golf, a few friends said. One of them, Ben Crenshaw, said, "I think 43 truly loves the game. If he could play more, he would. I can count on two hands how many times he has

President George W. Bush, "43," demonstrates his form off the tee during his August 2002 vacation near his ranch in Crawford, Texas. The president's father, "41," said his son is "long off the tee," and plays to about a 15 handicap.

played in the last three or four years."

Crenshaw met Bush in 1980 through mutual friends in Midland, Texas. He has played a few times with 43 at Barton Creek Country Club in Austin. When I asked him who was better, father or son, he said he thought 41 could still give 43 a run for his money.

Forty-three "can wind up and hit it," Crenshaw said. "He's very athletic and very strong. He's a pretty good driver, and he hits some good shots."

Crenshaw said that it is a workout playing with the Bushes. "You have to play ready golf—the ball is in the air nearly at all times," he said. "It's great. I've never seen two guys with more boundless energy in my life. They are just amazing. And that's the way they view life—they just charge right through."

George W. Bush plays golf aggressively, Crenshaw and others told me. He is not afraid of taking risks, always choosing to go for the green rather than playing it safe. He plays his politics the same way.

In the few weeks leading up to the mid-term elections in 2002, Bush, who hates to travel, went on an aggressive barnstorming tour for Republican candidates nationwide. It was a big bet by Bush, putting his own popularity on the line to help Republicans in congressional races. And it worked. The Republicans swept to a historic victory, taking control of the Senate and widening the gap over the Democrats in the House.

The Democrats were flabbergasted by Bush's aggressiveness, and they again scratched their heads and wondered how they could have underestimated him. His friends, however, told me that Bush is as competitive playing politics as he is playing golf. They were not the least bit surprised that he chose to go for the green in November 2002, and then did not regret it.

THE BUSH FAMILY CHARGES RIGHT THROUGH. The Bushes charge through their politics and their play time, racing to make the most of every moment. They are always together, helping each other, looking after each other, drawing strength from each other. They are like the Kennedys in that way. Political dynasties have a common ingredient of success: Family always comes first.

I asked 41 what he likes most about golf. "When I was POTUS [President of the United States]," he said, "golf was a great way to totally relax and play with friends or family." On the golf course, the Bush family demonstrates their love and solidarity, with Dad still enforcing the first tee rules and Mom keeping the current president's feet off the coffee table. Yet they move so fast, you have to pay attention or you will miss it.

"The moments with my sons on the links are very special," said George H. W. Bush. "Every moment with family out there is heaven."

EPILOGUE

THE ALLURE OF THE GAME

Playing golf with America's Presidents is a great denominator.
How a President acts in a sand trap is a pretty good barometer
of how he would respond if the hot line suddenly lit up.
—Bob Hope

NEARLY A CENTURY AGO, Theodore Roosevelt warned: Golf is fatal.

It certainly seemed that way at the time. William Howard Taft was dragging 300-plus pounds around America's golf courses, chasing comically after a little white ball, and the voters were convulsing with laughter. Roosevelt knew it could not be a good thing for people to laugh at a presidential candidate, and so he encouraged Taft to quit the game. Through the century that followed, whenever a president felt guilty about rushing from the White House to make a tee time, he could hear the whisper of Roosevelt's admonition.

Yet golf is not fatal to the president or the presidency. It is vital.

The game demonstrates that the most powerful man in the world can be just one of the guys. By playing golf, the president shows he is just as fanatical and flawed as a nation of weekend hackers.

The game even possesses the power to make the most inaccessible president seem accessible. In August 2002, George W. Bush went to his ranch in Crawford, Texas, for a monthlong "working vacation." Many nights, on the evening news, the President, wearing a sweat-soaked golf shirt and leaning on a golf club, appeared in a tee box or on a practice green as he discussed the possibility that the United States might invade Iraq or the administration's latest attempt to punish corporate crooks.

On many summer evenings in August 2002, Americans heard the latest pronouncements from their president from a tee box or fairway. George W. Bush usually wore a sweat-soaked golf shirt and often leaned on a golf club as he talked about the threat of terrorism or about corporate misbehavior. Many Americans found nothing wrong with that image or any message that it sent to the world.

The golf-course setting for such public pronouncements was not an accident. Bush's political strategists have determined that Americans no longer view a golfing president with alarm or mistrust. Golf is no longer perceived as an aristocratic pursuit; within the past decade, it has become America's game, with its ever-widening popularity leaping effortlessly across socioeconomic boundaries. So why shouldn't America's president play the game that millions of Americans are playing?

This sentiment is a dramatic shift from the early days of Bill Clinton's administration, when White House adviser Dick Morris conducted a poll to determine the most constituent-friendly vacation destinations and activities for the President. At that time, golf was polling as a definite no-no, especially for a Democrat. The numbers showed that Clinton should go to the mountains, preferably spending his time camping and hiking to curry the favor of swing voters who apparently preferred camping and hiking.

"Can I golf?" Clinton sarcastically asked Morris, who glowered at the query. Then the President offered a concession that might make the image more mainstream: "Maybe if I wear a baseball cap?"

"You're going to golf anyway," Morris answered glumly.

Everything—even vacation pursuits—was poll-tested in the Clinton White House. No golf? It may have been the only time that the poll numbers did not matter to Bill Clinton.

So Clinton did what the poll advised by relaxing for a week in Yellowstone National Park and Grand Teton National Park in the Rocky Mountains, where he went through the tent-pitching and trail-hiking motions. But he rejected Morris's advice about golf and played thirty-seven holes in a single day.

"He did camp in a tent," Morris said in his book *Behind the Oval Office*. "He did hike in the national parks. But, damn, he also golfed!"

A s IT TURNS OUT, golf is fatal only to the presidential aspirants who dare *not* play it.

The list of recent Presidential nominees who are nongolfers is a losers' roll: Al Gore, Bob Dole, Michael Dukakis, and Walter Mondale. None of those men played the game, and all four were defeated in presidential elections by candidates whose affection for the game was well known to the electorate.

After all, it is impossible to imagine Al Gore yelling "Fore!" off the tee or soaking up an eighteen-hole lesson from Greg Norman. Michael Dukakis would look as ridiculous piloting a golf cart as he looked at the helm of an army tank wearing that oversized helmet. Can you imagine Walter Mondale laughing gleefully as he sneaked away for eighteen holes in the middle of a workday afternoon?

But you can envision George H. W. Bush and George W. Bush needling each other as they catapult the cart through a two-hour round of eighteen. You can hear Ronald Reagan joking about melting his metal iron shafts into an ashtray. And it is easy to see Clinton writing a "4" on his scorecard after shooting a "6." On the golf course, these presidents have acted the way we have come to expect them to act.

The golfing presidents are guys you can imagine relaxing with after playing a round. Over a few beers, it is easy to imagine replaying that awful hole with Taft or Harding or Ike or Ford.

In life and in politics, there are golfers and there are nongolfers. The American people have spoken: We prefer golfers.

Granted, this amounts to absurd political analysis, but it is hard to argue with these facts: In the past century, Jimmy Carter was the only nongolfer to defeat a golfer, Gerald Ford, on Election Day. Ford's pardon of another golfer, Nixon, did him in, though another golfer, Ronald Reagan, made sure that Carter served a single term. In fact, the three nongolfing chief executives in the past century— Herbert Hoover, Harry S Truman, and Jimmy Carter—were all elected to single terms in office.

What does this phenomenon say about the state of the game and the state of presidential politics?

If you are a potential president, it is wise to play golf and wiser still to publicly embrace that passion. (William Howard Taft was exactly right, after all.) But be warned: Do not play too well. Dan Quayle was the most talented golfer to serve in the executive branch, but his single-digit handicap became a national punch line. If an elected official can make Nicklaus or Norman sweat, Americans will assume that he is spending too much time golfing and not enough time governing.

We want presidents who play as poorly and recklessly as we do. We would even prefer a golf cheat to a scratch golfer.

IN TWENTY-FIRST-CENTURY AMERICA, golf is no longer the blue-blooded sport of the gilded gentry, played behind country club gates that bar entry to nearly all Americans. Augusta (along with twenty-three other American country clubs) still stubbornly keeps its doors slammed shut to women members. And it still takes big money to buy your way into the best and most elite country clubs. But the game no longer belongs exclusively to the wealthiest Americans. Visit any driving range today and you'll see African Americans, Asian Americans, Hispanics, middle class and poor, banging away at thousands of scuffed-up range balls and marveling at that occasional shot that resembles perfection. These days, you would have to search a dozen driving ranges and public courses before you stumbled on your first wealthy, preppy golfer wearing an Izod polo shirt with the little green alligator.

It is no coincidence that in the summer of 2002, George W. Bush felt comfortable looking like nothing more than another weekend hacker. Two months earlier, the U.S. Open in Bethpage, New York, was played on a public golf course for the first time.

Tiger Woods deserves most of the credit for the gargantuan popularity of today's game. The bookmakers in Great Britain have recognized the natural connection between golf and politics. In 2000, they installed Tiger as a 500-1 shot that he would someday be elected to public office. He was made a long shot only because he has insisted that he has no interest in running. "I'd rather go out there and play golf," Woods said. "And when you're President, it's kind of hard to get away and play a nice round of golf."

It may seem that way. But the fourteen golfing presidents managed to have fun on the links despite the hazards of the Secret Service agents, nosy photographers, gawking spectators, and humorless reporters tabulating the mulligans. Any one of those things would ruin the afternoon of an amateur golfer. Golf allowed the presidents to forget who they were and what they were expected to do, if only for a few blessed hours.

Almost everything the president does is reported, gauged, weighed, analyzed, dissected, repeated, badmouthed, and second-guessed. The president's golf game must withstand that same degree of scrutiny, but it gets only the slightest reprieve because the public cannot watch. Golf remains one of the few public things that the president can do with some degree of privacy. After the president hits his drive off the first tee, he will not see another photographer or field another question until he steps on the 18th green.

For the president, this translates into a three-hour reprieve with the blinds closed, a three-hour escape from the fishbowl. This is bliss.

THE GAME SAYS NO, which is why the president is naturally drawn to it. But golf is one of the few things the president does only for himself. The president does have *choices*. No aide can script a round. No strategist can blast out of the trap for him. The golf course is one of the few places left on earth where a president can let down his guard and not worry about the consequences. The game is his and his alone.

No matter what anyone says about how he plays or how he records his score, only the president determines whether he will allow the game to lift his spirits or break his heart.

He can scream at the game's cruelty, or just laugh out loud.

He can cheat on every hole, or count every stroke.

He can yell at a caddy's bad advice, or blame himself for taking it.

He can ban photographers from the course, or invite them to come along for all eighteen holes.

He can play only when the sun shines, or play in the dark, in the rain, alone.

He can fume about being called a cheater, or laugh and say, "Who isn't?"

He can tear up his scorecard, or have it framed.

He can pretend he is better than he is, or acknowledge he is worse than we thought.

He can let the game mean everything, or nothing.

The only thing the president cannot control is how the game plays—and, thus, reveals—him.

A NOTE ON SOURCES

O N A MARCH DAY IN 2002, my researcher, John Files, and I rifled through the voluminous archives at the United States Golf Association headquarters in Far Hills, New Jersey. We thumbed past millions of words lauding the heroics of Jones, Palmer, Nicklaus, and Woods, hunting instead for the few buried nuggets about the golfing high jinks of Taft, Wilson, Harding, and Coolidge. After a long day culling a few dozen modestly helpful clips from the *American Golfer* and *Golf Digest*, we began to pack up our things for the drive home to Washington, D.C., when I yanked open a bottom metal storage drawer in a back corner of the USGA library. Jammed inside were dozens of clipped magazine articles from the 1950s about Dwight D. Eisenhower's golf game. An embarrassment of riches popped out of the drawer and fell at our feet—detailed articles about Ike's golf obsession, published by *Look, Life,* and *This Week*. There was one problem. In a matter of minutes, the USGA was scheduled to close shop and show its two remaining guests to the door. But the archivists were kind enough to keep the lights on, allowing us to frantically copy a backpack full of golden clips that helped bring Ike to life.

Whether you are knee-deep in a sand trap or knee-deep in musty, long-forgotten periodicals, a little luck goes a long way. More than once during the research for *First Off the Tee*, we were fortunate enough to stumble upon this perfect anecdote or that priceless quotation. Almost always, a gem arrived unannounced, startling us like a twenty-five-foot shot blasted out of the sand that miraculously rolls into the cup.

We interviewed more than 100 people with knowledge of a golfing president's game. This group, many of whom spoke only on condition of anonymity, ranged from former Secret Service agents who had rare, greens-side seats to current White House aides and congressmen who played a round or two with a sitting president. We extracted details about the presidents' golf games from history books, biographies, and memoirs.

We unearthed anecdotes from faded newspaper clippings and long-forgotten golf periodicals. We found countless gems inside the archives of more than a dozen presidential libraries and historical societies. In all, we scoured more than 1,000 books and tens of thousands of newspaper and magazine articles—most of them clips located in the Library of Congress, the USGA library, and the archives inside the Washington bureau of the *New York Times*.

There are several books that deserve to be singled out. First and foremost, I am grateful to Shepherd Campbell and Peter Landau, the authors of *Presidential Lies: The Illustrated History of White House Golf* (New York: Macmillan, 1996), the first book devoted to the golfing American presidents. I was fortunate enough to find a copy of a wonderful, out-of-print book entitled *White House Sportsmen* (Boston: Houghton Mifflin Company, 1964), written by Edmund Lindop and Joseph Jares. I also relied on Harry B. Martin's *Fifty Years of American Golf* (New York: Dodd Mead, 1936), which describes the early years of the game in America as well as the earliest golfing presidents' devotion to the game.

I was wowed by the keenly perceptive observations of Colonel Edmund W. Starling, a security man to five presidents who is buried at Arlington National Cemetery. His compulsively readable autobiography, *Starling of the White House* (as told to Thomas Sugrue, New York: Simon and Schuster, 1946), helped shape my understanding of the behavior, both on and off the links, of the twentieth century's first three golfing presidents.

Among the thousands of newspaper and magazine articles, none was better than "The Hidden Scorecards of Pennsylvania Avenue," by Robert L. Caleo, published in the September 1969 edition of *Golf* magazine.

I also consulted these articles and books for at least two chapters:

Aherns, Frank. "The First Golfers." *Washington Post*, June 11, 1997.

Barber, James David. *The Presidential Character: Predicting Performance in the White House*. New York: Pearson Education (paperback edition), 1992.

Barkow, Al. *The Golden Era of Golf: How America Rose to Dominate the Old Scots Game*. New York: St Martin's Press, 2000.

Boller, Paul F. *Presidential Anecdotes*. New York: Oxford University Press, 1981.

Brallier, Jess, and Sally Chabert. *Presidential Wit and Wisdom: Maxims, Mottoes, Sound Bites, Speeches, and Asides, Memorable Quotes from America's Presidents*. New York: Penguin Books, 1996.

Burning Tree Club (Bethesda, Md.). *The Fifth Decade, 1963–1972*. Bethesda, Md.: Privately published, 1972.

———. *A History, 1922–1962*. Bethesda, Md.: Privately published, 1962.

Chevy Chase Club (Chevy Chase, Md.). *The Club History*. Chevy Chase, Md.: Privately published, n.d.

Congressional Country Club (Bethesda, Md.). *A History*. Bethesda, Md.: Privately published, n.d.

Dolan, Anne Reilly. *Congressional Country Club, 1924–1984*. Washington, D.C.: Privately published, n.d.

Gilleece, Dermot. "Presidents Getting the Rub of the Green on the White House Lawn." *Irish Times*, September 18, 2001.

"Golfers Prominent on Roster of World Leaders: Many Presidents Played."
U.S.G.A. Journal and Turf Management, February 1961.

Hawkins, John. "Fore More Years? Most Recent Presidents Way Above Par."
Washington Times, September, 13, 1994.

Hodges, Jim. "Capitol Games." *Los Angeles Times,* June 12, 1997.

Hope, Bob, with Dwayne Netland. *Confessions of a Hooker: My Lifelong Love Affair with Golf.* Garden City, N.Y.: Doubleday, 1985.

Ladowsky, Ellen, "As They Golf, So Shall They Govern." *Washington Post,* September 4, 1994.

Lynham, John M. *The Chevy Chase Club: A History, 1885–1957.* Chevy Chase, Md.: Privately published, 1958.

MacRury, Downs. *Golfers on Golf: Witty, Colorful, and Profound Quotations on the Game of Golf.* New York: B&N Books, 2001.

McGrory, Brian. "A Slice of Presidential Life." *Boston Globe,* August 17, 1996.

Miller, Hope Ridings. *Scandals in the Highest Office: Facts and Fictions in the Private Lives of Our Presidents.* New York: Random House, 1973.

Palmer, Arnold, with James Dodson. *A Golfer's Life.* New York: Ballantine Publishing Group, 1999.

Parascenzo, Marino. "Capital Golf." *Golf,* November 1980.

Perry, Enos J. *The Boyhood Days of Our Presidents.* N.p.: Self-published, 1971.

Sidey, Hugh. *Hugh Sidey's Profiles of the Presidents: From FDR to Clinton with Time Magazine's Veteran White House Correspondent.* New York: Little, Brown and Company, 2001.

Slay, Dick. "The Golfing Presidents." *Washington Star-News,* September 1, 1974.

Snead, Sam, with George Mendoza. *Slammin' Sam.* New York: Donald I. Fine, 1986.

Travers, Jerome D., and James R. Crowell. *The Fifth Estate: Thirty Years of Golf.* New York: Alfred A. Knopf, 1926.

United States Golf Association. *Golf: The Greatest Game.* New York: Harper-Collins, 1994.

Watters, Susan. "Power Golf." *M,* August 1989.

Wind, Herbert Warren. *The Story of American Golf.* New York: Farrar Straus, 1948.

Windeler, Robert. *The Quotable Golfer: The Greatest Things Ever Said about the Greatest @*!!#! Game Ever Played.* New York: Running Press, 1998.

We found wonderful anecdotes inside the privately published club histories, particularly for Burning Tree Country Club, the Chevy Chase Club, and Congressional Country Club. Those three clubs are proud that so many American presidents were able to enjoy their fine golf courses, and their publications were packed with revealing anecdotes, especially about the earliest golfing presidents.

I relied on pool reports for presidential golf course scenes witnessed by members of the White House press corps. There are far too many reporters to mention here whose pool reports helped set a scene in this book, but I am especially grateful for the sharp and often witty observations of Maureen Dowd, Frank Bruni, John M. Broder, Gerald Seib, John F. Harris, and Anne Kornblut.

For the "average" Presidential scorecards that begin each of this book's four sections, my researcher, John Files, designed an "imaginary" nine-hole golf course that includes exact replicas of selected holes on the favorite golf courses of the Presidents: Burning Tree, Congressional, Chevy Chase, and Cape Arundel. The par, handicap, and distances from the white tees are all exact. The holes are:

First Off the Tee 1: Burning Tree's Hole 1
First Off the Tee 2: Congressional's Hole 2
First Off the Tee 3: Chevy Chase's Hole 5
First Off the Tee 4: Congressional's Hole 15
First Off the Tee 5: Cape Arundel's Hole 4
First Off the Tee 6: Cape Arundel's Hole 16
First Off the Tee 7: Burning Tree's Hole 7
First Off the Tee 8: Chevy Chase's Hole 10
First Off the Tee 9: Chevy Chase's Hole 13

For each of *First Off the Tee*'s fifteen chapters, I have listed the books or articles that were used as source material or helped shape my understanding of the man and his game. Some interviews with people quoted in this book were taken from other sources. In those instances, they are listed below if their origin was not identified in the text. Any quotations not identified in the text or in this chapter were given directly to the author or John Files during interviews conducted from August 1999 to December 2002.

Prologue

Alas, I did not attend the famous presidential threesome round at the Bob Hope Chrysler Classic on February 15, 1995. However, I watched the NBC videotape of the round and relied on the White House transcript of Dick Enberg's interview of the three presidents and Bob Hope and dozens of newspaper and magazine articles recounting the match. Among them:

Broder, John M. "The Green Party: Clinton, Ford, and Bush a Fearsome Threesome at Golf." *Los Angeles Times*, February 16, 1995.

Downey, Mike. "Their Fivesome Lacks the Writer's Touch." *Los Angeles Times*, February 13, 1995.

Guest, Larry. "Hoch 'Thrilled' Playing Golf with 3 Presidents." *Orlando Sentinel,* February 16, 1995.

Harris, John F. "Golfing with Hope, Presidents Laughable Errant Shots Zing Tourney Spectators." *Washington Post*, February 16, 1995.

Hershey, Steve. "Clinton: Thanks for the Memory." *USA Today*, February 16, 1995.

———. "Historic Fivesome Adds Complications." *USA Today*, February 15, 1995.

Kornheiser, Tony. "The Bogey Men." *Washington Post*, February 19, 1995.

Lindlaw, Scott. "Clinton Closes Out Brief California Trip with Golf." Associated Press, February 15, 1995.

Moss, J. Jennings. "Clinton Golf Buddies Are Terror on Fairways." *Washington Times*, February 16, 1995.

Reinman, T. R. "All the Presidents' Bogeys." *San Diego Union-Tribune*, February 16, 1995.

Romano, Lois. "The Reliable Source: A Presidential Handicap." *Washington Post*, February 15, 1995.

Ventre, Michael. "Chiefs Play with Hope, Not Skill." *Los Angeles Daily News*, February 16, 1995.

The Eisenhower Augusta anecdote is a wonderful piece of golfing lore. See Al Ludwick, "General Very Nearly Eliminated That Tree," *Augusta Herald*, April 10, 1969.

George H. W. Bush described the experience of playing the Bob Hope Chrysler Classic, both in written answers to me and in a piece published in *Golf Digest*. Many of Bush's recollections of that afternoon appear in italics as his thoughts as he survived that chaotic day.

All the quotations in the Prologue's third section describing the origin of the book were given to me. During Terry McAuliffe's phone call to me in early September 1999 about my original *New York Times* article about Bill Clinton and mulligans, I scribbled every scolding word that McAuliffe shouted into the phone.

Golf round quotations of Norma Earley and John Rynd are from David Grimes, "Goofy Golf When Presidents Hit the Links," *Sarasota Herald-Tribune*, February 25, 1995.

Post-round quotations of Norma Earley are from L. Erik Bratt, "Golf Spectator's Sudden Celebrity a Consequence of Bush's Stroke of Bad Luck," *San Diego Union-Tribune*, February 21, 1995.

The quotation from Geoff Russell of *Golf World* magazine comes from "Hail from the Chiefs," *Patriot Ledger*, February 16, 1995.

JOHN F. KENNEDY

Bradlee, Benjamin C. *Conversations with Kennedy*. New York: W. W. Norton, 1975.

Caleo, Robert L. "Hidden Scorecards of Pennsylvania Avenue," *Golf*, September 1969.

Campbell, Shepherd, and Peter Landau. *Presidential Lies: The Illustrated History of White House Golf*. New York: Macmillan, 1996.

Fay, Paul B. Jr. *The Pleasure of His Company*. New York: Harper and Row, 1966.

Graham, Dillon. "Big Golf Day A-Coming, Eisenhower Vs. Kennedy." *Washington Evening Star*, April 10, 1961.

Hunter, Marjorie. "Kennedy Course Is Like Politics: Lots of Obstructions and Traps." *New York Times*, July 15, 1963.

"Kennedy at Church, Pool, Yacht, Links." *New York Times*, September 16, 1963.

"Kennedy Could Play Golf in 70's with Practice, Says Family Pro." Associated Press, February 20, 1961.

"Kennedy Golf Ball Hits Secret Service Agent." *New York Times*, April 6, 1961.

"Kennedy Like Old Self in Three Golf Rounds." Associated Press, *Washington Evening Star*, July 15, 1963.

"Kennedy Now Hopes to Be Golfing Soon." Associated Press, December 14, 1961.

"Kennedy Permits First Golf-Course Photographs." *New York Times*, April 5, 1961.

"Kennedy Plays Golf Under Florida Sun." *New York Times*, May 13, 1961.

"Kennedy Slips Off for 6 Holes of Golf." Associated Press, February 23, 1961.

"Kennedy Will Forgo Golf Once He's in White House." United Press International, December 27, 1960.

"Kennedy Suffers a Back Relapse." *New York Times*, August 28, 1963.

Lannan, John. "Kennedy Was Quite an Athlete, Now Prefers Swimming, Sailing." Associated Press, July 15, 1960.

Lasky, Victor. *JFK: The Man and the Myth*. New York: Crown, 1966.

Lawrence, W. H. "President-Elect Host to Ribicoff." *New York Times*, November 16, 1960.

Lindop, Edmund, and Joseph Jares. *White House Sportsmen*. Boston: Houghton Mifflin Company, 1964.

Loftus, Joseph A. "Diversions Ease President's Load." *New York Times*, September 18, 1961.

Manchester, William, *Portrait of a President: John F. Kennedy in Profile*. Boston: Little, Brown & Company, 1962.

"Mrs. Kennedy Watches as Husband Plays Golf." *New York Times*, December 31, 1960.

Palmer, Arnold, with James Dodson. *A Golfer's Life*. New York: Ballantine Publishing Group, 1999.

Phillips, R. Hart. "Cuban Golfs, Boasts He Could 'Easily' Beat Kennedy." *New York Times*, March 31, 1961.

"President Plays 5 Holes of Golf." *Washington Post*, July 8, 1963.

Presidential Golf. The Golf Channel's sixty-minute documentary that first aired in January 2001: quotation from Ethel Kennedy.

Reeves, Richard. *President Kennedy: Profile of Power*. New York: Simon and Schuster, 1993.

Reeves, Thomas C., *A Question of Character: A Life of John F. Kennedy*. New York: Free Press, 1991.

Rosaforte, Tim. "Kennedy Kept His Passion for the Game Under Wraps." *Sports Illustrated*, May 6, 1996.

Salinger, Pierre. *With Kennedy*. Garden City, N.Y.: Doubleday, 1966.

Schlesinger, Arthur Jr. *A Thousand Days: John F. Kennedy in the White House*. Boston: Houghton Mifflin Company and Cambridge, Mass.: Riverside Press, 1965.

From the John F. Kennedy Library and Museum in Boston: photographs, papers, schedules, and correspondence.

DWIGHT D. EISENHOWER

Armour, Tommy. "Mr. President: Here's What's Wrong with Your Golf Game . . . ." *This Week*, May 10, 1953.

Baker, Russell. "Eisenhower Tries a Few Golf Shots." *New York Times*, July 4, 1956.

Belair, Felix Jr. "President Golfs with Palmer, Winner of Masters." *New York Times*, April 12, 1960.

———. "President Starts Golfing Vacation." *New York Times*, July 8, 1960.

Burning Tree Club (Bethesda, Md.). *The Fifth Decade, 1963–1972*. Bethesda, Md.: Privately published, 1972.

———. *A History, 1922–1962*. Bethesda, Md.: Privately published, 1962.

Boller, Paul F. *Presidential Anecdotes*. New York: Oxford University Press, 1981.

Brendon, Piers. *Ike: His Life and Times*. London: Secker and Warburg, 1987.

Caleo, Robert L. "Hidden Scorecards of Pennsylvania Avenue," *Golf*, September 1969.

Campbell, Shepherd, and Peter Landau. *Presidential Lies: The Illustrated History of White House Golf.* New York: Macmillan, 1996.

Daley, Arthur. "3,265,000 Reasons for Playing Golf." *New York Times Magazine,* May 31, 1953.

Eisenhower, David. *Strictly Personal.* Garden City, N.Y.: Doubleday and Company, 1981.

"Eisenhower and Arnold Palmer Win a Golf Match." Associated Press, September 10, 1960.

"Eisenhower and Sports." *Overview: Eisenhower Foundation Newsletter,* vol. 10, no. 1, Spring 1984.

"Eisenhower Plays Four Holes of Golf and He Feels 'Fine.'" *New York Times,* August 5, 1956.

"Golf and Grandchildren Divert President on Holiday." United Press International, September 4, 1960.

Greenbrier Club History. N.p.: Privately published, n.d.

Gustafson, Merlin. "President Eisenhower's Hobby." *Presidential Studies Quarterly,* vol. 13, no. 1, Winter 1983.

Hinton, Harold. "How Presidents Get Away from It All." *New York Times Magazine,* April 19, 1953.

Hogan, Ben, as told to Tim Cohane. "How Ike Can Play in the 80's." *Look,* June 2, 1953.

Hope, Bob. "My Fifty Years in Golf." *Golf,* March 1980.

Husar, John. "Augusta Remembers Ike's Golf." *Chicago Tribune,* August 10, 1969.

"Ike Finds a Fairway." *Life,* February 23, 1953.

"Ike to Play More Golf, He Tells Labor Critic." *Washington Post,* January 28, 1955.

"Johnson Takes Stand for Presidential Golf." United Press International, June 21, 1960.

Kahn, Roger. "Take That Mulligan, Mr. President!" *Golf,* 1958.

Kinkead, Eugene. "Caddy to a President." *Life,* May 11, 1953.

Lawrence, W. H. "Sun Alone Hits Par as President Golfs." *New York Times,* February 28, 1953.

Leviero, Anthony. "Eisenhower and Nixon Are Partners on Links, Too." *New York Times,* September 12, 1953.

Lindop, Edmund, and Joseph Jares. *White House Sportsmen.* Boston: Houghton Mifflin Company, 1964.

Ludwick, Al. "General Very Nearly Eliminated That Tree." *Augusta Herald,* April 10, 1969.

Lyon, Peter. *Eisenhower: Portrait of a Hero.* Boston: Little, Brown and Company, 1974.

McCormack, Mark H. *Arnie, The Evolution of a Legend.* New York: Simon and Schuster, 1967.

McLemore, Henry. "The Lighter Side . . . ." Column distributed by *McNaught Syndicate.*

"My Colorado Golf Cronies." *Life,* August 24, 1953.

Palmer, Arnold, with James Dodson. *A Golfer's Life.* New York: Ballantine Publishing Group, 1999.

Palmer, Norman, and William V. Levy. *Five Star Golf.* New York: Dell, Sloan, and Pierce, 1964.

"Portrait by the President." *Life,* March 23, 1953.

"President's Caddy Says He Keeps You Laughing." Associated Press, April 30, 1957.

"President vs. Squirrels and Senator." *New York Times.*

Presidential Golf. The Golf Channel's sixty-minute documentary that first aired in January 2001: quotation from Arnold Palmer about his friendship with Ike.

"President's Copter Trip Recalls Old Flareup." Associated Press, June 10, 1960.

"Pro to the presidents." *Golf,* 1967 annual.

Reston, James. "President Putts the Party in an Impossible Dilemma." *New York Times,* April 23, 1953.

Rubenstein, Lorne. "When Everything's Said and Done, Golf Is Just a Game." *Globe and Mail,* December 29, 1988.

Salisbury, Harrison E. "Hawaii Caddy Bares the Score: 85." *New York Times,* June 22, 1960.

Smith, Merriman. "Does Eisenhower Play Too Much Golf?" *This Week,* May 30, 1954.

————. *Meet Mister Eisenhower.* New York: Harper and Brothers, 1954.

Snead, Sam, with George Mendoza. *Slammin' Sam.* New York: Donald I. Fine, 1986.

Snead, Sam, with Al Stump. *The Education of a Golfer.* New York: Simon and Schuster, 1988.

Summersby, Kay, *Eisenhower Was My Boss.* Englewood Cliffs, N.J.: Prentice-Hall, 1948.

Werden, Lincoln A. "Eisenhower Recalled as Anxious Golfer." *New York Times,* April 10, 1969.

From the Dwight D. Eisenhower Library and Museum, Abilene, Kansas: memos, schedules, dozens of letters about golf written by Ike, photographs and transcripts of press conferences, including the October 15, 1958, press conference when Ike was asked about his love of golf by Laurence H. Burd of the *Chicago Tribune.*

Gerald R. Ford

Boller, Paul F. *Presidential Anecdotes.* New York: Oxford University Press, 1981.

Buchanan, Rob. *Eighteen Holes with . . . Gerald Ford. Golf,* June 1991.

Campbell, Shepherd, and Peter Landau. *Presidential Lies: The Illustrated History of White House Golf.* New York: Macmillan, 1996.

Ford, Gerald R., with John Underwood. "In Defense of the Competitive Urge." *Sports Illustrated,* July 8, 1974.

"Gallery Is Charitable Toward Ford's Golfing." Associated Press, February 27, 1975.

Gildea, William. "Slicing It Up with the Congressmen." *Washington Post,* September 17, 1974.

Halley, Patrick S. *Five Presidents and a Funeral. Washingtonian,* August 2002.

Herbers, John. "Ford to Play Today in Gleason Golf Classic." *New York Times,* February 24, 1975.

Hope, Bob. "My Fifty Years in Golf." *Golf,* March 1980.

Hope, Bob, with Dwayne Netland. *Confessions of a Hooker—My Lifelong Love Affair with Golf.* New York: Doubleday, 1985.

Hunter, Marjorie. "Ford, on First Day of Private Life, Draws Crowds as He Plays Golf." *New York Times,* January 22, 1977.

Naughton, James M. "Two Miles up, Ford Relaxes with Golf." *New York Times,* August 13, 1975.

Palmer, Arnold, with James Dodson. *A Golfer's Life.* New York: Ballantine Publishing Group, 1999.

Richman, Milton. "The President Was a Center." United Press International, August 11, 1974.

Ross, John M. "Plain Talk on Weekdays, Golf on Sunday." *Golf,* December 1974. For the scenes at Pinehurst, I am grateful for Ross's wonderfully detailed account in *Golf* magazine. I also relied on articles published in the *New York Times,* the *Washington Post,* and other golf publications.

Slay, Dick. "The Golfing Presidents." *Washington Star-News,* September 1, 1974.

Udall, Morris K., *Too Funny to be President.* New York: Henry Holt, 1988.

From the Gerald R. Ford Library and Museum in Ann Arbor, Michigan: papers, schedules, correspondence, memos, and photographs.

Franklin D. Roosevelt

Burning Tree Club (Bethesda, Md.). *The Fifth Decade, 1963–1972.* Bethesda, Md.: Privately published, 1972.

———. *A History, 1922–1962.* Bethesda, Md.: Privately published, 1962.

Busch, Noel F. *What Manner of Man?* New York: Harper, 1944.

Campbell, Shepherd, and Peter Landau. *Presidential Lies: The Illustrated History of White House Golf.* New York: Macmillan, 1996.

Lindop, Edmund, and Joseph Jares. *White House Sportsmen.* Boston: Houghton Mifflin Company, 1964.

Maine, Basil. *Franklin Roosevelt: His Life and Achievements.* London: John Murray, 1938.

McCallum, Walter R. "The Washington Swing: Looking Over the Golfing Ratings of the Men Who Are in the Spotlight in the National Capital." *American Golfer,* June 1933.

Nelson, Ron. "The Game That Seized the President's Soul." *Golf,* October 1, 1995.

Roosevelt, James. *My Boy, Franklin.* Ray Long and Richard R. Smith, 1933.

Roosevelt, James, with Sidney Shalett. *Affectionately, F.D.R.: A Son's Story of a Lonely Man.* New York: Harcourt, Brace, 1959.

Ross, Leland M., and Allen W. Grobin. *This Democratic Roosevelt: The Life Story of "F.D."* New York: E. P. Dutotn, 1932.

Smith, Gene. *When the Cheering Stopped: The Last Years of Woodrow Wilson.* New York: Morrow, 1964.

From the Franklin D. Roosevelt Presidential Library and Museum in Hyde Park, New York: papers and photographs, including internal White House memos about golf and golf course spending, and letters written to the President and from the President about golf.

William Howard Taft

Anderson, Judith Icke. *William Howard Taft: An Intimate History.* New York: W. W. Norton, 1981.

Barker, Charles E. *With President Taft in the White House, Memories of William Howard Taft.* Chicago: A. Kroch and Son, 1947.

Boller, Paul F. *Presidential Anecdotes.* New York: Oxford University Press, 1981.

Butt, Archibald. *Taft and Roosevelt: The Intimate Letters of Archie Butt.* Garden City, N.Y.: Doubleday, Doran and Company, 1930.

Caleo, Robert L. "Hidden Scorecards of Pennsylvania Avenue," *Golf,* September 1969.

"Chevy Chase Club Where President Taft Plays Golf." *American Golfer,* 1909.

Cotton, Edward H. *William Howard Taft: A Character Study.* Boston: Beacon Press, 1932.

Duffy, Herbert S. *William Howard Taft: The President Who Became Chief Justice.* New York: Minton, Balch, 1930.

Lauder, Sir Harry. *Roamin' in the Gloamin'.* London: Hutchinson, 1928.

Lynham, John M. *The Chevy Chase Club: A History, 1885–1957*. Chevy Chase, Md.: Privately published, 1958.

Parks, Lillian Rogers, with Frances Spatz Leighton. *My Thirty Years Backstairs at the White House*. New York: Fleet Publishing Corp., 1961.

"President Taft Plays Golf with Advertisers." *American Golfer*, September 1, 1909.

Pringle, Henry F. *The Life and Times of William Howard Taft*. Norwalk, Conn.: Eastern Press, 1986.

Severn, Bill. *William Howard Taft*. New York: David McKay and Co., 1970.

Travers, Jerome D., and James R. Crowell. *The Fifth Estate: Thirty Years of Golf*. New York: Alfred A. Knopf, 1926.

Travis, Walter J. "Mr. Taft as a Golfer." *American Golfer*, April 1909.

———. "The President and the Vice President at Chevy Chase." *American Golfer*, July 1909.

———. "President Taft as a Golfer: A Four-ball Match at Chevy Chase." *American Golfer*, April 1909.

From William Howard Taft National Historic Site, Cincinnati, Ohio: papers and photographs.

WOODROW WILSON

Booth, Mooney. *Woodrow Wilson*. New York: Follett Publishing Co., 1968.

Caleo, Robert L. "Hidden Scorecards of Pennsylvania Avenue," *Golf*, September 1969.

Campbell, Shepherd, and Peter Landau. *Presidential Lies: The Illustrated History of White House Golf*. New York: Macmillan, 1996.

Grayson, Rear Admiral Cary T. *Woodrow Wilson: An Intimate Memoir*. New York: Holt, Rinehart and Winston, 1960.

Hardin, Craig. *Woodrow Wilson at Princeton*. Oklahoma City: University of Oklahoma Press, 1960.

Lauder, Sir Harry. *Roamin' in the Gloamin'*. London: Hutchinson, 1928.

Lewis, McMillan. *Woodrow Wilson of Princeton*. Narbeth, Pa.: Livingston Publishing Co., 1952.

Lindop, Edmund, and Joseph Jares. *White House Sportsmen*. Boston: Houghton Mifflin Company, 1964.

Lynham, John M. *The Chevy Chase Club: A History, 1885–1957*. Chevy Chase, Md.: Privately published, 1958.

McAdoo, Eleanor Wilson. *The Woodrow Wilsons*. New York: Macmillan, 1937.

Miller, Hope Ridings. *Scandals in the Highest Office: Facts and Fictions in the Private Lives of Our Presidents*. New York: Random House, 1973.

Reid, Edith Gittings. *Woodrow Wilson: The Caricature, The Myth, and the Man.* London: Oxford University Press, 1934.

Ross, Ishbel. *Power with Grace: The Story of Mrs. Woodrow Wilson.* New York: Putnam, 1975.

Smith, Gene. *When the Cheering Stopped: The Last Years of Woodrow Wilson.* New York: Morrow, 1964.

Starling, Colonel Edmund W. *Starling of the White House.* New York: Simon and Schuster, 1946.

Travers, Jerome D., and James R. Crowell. *The Fifth Estate: Thirty Years of Golf.* New York: Alfred A. Knopf, 1926.

Tumulty, Joseph P. *Woodrow Wilson As I Knew Him.* Garden City, N.Y.: Doubleday, 1921.

Wilson, Edith Bolling. *My Memoir.* Indianapolis: Bobbs-Merrill, 1938.

Wilson, Woodrow, and A. S. Link, ed. *The Papers of Woodrow Wilson.* Vol. 9. Princeton: Princeton University Press, 1970.

Wind, Herbert Warren. *The Story of American Golf: Volume One.* New York: Callaway Editions, 2000.

From the Woodrow Wilson House, Washington, D.C.: papers, memos, letters, and photos.

Calvin Coolidge

Caleo, Robert L. "Hidden Scorecards of Pennsylvania Avenue," *Golf*, September 1969.

Campbell, Shepherd, and Peter Landau. *Presidential Lies: The Illustrated History of White House Golf.* New York: Macmillan, 1996.

Lindop, Edmund, and Joseph Jares. *White House Sportsmen.* Boston: Houghton Mifflin Company, 1964.

Starling, Colonel Edmund W. *Starling of the White House.* New York: Simon and Schuster, 1946.

Ronald Reagan

Adler, Bill, with Bill Adler Jr. *The Reagan Wit.* Aurora, Ill.: Caroline House Publishers, 1981.

Boller, Paul F. *Presidential Anecdotes.* New York: Oxford University Press, 1981.

Campbell, Shepherd, and Peter Landau. *Presidential Lies: The Illustrated History of White House Golf.* New York: Macmillan, 1996.

Cannon, Lou. "A Letter from Palm Springs: President's Aides Shine the Saddle After Rough Ride." *Washington Post*, January 1, 1987.

———. *President Reagan: The Role of a Lifetime.* New York: Simon and Schuster, 1991.

Edwards, Anne. *Early Reagan: The Rise to Power.* New York: William Morrow, 1987.

Lakeside Country Club. *Club History.* N.p.: Privately published, n.d.

Lowitt, Bruce. "Presidents at Play." *St. Petersburg Times,* November 3, 1996.

Palmer, Arnold, with James Dodson. *A Golfer's Life.* New York: Ballantine Publishing Group, 1999.

Sherill, Martha. "Power Golf: Out on the Greens with the Men of Driving Ambition." *Washington Post,* June 6, 1989.

Udall, Morris K., *Too Funny to be President.* New York: Henry Holt, 1988.

Van der Linden, Frank, *The Real Reagan: What He Believes, What He Accomplished, What We Can Expect From Him.* New York: William Morrow, 1981.

Watters, Susan. "Power Golf." *M,* August 1989.

Wills, Garry. *Reagan's America: Innocents at Home.* New York: Doubleday, 1986.

From the Ronald Reagan Presidential Library and Museum, Simi Valley, California: correspondence and photographs.

BILL CLINTON

I played golf with President Clinton on August 13, 2002, at the Golf Club of Purchase in Purchase, New York. All of President Clinton's quotes during my round with him, and the quotations of our playing partners, Barry Baker and Michael Bronfein, were on the record. Nearly all the President's quotations were tape-recorded by me, including Clinton's angry exchange with a caddy. Several of his quotations were transcribed by John Files, my researcher.

Several quotes in the Clinton chapter were taken from an interview that he gave to Thomas L. Friedman in August 2000, for a piece published in the fall of 2000 by *Golf Digest.* The quotes are Clinton's observation that "mulligans are way overrated," his remark that Americans did not begrudge him his golf playing, and one of his remarks about playing while growing up in Little Rock.

The accounts of Clinton's golf games during his presidency are taken from a variety of sources, including eyewitness accounts, press reports, and White House pool reports.

Clinton has played a round only a handful of times with journalists. The most famous round was with Rick Reilly of *Sports Illustrated* in May 1995. Clinton played with Reilly at Congressional Country Club in Bethesda, Maryland; Reilly's article was entitled "Perfect Pard," and Reilly raised, then knocked down, the accusation that the President cheats at golf. Reilly was suspicious of Clinton's then-claimed handicap of 13: "I'd also heard that the 13 was phonier than Cheez Whiz and that he would probably go out and shoot himself a radio station—a Magic 102 or a Zoo 105." In the *Sports Illustrated* article and an interview with the author in August 1999, Reilly reported that the President took some practice shots, but always played his first ball. Reilly reported, though, that Clinton received a handful of gimmes.

Several other press accounts point out Clinton's habit of playing practice shots and often asking his playing partners to remind him which is his first ball. During my round with him, he also asked for help finding his first ball. More often than not, Clinton chose to play his *best* ball, and it was usually not the first ball that he had hit off the tee or off the fairway.

Clinton played a less famous round with Bill Nichols of *USA Today* in August 1995. Nichols played with Clinton at the Jackson Hole Golf and Tennis Club in Jackson, Wyoming. Nichols reported that Clinton shot "a legit" 81. Addressing "the mulligan question," Nichols wrote, "Cynical reporters, myself included, have suspected that the president takes more than his share of these re-hits. Not true. He does grant other plays rather long putts. And if the president tells you to pick up a 5-footer for par, what's a guy to do? You can't insult him. But the extra shots Clinton hits are for practice. His score, on this day, was legit."

On November 2, 1997, Glenn F. Bunting of the *Los Angeles Times* played in a foursome that trailed a Clinton foursome at the Golf Club at Amelia Island, Florida, during a Democratic National Committee "autumn retreat." The President was joined on the front nine and back nine by different groups of corporate executives who each ponied up $50,000 for the privilege to play with him. From his vantage point on neighboring holes, Bunting reported that Clinton "took a lot of practice shots on the course. On all but a few occasions, though, he played his original ball." On the par-5, 15th hole, Bunting watched (from the nearby 12th fairway) as Clinton sliced a ball into the woods, then took a second shot that landed in the fairway. Richard Lawrence, a Cincinnati medical malpractice lawyer who played with Clinton that day, told Bunting, "He would yank his drive out of bounds, turn to me and say, 'Look, you let me hit another one, I'll let you hit another one.'"

Clinton claimed to shoot 83 that day. John Palmer, the longtime NBC Washington correspondent, also joined Clinton for nine holes at Amelia Island. Palmer denied that he saw the President cheat, saying, "What he does is hit a lot of balls, because he wants to get it right."

Andersen, Harold W. "With Clinton and Co. on the Links." *Omaha World-Herald*, June 10, 2001.

Barnicle, Mike. "Clinton, Golf: A Poor Match." *Boston Globe*, September 8, 1994.

Bedard, Paul. "No More Slick Shots? Teased into Playing It As It Lies, Clinton Has a Dismal Day." *Washington Times*, August 23, 1997.

Bunting, Glenn F. "Game Fits the President to a T-er." *Los Angeles Times*, November 13, 1997.

Callahan, Gerry. "Hail to the Cheat." *Boston Herald*, September 8, 1994.

Campbell, Shepherd, and Peter Landau. *Presidential Lies: The Illustrated History of White House Golf*. New York: Macmillan, 1996.

Cannon, Carl M. "Clinton Finds Golfing a Great Escape." *Baltimore Sun*, August 24, 1993.

Carr, Howie. "Go Home, Bill, and Take the Oliphants with You." *Boston Herald*, August 29, 1994.

Cuniberti, Betty. "Mulligan-Taking Can Lead to Larger Evils on the Course." *Kansas City Star*, June 18, 1994.

Ditota, Donna. "Par for the President." *Syracuse Post-Standard*, August 31, 1999.

Farrell, John Aloysius. "On Public Links, Clinton Reveals His Hacking Ways." *Boston Globe*, August 16, 1993.

Friedman, Thomas L. "Bill Clinton: The First Golfer on the Game He Loves, and Why He's Like Any Other Guy on the Tee." *Golf Digest*, November 2000. The chapter's epigraph is from this interview with Friedman, as are several other quotations.

Gilleece, Dermot. "Ballybunion Sure to Be a Test of Clinton's Drive." *Irish Times,* September 5, 1998.

Goldman, John J. "This Détente Is Down to a Tee." *Los Angeles Times*, May 21, 2001.

"Golf as Life: Revised Edition." Editorial, *Globe and Mail*, September 4, 1999.

Grimsley, Edward. "Alas, President Clinton Is Giving Golf a Bad Name." *Richmond Times-Dispatch*, November 17, 1995.

Gurdon, Hugo. "Clinton on Course to Match Ike in Escape from Reality." *Daily Telegraph,* December 12, 1997.

Hubbell, Webb. *Friends in High Places: Our Journey from Little Rock to Washington, D.C.* New York: William Morrow and Co., 1997.

Huxley, John. "Bill Cheats and Greg Chokes. It's Par for the Course." *Sydney Morning Herald,* November 21, 1996.

Larocca, Amy. "The Golfer." *New York Observer*, June 7, 1999.

Latimer, Clay. "Nicklaus Says Clinton Has Potential." *Rocky Mountain News*, August 18, 1993.

Macintyre, Ben. "Clinton's Dark Side Emerges on Golf Course." *Times* (London), October 19, 1999.

Maraniss, David. *First in His Class: The Biography of Bill Clinton*. New York: Simon and Schuster, 1995.

Marcus, Ruth. "Bill's Bunker Mentality: Adventures of the First Duffer." *Washington Post*, August 26, 1993.

McGrory, Brian. "A Slice of Presidential Life: Different Strokes Mark the Courses of Chief Executives." *Boston Globe*, August 17, 1996.

Mell, Randall. "Inverrary GM Helps Clinton with Swing." *Sun-Sentinel*, December 19, 1999.

Morris, Dick. *Behind the Oval Office: Getting Reelected Against All Odds.* Los Angeles: Renaissance Books, 1999.

Omicinski, John. "Clinton Plays Golf the Way He Plays the Presidency." *Gannett News Service*, August 30, 1997.

Palmer, Arnold, with Steve Eubanks. *Playing by the Rules: All the Rules of the Game, Complete with Memorable Rulings from Golf's Rich History*. New York: Pocket Books, 2002.

Press briefing. Office of the Press Secretary, The White House, transcript of Mike McCurry's daily press briefing, June 19, 1995.

Seelye, Katharine Q. "President Hits the Golf Course, and the Books." *New York Times*, August 24, 1999.

Sullivan, Robert. "Teeing Off: Your Cheatin' Heart." *Sports Illustrated*, August 31, 1998.

Reilly, Rick. "Perfect Pard." *Sports Illustrated*, June 12, 1995.

Rosaforte, Tim. "Kennedy Kept His Passion for the Game Under Wraps." *Sports Illustrated*, May 6, 1996.

Russert, Tim. *Meet the Press* transcript of interview with the President, NBC News, November 10, 1997.

Sarasohn, David. "Clinton into the Rough." *Portland Oregonian*, December 12, 1997.

Scarborough, Rowan. "Master of the Mulligan." *Washington Times*, October 31, 1996.

Spear, Joseph. "Clinton Got the Golf Vote." *Las Vegas Review-Journal*, November 14, 1996.

St. John, Lauren. *Shark: The Biography of Greg Norman*. London: Rutledge Hill Press, 1998.

Stephanopoulos, George. *All Too Human: A Political Education*. New York: Macmillan, 1999.

Thomma, Steven. "Dole: Clinton a Liberal with his Golf Scores." *Knight-Ridder News Service*, October 19, 1996.

Tucker, Tim. "Shooting a 60 with President Mulligan." *Atlanta Journal and Constitution*, August 16, 1999.

Van Natta, Don Jr. "Par for Clinton's Course." *New York Times*, August 29, 1999.

Woodward, Bob. *Shadow: Five Presidents and the Legacy of Watergate, 1974–1999*. New York: Simon and Schuster, 1999.

York, Byron. "Bill's Bad Lie." *American Spectator*, October 1996.

White House pool reports, 1993 to 2000, helped inform all the scenes of Clinton playing golf during his two terms as president.

RICHARD M. NIXON

Ambrose, Stephen E. *Nixon: The Education of a Politician, 1913–1962.* New York: Simon and Schuster, 1987.

Anson, Robert Sam. *Exile: The Unquiet Oblivion of Richard M. Nixon.* New York: Simon and Schuster, 1984.

Baltusrol Golf Club (Springfield, N.J.). *Club History.* N.p.: Privately published, n.d.

Bell, Harold. "He Wasn't A Great Golfer but . . . ." *Washington Post,* May 1, 1994.

Buchanan, Patrick J. *Right from the Beginning.* Boston: Little, Brown and Company, 1988.

Dodson, James. "Nixon Was One of Us." *Golf,* October 1, 1994.

Grizzard, Lewis. "Nixon's Credibility Is Gone with His Golf." *Atlanta Journal-Constitution,* April 18, 1990.

Hope, Bob. "My Fifty Years in Golf." *Golf,* March 1980.

Hughes, Arthur J. *Richard M. Nixon.* New York: Dodd, Mead, 1972.

Lakeside Country Club: A History. Los Angeles: Privately published, n.d.

Lowitt, Bruce. "Presidents at Play." *St. Petersburg Times,* November 3, 1996.

Nixon, Richard M. *In the Arena: A Memoir of Victory, Defeat, and Renewal.* New York: Simon and Schuster, 1990.

Palmer, Arnold, with James Dodson. *A Golfer's Life.* New York: Ballantine Publishing Group, 1999.

Presidential Golf. The Golf Channel's sixty-minute documentary that first aired in January 2001: quotations from Senator George A. Smathers of Florida and Max Elbin, longtime club professional at Burning Tree Country Club.

Sherill, Martha. "Power Golf: Out on the Greens with the Men of Driving Ambition." *Washington Post,* June 6, 1989.

Snead, Sam, with George Mendoza. *Slammin' Sam.* New York: Donald I. Fine, 1986.

Strober, Gerald S., and Deborah H. Strober. *Nixon: An Oral History of His Presidency.* New York: HarperCollins, 1994.

From the Richard Nixon Library and Birthplace, Yorba Linda, California: notes, memos, and photographs.

LYNDON B. JOHNSON

Caleo, Robert L. "Hidden Scorecards of Pennsylvania Avenue," *Golf,* September 1969.

Campbell, Shepherd, and Peter Landau. *Presidential Lies: The Illustrated History of White House Golf.* New York: Macmillan, 1996.

Clifford, George, and Tom Kelly. "A Rest for LBJ." *Washington Star,* January 20, 1964.

Finney, John W. "Johnson, for Fun, Has a Hideaway Ranch." *New York Times,* July 7, 1964.

Frankel, Max. "Johnson Takes a Whole Day Off." *New York Times,* March 4, 1968.

"Golf Bug Bites on Johnson." Associated Press, April 29, 1964.

"Johnson Likes to Chat at End of Day's Work." Associated Press, November 30, 1963.

"Johnson Putting Rusty on White House Green." Associated Press, May 10, 1968.

"Johnson Takes It Easy in Week End of Golf." Associated Press, *Washington Evening Star,* April 13, 1964.

"LBJ Golfing Again." *Washington Post,* September 27, 1967.

Lindop, Edmund, and Joseph Jares. *White House Sportsmen.* Boston: Houghton Mifflin Company, 1964.

Lowitt, Bruce. "Presidents at Play." *St. Petersburg Times,* November 3, 1996.

"President Goes Golfing, and Club Pro Is Impressed." Associated Press, November 13, 1967.

"The President Messes Up a Putt but Makes a Point at Navy Mess." *New York Times,* February 19, 1968.

Raymond, Jack. "President Goes for a Stroll and Pets His Beagles." *New York Times,* July 16, 1964.

Reedy, George. *Lyndon Johnson: A Memoir.* New York: Andrews and McMeels, 1982.

———. *The Twilight of the Presidency.* New York: World Publishing, 1970.

Reston, James. "Washington: Golf, Whisky, and Mr. Johnson." *New York Times,* September 29, 1967.

"White House Confirms It: Johnson Was Playing Golf." United Press International, April 7, 1964.

Worley, Eugene. "Golf Game with Lyndon Johnson." Lyndon Baines Johnson Library and Museum, Oral History Collection, Austin, Texas, 1968.

From the Lyndon Baines Johnson Library and Museum, Austin, Texas: correspondence, memos, oral history recollections, and photographs.

WARREN G. HARDING

Adams, Samuel Hopkins. *Incredible Era: The Life and Times of Warren Gamaliel Harding.* Boston: Houghton Mifflin, 1939.

Caleo, Robert L. "Hidden Scorecards of Pennsylvania Avenue," *Golf*, September 1969.

Campbell, Shepherd, and Peter Landau. *Presidential Lies: The Illustrated History of White House Golf*. New York: Macmillan, 1996.

"Getting in Trim for the Presidency." *American Golfer*, photograph of president-elect Harding, 1921.

Lindop, Edmund, and Joseph Jares. *White House Sportsmen*. Boston: Houghton Mifflin Company, 1964.

Mee, Charles L. Jr. *The Ohio Gang: The World of Warren G. Harding*. New York: M. Evans, 1981.

Miller, Hope Ridings. *Scandals in the Highest Office: Facts and Fictions in the Private Lives of Our Presidents*. New York: Random House, 1973.

Rice, Grantland. "The President's Golf Game: Wherein Your Correspondent and Ring Lardner Mingle in Fast Company over the Chevy Chase Links." *American Golfer*, April 23, 1921.

Russell, Francis. *The Shadow of Blooming Grove*. New York: McGraw Hill, 1968.

Starling, Colonel Edmund W. *Starling of the White House*. New York: Simon and Schuster, 1946.

I also relied on several undated and untitled articles published in the *American Golfer* about President Harding's game.

From the Ohio Historical Society, Columbus, Ohio: papers, letters, and photos.

George H. W. Bush and George W. Bush

Allen, Mike. "Before Golf, Bush Decries Latest Deaths in Mideast." *Washington Post*, August 5, 2002.

———. "Since September 11, Exerciser Bush Finds Himself on War Footing." *Washington Post*, August 22, 2002.

Balz, Dan. "The 18-Hole Drive to Play on Par with the President." *Washington Post*, September 3, 1990.

Bauer, Stephen M., with Frances Spatz Leighton. *At Ease in the White House: The Uninhibited Memoirs of a Presidential Social Aide*. New York: Caral, 1991.

Benedetto, Richard. "Bush Golfs with 'Bertha,' not Barbara." *USA Today*, August 16, 1991.

Bruni, Frank. *Ambling into History: The Unlikely Odyssey of George W. Bush*. New York: HarperCollins, 2002.

Burka, Paul. "The Revision Thing." *Texas Monthly*, November 1997.

"Bush and Son Golf Game Fast, Filled with Banter." Associated Press, August 23, 1989.

"Bush Breaks Own Speed Record on Maine Golf Course." Associated Press, August 18, 1990.

Callahan, Tom. "The Putting Green Stays." *Golf Digest*, May 1, 2001.

Campbell, Shepherd, and Peter Landau. *Presidential Lies: The Illustrated History of White House Golf*. New York: Macmillan, 1996.

Casstevens, David. "Every Bush Covered as George Plays Golf." *Dallas Morning News*, May 20, 1990.

Cocco, Marie. "Mr. Smooth Plays by His Own Rules." *Newsday*, August 23, 1989.

Doughtie, Charles. *From the Catbird Seat*. New York: Broken Hill Press, 1992.

Douglas, George A. *Our Little Golf Club in Maine, Cape Arundel: The History of Cape Arundel Golf Club of Kennebunkport*. Kennebunkport, Me: Cape House Book Publishers, 2001.

Dowd, Maureen. "Adrift in Bush's Circle Seeking the Common Man." *New York Times*, December 1, 1991.

————. "As Golf Duo, First Family Becomes Average Family." *New York Times*, August 18, 1991.

————. "Bush Is Yipping and Chipping in Wedge City." *New York Times*, August 24, 1989.

————. "Bush Seldom Met a Sport He Didn't Like." *New York Times*, January 2, 1989.

————. "A Grim Bush Golfs and Boats as Aides Fret About Image." *New York Times*, August 20, 1990.

————. "This President Relaxes by Wearing Others Out." *New York Times*, July 4, 1989.

Ferraro, Thomas. "Bush Plays 'Aerobic' Golf." United Press International, September 3, 1989.

————. "Bush's Pro Helps Avoid Golf Crisis Recreation." United Press International, October 14, 1990.

Fournier, Ron. "Bushes Square Off in Vacation Play." Associated Press, July 7, 2001.

Gerstenzang, James. "President Bush Is No Mulligan Man." *Los Angeles Times*, August 20, 2001.

Gold, Victor. "The Itch Bush Just Has to Scratch." *Washington Times*, September 15, 1991.

Gordon, Joe. "Prez on Top of His Game." *Boston Herald*, September 23, 2001.

Hillman, G. Robert. "Golf Doesn't Thrill First Lady." *Dallas Morning News*, August 18, 1991.

Hurt, Harry III. "Tackling the Bush Pentathlon." *Newsweek*, August 21, 1989.

Lowry, Joan. "Bush a Golf Cheat?" *Seattle Post-Intelligencer*, February 29, 2000.

Macintyre, Ben. "Bush Follows Clinton down Fairway to Cheating." *Times* (London), July 5, 2001.

Martzke, Rudy. "Bush Relishes Role of Golf Ambassador for Cup Play." *USA Today*, May 7, 1996.

McFeatters, Ann. "Golf Links Are a President's Best Friend, Of Course." *Pittsburgh Post-Gazette*, December 31, 2000.

Moore, David Leon, and Jessica Lee. "Sportsman in the White House." *USA Today,* December 20, 1988.

Reid, Tim. "President Discovers Joys of a Good Walk Spoiled." *Times* (London), August 6, 2002.

Rosenthal, Harry F. "Jog, Tennis, Swim, Golf, Fish: If It Involves Sweat, It's for Bush." Associated Press, August 8, 1992.

Sheehan, Jack. "Eighteen Holes with . . . George Bush." *Golf,* June 1, 1995.

Sherill, Martha. "Power Golf: Out on the Greens with the Men of Driving Ambition." *Washington Post,* June 4, 1989.

Smits, Garry. "Governor Bush Shares Family Links to Golf." *Florida Times-Union*, November 25, 2001.

Sweda, George. "No Presidential Pardons Here, Sir Firestone Takes Toll on Bush." *Cleveland Plain Dealer*, August 25, 1994.

Venezia, Todd. "It's Bush League on Links." *New York Post*, July 8, 2001.

Wischnia, Bob, and Paul Carrozza. "Twenty Questions for President George W. Bush: A Running Conversation." *Runner's World*, October 2002.

White House pool reports, 1989–1991, 2001, 2002.

Epilogue

Hope, Bob, with Dwayne Netland. *Confessions of a Hooker: My Lifelong Love Affair with Golf.* Garden City, N.Y.: Doubleday, 1985.

Morris, Dick. *Behind the Oval Office: Getting Reelected Against All Odds.* Los Angeles: Renaissance Books, 1999.

ACKNOWLEDGMENTS

Writing a book is a lonely and at times aggravating endeavor that renews a writer's fondness for the 900-word article needed in forty-five minutes for publication in tomorrow's newspaper. Yet it is also the most rewarding privilege a writer can have. This book would not have been possible without the help, support, encouragement, and enthusiasm of hundreds of friends, colleagues, and strangers.

I first want to thank my agent, Christy Fletcher, who, on a whim, wrote me an e-mail on August 30, 1999, wondering if I would be interested in writing a book about presidents and golf. Without Christy's boundless enthusiasm for this project, I never would have been able to navigate the three-and-a-half-year obstacle course that led to that golden hour when this book was finally grasped by a reader.

I also want to extend my sincere gratitude to John Files, my researcher, who is a first-class journalist, a fine golfer, and a good friend. John excavated revealing anecdotes from the United States Golf Association archives, the Library of Congress, and a dozen presidential libraries and archives. He accompanied me during my round with Bill Clinton on Tuesday, August 13, 2002, in Purchase, New York. John first noticed that Clinton was playing his second and even third "practice" shots hit from the tee boxes and the fairways. (I was too busy trying to keep my ball in play.) John thanks his wife, Susannah N. Files.

I am extremely grateful to the subjects themselves—the presidents who generously gave me their time and patience. I was honored that they were so eager and willing to assist this project. Each man's candor and humor immeasurably improved the book.

Most of all, I thank Bill Clinton. He graciously agreed to play eighteen holes with me on that blistering summer day in August 2002. Even though he was busy at the time writing his own political memoir, Clinton spent nearly seven hours with me, telling wonderful golf stories and trying, in vain, to help me improve my swing. During our round, Clinton, who knew I was there to see if he bends the rules, was able to abide by the rulebook for nearly two holes. And then, he let down his guard and played his customary round, Billigans and all. If Bill Clinton comes to life more than the other presidents in this book, it is because he enthusiastically agreed to reveal himself on the links, even knowing (as he must have) that some of the things I witnessed that afternoon would not necessarily enhance his golfing legacy.

I also want to extend my warm thanks to George H. W. Bush, who responded to my many meandering, multipart questions with sharp volleys of witty and revealing retorts. And I thank Gerald R. Ford, who over the course of an interview patiently and carefully answered my prying questions about long-ago golf shots and the emotions they left in their wake.

Thank you to the presidents' friends, aides, and spokespersons, who helped gather information for me as well as persuade the presidents to cooperate. Thank you to the members of "Team Clinton"—Terry McAuliffe, Doug Sosnik, Julia Payne, John Podesta, Joe Lockhart, and Jim Kennedy. And thank you to the members of "Team Bush"—Jean Becker, Dorrance Smith, Ken Raynor, Paul Marchand, and Wayne Berman. A special thanks also to Anne Womack and Georgia Godfrey at the White House.

I thank the great people at PublicAffairs, a six-year-old publishing house whose publisher, Peter Osnos, envisioned *First Off the Tee* on a bookstore table when most editors did not bother to read my proposal. It was Peter Osnos who advised, very early on, "Have fun. Whip up a wonderful dessert." Thank you to Paul Golob, an insatiably curious editor and a meticulous wordsmith who helped improve so much of the manuscript. Thanks also to his talented assistant, David Patterson, as well as to Gene Taft, Lisa Kaufman, Robert Kimzey, and Melanie Peirson Johnstone.

Thank you to the professional golfers who granted me interviews or answered my written questions. They comprise a fivesome for the ages: Arnold Palmer, Jack Nicklaus, Greg Norman, Ben Crenshaw, and Ray Floyd. Thanks also to Doc Giffin, the spokesman for Palmer, and to Scott Tolley, the spokesman for Nicklaus.

I am deeply indebted to the research assistance provided by E. Ray Henderson at the William Howard Taft National Historic Site; Meg Nowack at the Woodrow Wilson House in Washington, D.C.; Duryea Kemp at the Ohio Historical Society; Raymond Teichman at the Franklin Delano Roosevelt Library; Kathleen Struss and Barbara Constable at the Dwight D. Eisenhower Library; James Hill at the John Fitzgerald Kennedy Library; Shannon Jarrett and Kyla Wilson at the Lyndon Baines Johnson Library; James R. Jones, a chief of staff to LBJ; Arianna Barrios Lochrie and Susan Naulty at the Richard Nixon Library and Birthplace; William McNitt and Kenneth Hafeli at the Gerald R. Ford Library and Museum; Josh Tenenbaum at the Ronald Reagan Presidential Library; and Mary Finch and Deborah Wheeler at the George Bush Presidential Library and Museum. Thanks also to Doug Stark and Rand Jerris at the United States Golf Association, Eric Bartels of The Golf Channel, Judy Thompson of the National Golf Foundation, the staff at the United

States Library of Congress, Jemal Creary at Corbis, and Joan Carroll at AP/Wide World Photos.

Bob Hope and his spokesman, Ward Grant, were early and enthusiastic supporters of this project. Their assistance was invaluable.

Thank you so much to my friends at the *New York Times*. They encouraged me, picked up my slack, and tolerated my telling and retelling of the golfing heroics of long-dead presidents. There is not enough room to mention them all, and I apologize to anyone I have forgotten. I owe a special thanks to Joe Sexton, David Johnston, Chris Drew, Jim Risen, Doug Frantz, John Broder, Frank Rich, David Firestone, Adam Clymer, Nick Lewis, Robin Toner, Linda Greenhouse, Frank Clines, Alison Mitchell, Carl Hulse, Todd Purdum, Steve Labaton, Dick Stevenson, David Gonzalez, Kit Seelye, Elisabeth Bumiller, Rick Berke, Michael Gordon, Rick Bragg, Jim Yardley, Dan Barry, David Barstow, Philip Shenon, Adam Nagourney, Elaine Sciolino, Jim Roberts, James Bennet, and Julie Bosman.

The research was made considerably easier by the terrific talents of Barclay Walsh and Monica Borkowski, who work wonders inside the library in the Washington bureau of the *Times*.

I signed the contract for this book shortly before two monumental news events consumed many months of my professional life—the deadlocked presidential election in Florida and the 9/11 terrorist attacks. Despite those responsibilities, my editors at the *Times* generously allowed me the time and space to research and write this book. I extend my sincere thanks and admiration to Joe Lelyveld, Bill Keller, Andy Rosenthal, Michael Oreskes, Gerald Boyd, and Howell Raines.

This is a book of foursomes, and there were four wonderful friends at the *Times* who contributed in so many ways:

First, my sincere thanks to the indomitable Jill Abramson, the Washington bureau chief, my coauthor on countless stories about "that woman" and one of my closest friends. She generously allowed me the time and room that I needed, especially during the homestretch.

Then there is the incomparable Maureen Dowd, who pushed me to get the Bushes exactly right, flooded me with hilarious anecdotes and invented ways to keep me howling with laughter.

Then there is the inimitable Frank Bruni, a graceful writer, dynamo reporter and good friend whose gentle encouragement, at several important moments, helped me cross the finish line.

Finally, I thank the indefatigable Jeff Gerth, a near-scratch golfer and outstanding journalist who inspired me every day I had the honor to work by his side.

There are few sportswriters in America as gifted as Scott Price, a senior writer at *Sports Illustrated* and the author of a first-class book about sports in Cuba. I am blessed that he is also one of my best friends. Scott embraced *First Off the Tee* when it did not have a name and was nothing more than a lark. He was the first person to read the prologue's opening scene, and his spontaneous gush of enthusiasm, delivered over a few cold beers in a dark bar just a few blocks from the White House, helped me clear the first and highest hurdle. Thanks also to Fran Brennan, Scott's wife, a first-rate journalist and a great friend who made several important contributions to this book.

Thank you to Pete Cross, one of my closest friends, whose beautiful photograph of an authentic Bill Clinton presidential seal golf ball graces the cover. And thanks to Pete's wife, Christine Evans, a graceful, prize-winning writer and good friend.

Thank you to Paquita Madariaga, Mariana Alvarez and Terri and Frank Alvarez, for ten years of love and support. And a sincere thanks to my good friends Mari Beth McCarthy and Rich Heilman, Ann O'Hanlon and John Harris, Lisa Getter and John Peterson, Beth and Ian MacPhail, Cindy and Mark Sloan, and Debra Ellis.

I am so fortunate that my family supported me through this long project with love and patience. My mother, Liette Van Natta, is the most generous person I know. She has always given me so much, but her love is the world's greatest gift.

Thanks also to my brothers, Steve and Dean, whose love and friendship mean everything to me.

My wife, Lizette Alvarez, is the most talented and generous writer I know. Not only did she help polish the manuscript, she gave me the time, space, and encouragement that I needed to complete it. Lisi, thanks for making sure our life together is the greatest adventure.

Thanks also to my young daughters, Isabel and Sofia, for being so understanding when Daddy had to keep typing.

Finally, this book is dedicated, in large part, to the memory of my father, Don Van Natta Sr., a generous, big-hearted man who taught his three sons—and hundreds of other men and women who had the pleasure to know him—all the big lessons of business and life. I regret that my father did not live to see this book published. Ask anyone who knew my dad, and they will tell you that he lived his life the way he hit the ball off the first tee—straight and fair and true.

Don Van Natta Jr.
Alexandria, Virginia
January 2, 2003

PHOTO CREDITS

PHOTO CREDITS

INDEX

ABOUT THE AUTHOR

Don Van Natta Jr. is an investigative correspondent for the *New York Times*, where he has worked since 1995. Prior to that, he worked for eight years at the *Miami Herald*. He has been a member of three Pulitzer Prize–winning teams—two at the *Times*, and one at the *Herald*. As an investigative reporter at the *Times*, he has covered a wide range of subjects, including terrorism, the impeachment of Bill Clinton, and the deadlocked 2000 presidential election. He is a 100-plus golfer who managed to shoot an ugly hole-in-one (the ball ricocheted off a tree, rolled down an embankment, and somehow ended up in the cup). He lives in London with his wife, Lizette Alvarez, who is also a *Times* correspondent, and their two daughters, Isabel and Sofia.

PublicAffairs is a publishing house founded in 1997. It is a tribute to the standards, values, and flair of three persons who have served as mentors to countless reporters, writers, editors, and book people of all kinds, including me.

I. F. Stone, proprietor of *I. F. Stone's Weekly,* combined a commitment to the First Amendment with entrepreneurial zeal and reporting skill and became one of the great independent journalists in American history. At the age of eighty, Izzy published *The Trial of Socrates,* which was a national bestseller. He wrote the book after he taught himself ancient Greek.

Benjamin C. Bradlee was for nearly thirty years the charismatic editorial leader of *The Washington Post.* It was Ben who gave the *Post* the range and courage to pursue such historic issues as Watergate. He supported his reporters with a tenacity that made them fearless, and it is no accident that so many became authors of influential, best-selling books.

Robert L. Bernstein, the chief executive of Random House for more than a quarter century, guided one of the nation's premier publishing houses. Bob was personally responsible for many books of political dissent and argument that challenged tyranny around the globe. He is also the founder and was the longtime chair of Human Rights Watch, one of the most respected human rights organizations in the world.

.   .   .

For fifty years, the banner of Public Affairs Press was carried by its owner, Morris B. Schnapper, who published Gandhi, Nasser, Toynbee, Truman, and about 1,500 other authors. In 1983 Schnapper was described by *The Washington Post* as "a redoubtable gadfly." His legacy will endure in the books to come.

Peter Osnos, *Publisher*